eight™

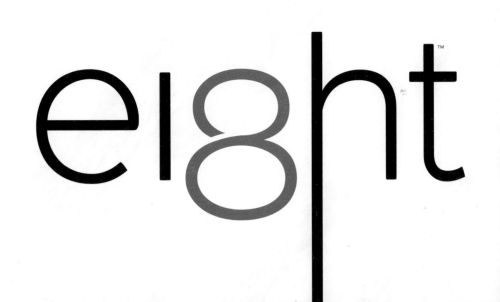

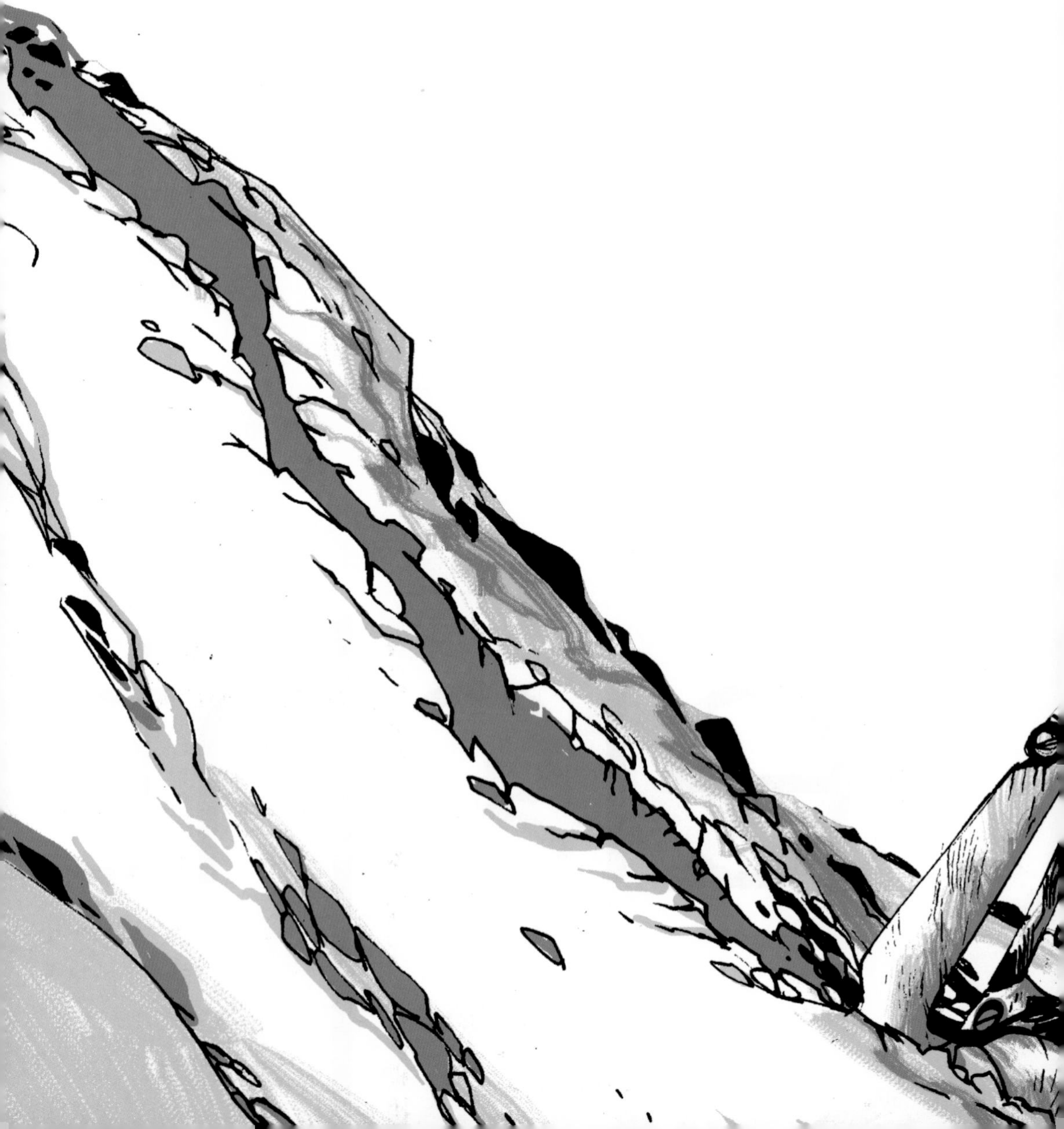

STORY AND ART **RAFAEL ALBUQUERQUE**
SCRIPT **MIKE JOHNSON**
LETTERS **NATE PIEKOS OF BLAMBOT®**

ei8ht™
OUTCAST

Dark Horse Books

PRESIDENT & PUBLISHER **MIKE RICHARDSON**

EDITOR **SIERRA HAHN**

ASSISTANT EDITOR **SPENCER CUSHING**

COLLECTION DESIGNER **BRENNAN THOME**

DIGITAL ART TECHNICIAN **ALLYSON HALLER**

NEIL HANKERSON Executive Vice President **TOM WEDDLE** Chief Financial Officer **RANDY STRADLEY** Vice President of Publishing **MICHAEL MARTENS** Vice President of Book Trade Sales **SCOTT ALLIE** Editor in Chief **MATT PARKINSON** Vice President of Marketing **DAVID SCROGGY** Vice President of Product Development **DALE LaFOUNTAIN** Vice President of Information Technology **DARLENE VOGEL** Senior Director of Print, Design, and Production **KEN LIZZI** General Counsel **DAVEY ESTRADA** Editorial Director **CHRIS WARNER** Senior Books Editor **DIANA SCHUTZ** Executive Editor **CARY GRAZZINI** Director of Print and Development **LIA RIBACCHI** Art Director **CARA NIECE** Director of Scheduling **MARK BERNARDI** Director of Digital Publishing

PUBLISHED BY DARK HORSE BOOKS
A DIVISION OF DARK HORSE COMICS, INC.
10956 SE MAIN STREET
MILWAUKIE, OR 97222

FIRST EDITION: OCTOBER 2015
ISBN 978-1-61655-637-2

1 2 3 4 5 6 7 8 9 10
PRINTED IN CHINA

INTERNATIONAL LICENSING: (503) 905-2377
COMIC SHOP LOCATOR SERVICE: (888) 266-4226

EI8HT VOLUME 1: OUTCAST

THIS VOLUME COLLECTS AND REPRINTS THE COMIC BOOK SERIES EI8HT #1–#5.

THE PAST IS **GREEN**

THE PRESENT IS **PURPLE**

THE FUTURE IS **BLUE**

THE MELD IS SOMETHING ELSE ENTIRELY

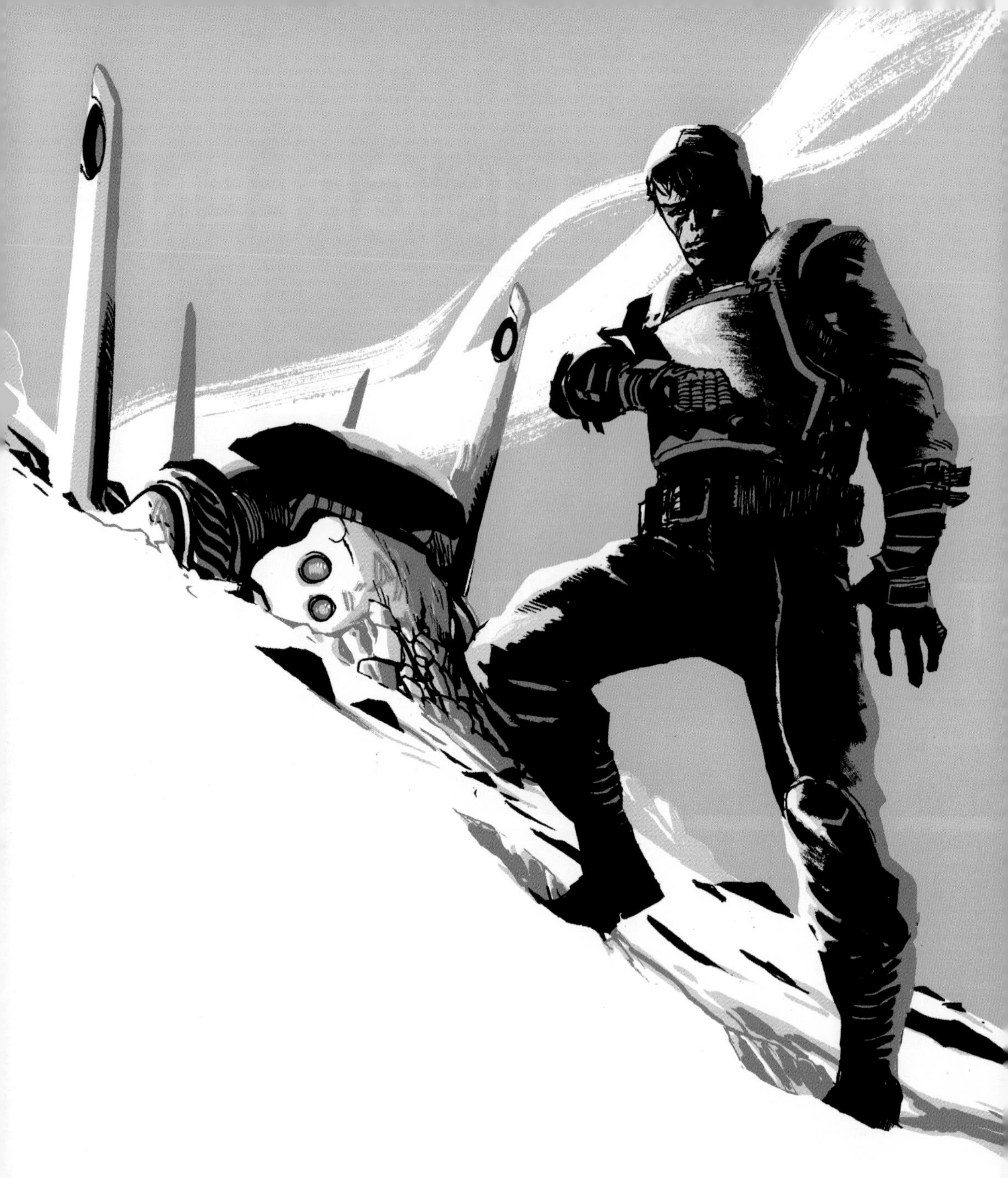

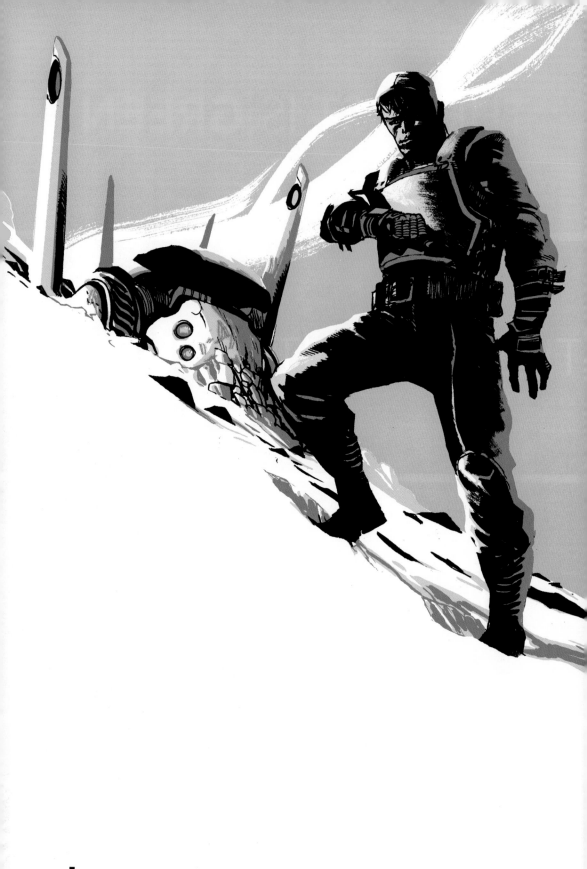

chapter 1

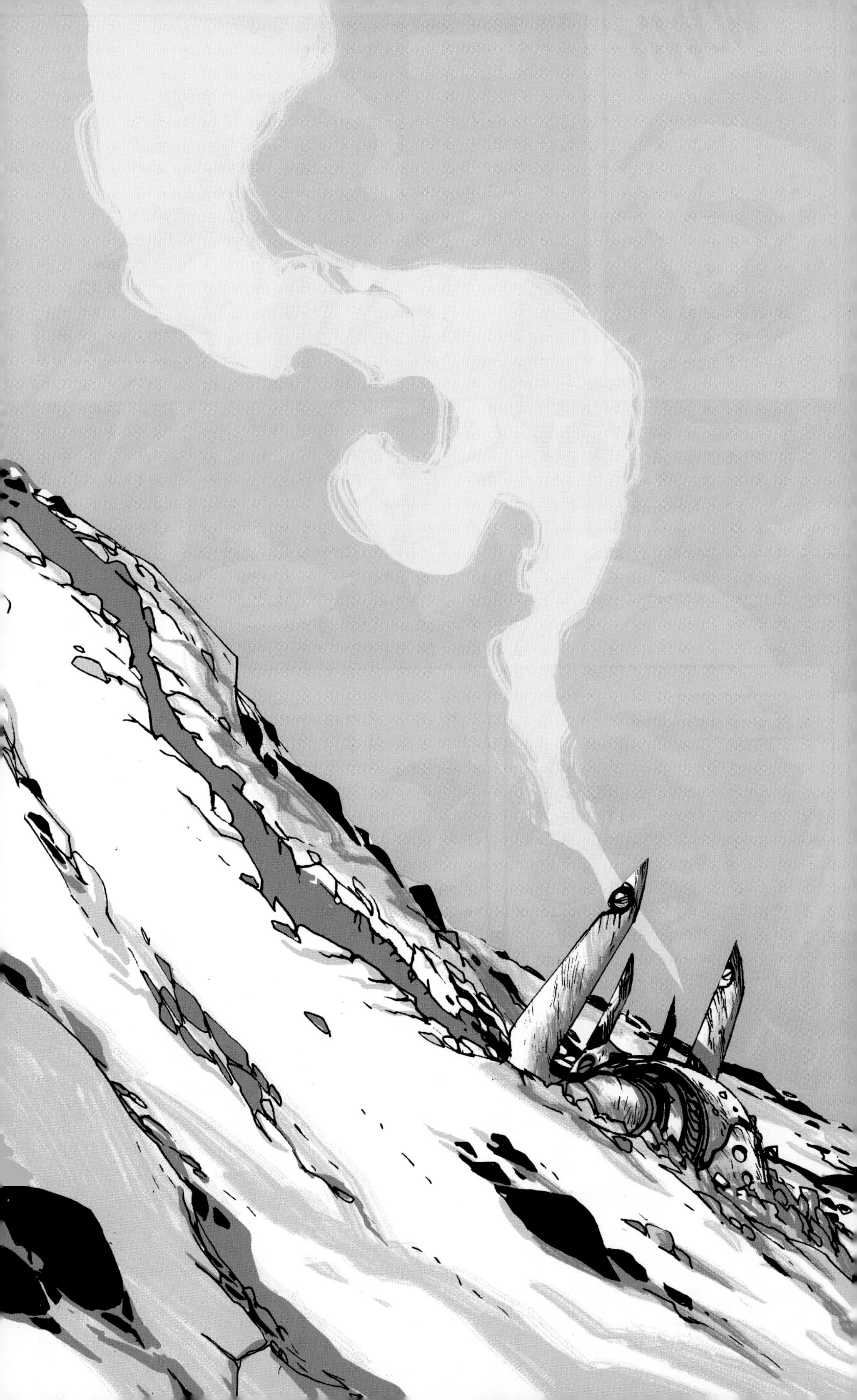

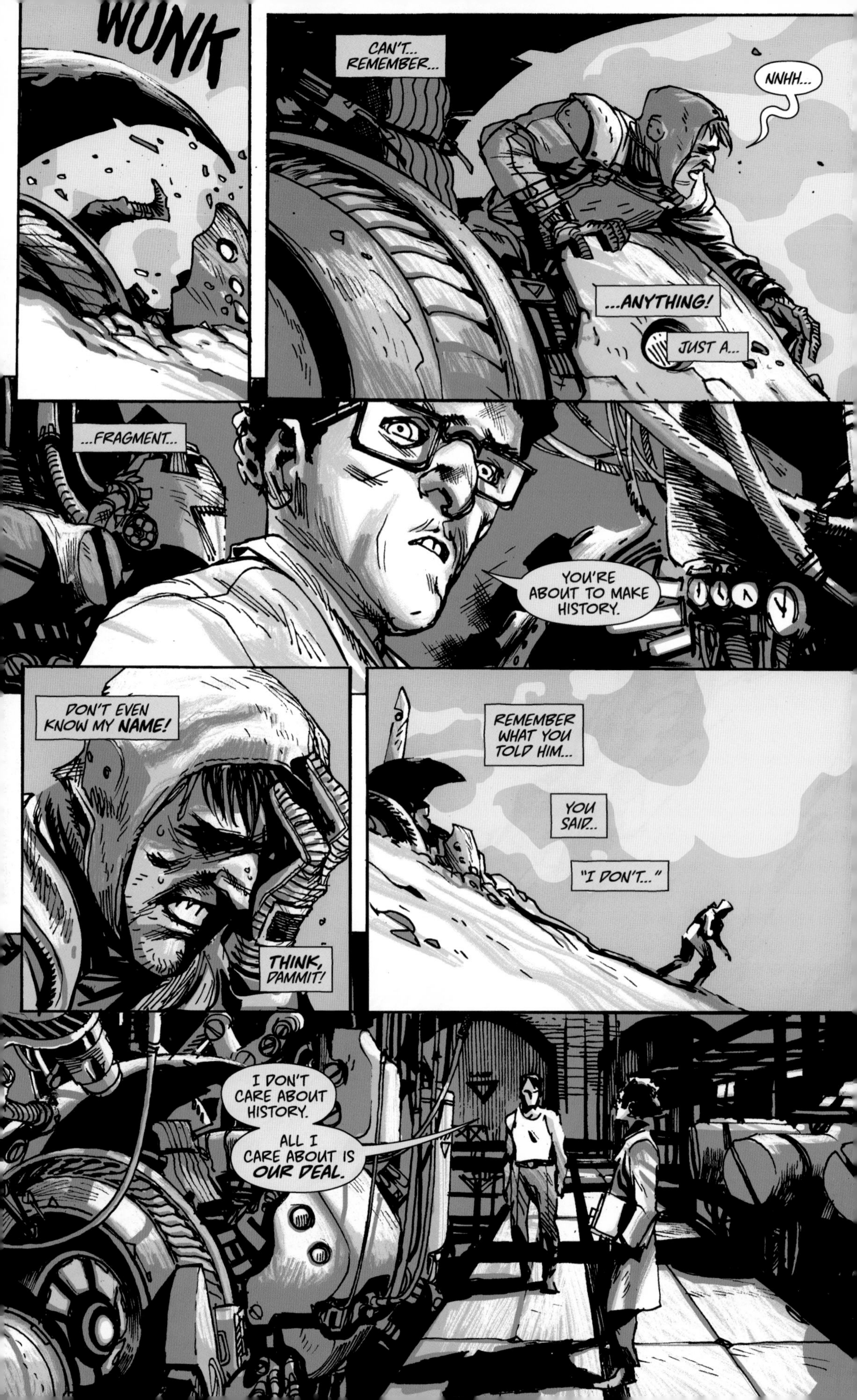
WUNK
CAN'T... REMEMBER...
NNHH...
...ANYTHING!
JUST A...
...FRAGMENT...
YOU'RE ABOUT TO MAKE HISTORY.
DON'T EVEN KNOW MY NAME!
THINK, DAMMIT!
REMEMBER WHAT YOU TOLD HIM...
YOU SAID...
"I DON'T..."
I DON'T CARE ABOUT HISTORY.
ALL I CARE ABOUT IS OUR DEAL.

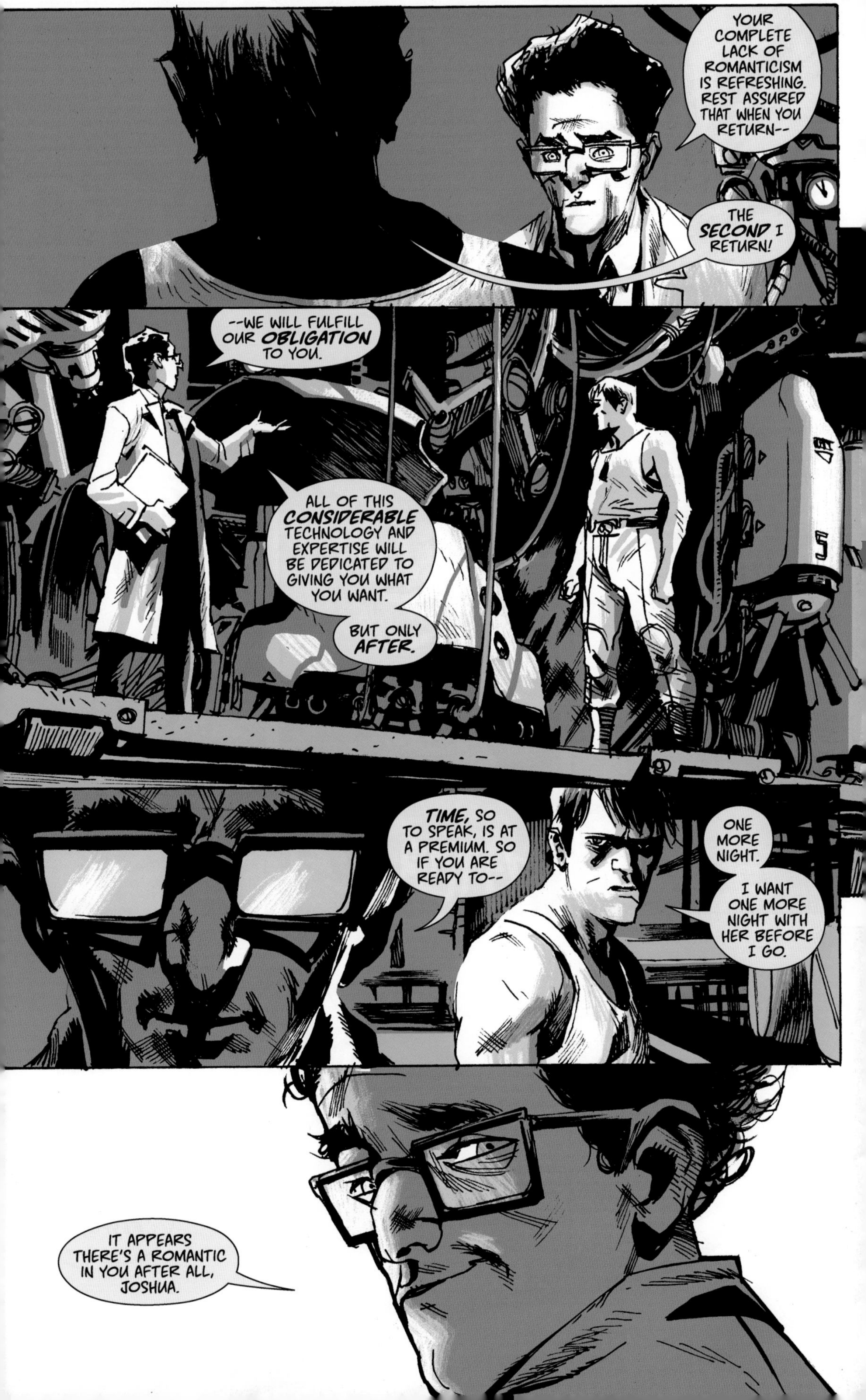
YOUR COMPLETE LACK OF ROMANTICISM IS REFRESHING. REST ASSURED THAT WHEN YOU RETURN--
THE SECOND I RETURN!
--WE WILL FULFILL OUR OBLIGATION TO YOU.
ALL OF THIS CONSIDERABLE TECHNOLOGY AND EXPERTISE WILL BE DEDICATED TO GIVING YOU WHAT YOU WANT.
BUT ONLY AFTER.
TIME, SO TO SPEAK, IS AT A PREMIUM. SO IF YOU ARE READY TO--
ONE MORE NIGHT.
I WANT ONE MORE NIGHT WITH HER BEFORE I GO.
IT APPEARS THERE'S A ROMANTIC IN YOU AFTER ALL, JOSHUA.

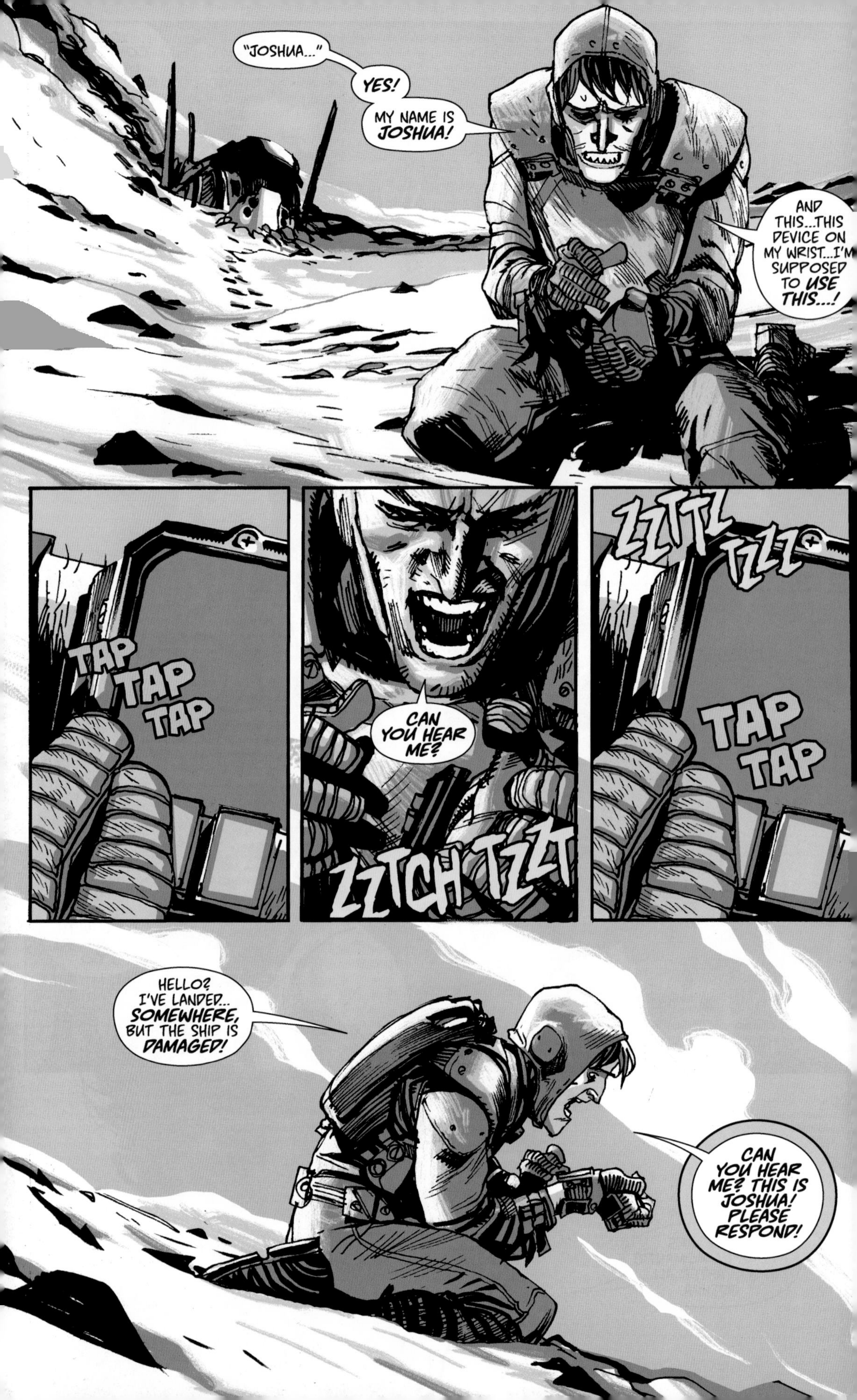
"JOSHUA..."
YES!
MY NAME IS JOSHUA!
AND THIS...THIS DEVICE ON MY WRIST...I'M SUPPOSED TO USE THIS...!
TAP TAP TAP
CAN YOU HEAR ME?
ZZTCH TZZT
ZZTTZ TZZZ
TAP TAP
HELLO? I'VE LANDED... SOMEWHERE, BUT THE SHIP IS DAMAGED!
CAN YOU HEAR ME? THIS IS JOSHUA! PLEASE RESPOND!

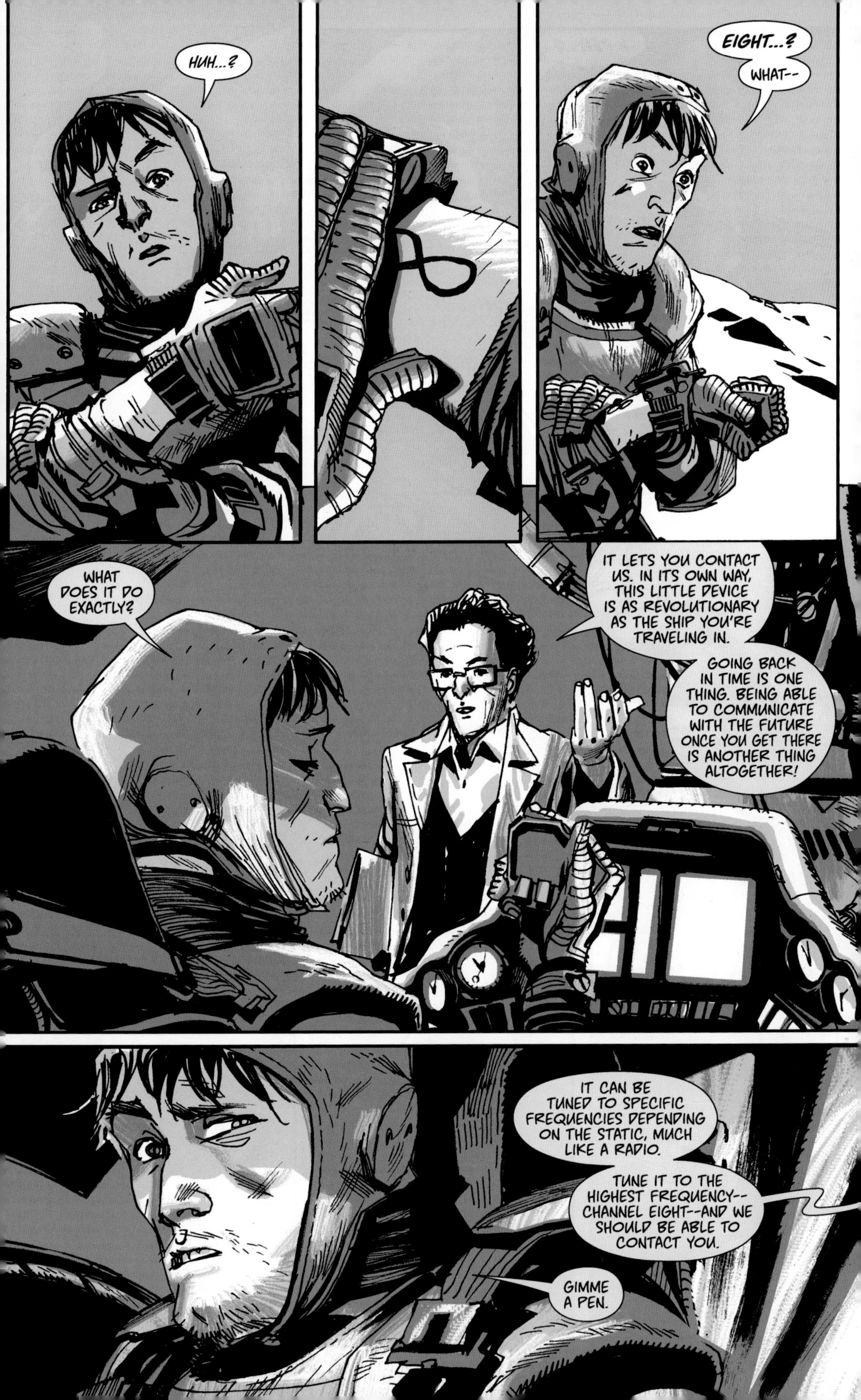
HUH...?
EIGHT...?
WHAT--
WHAT DOES IT DO EXACTLY?
IT LETS YOU CONTACT US. IN ITS OWN WAY, THIS LITTLE DEVICE IS AS REVOLUTIONARY AS THE SHIP YOU'RE TRAVELING IN.
GOING BACK IN TIME IS ONE THING. BEING ABLE TO COMMUNICATE WITH THE FUTURE ONCE YOU GET THERE IS ANOTHER THING ALTOGETHER!
IT CAN BE TUNED TO SPECIFIC FREQUENCIES DEPENDING ON THE STATIC, MUCH LIKE A RADIO.
TUNE IT TO THE HIGHEST FREQUENCY--CHANNEL EIGHT--AND WE SHOULD BE ABLE TO CONTACT YOU.
GIMME A PEN.

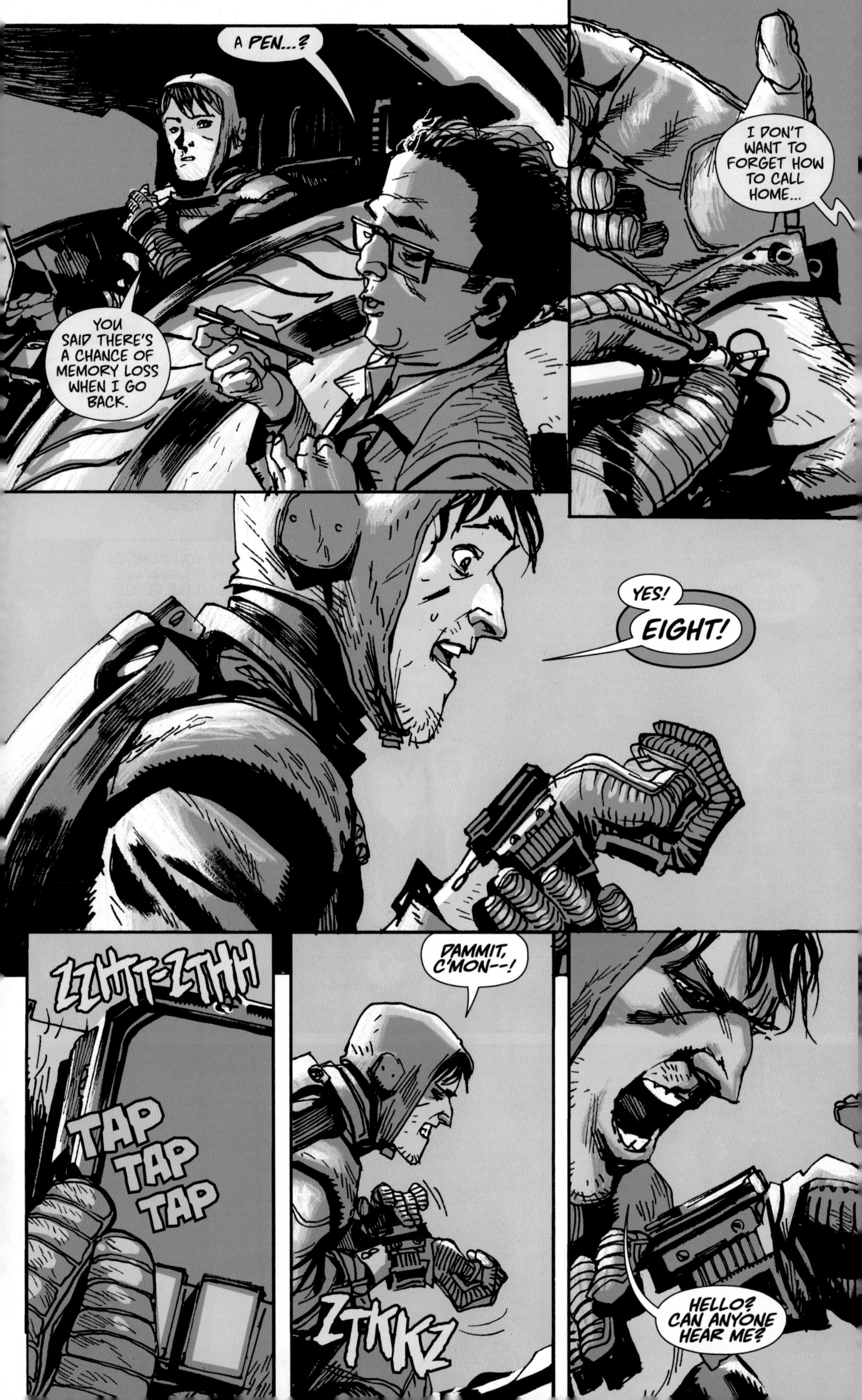
A PEN...?
YOU SAID THERE'S A CHANCE OF MEMORY LOSS WHEN I GO BACK.
I DON'T WANT TO FORGET HOW TO CALL HOME...
YES!
EIGHT!
ZZHTT-ZTHH
TAP TAP TAP
DAMMIT, C'MON--!
ZTKKZ
HELLO? CAN ANYONE HEAR ME?

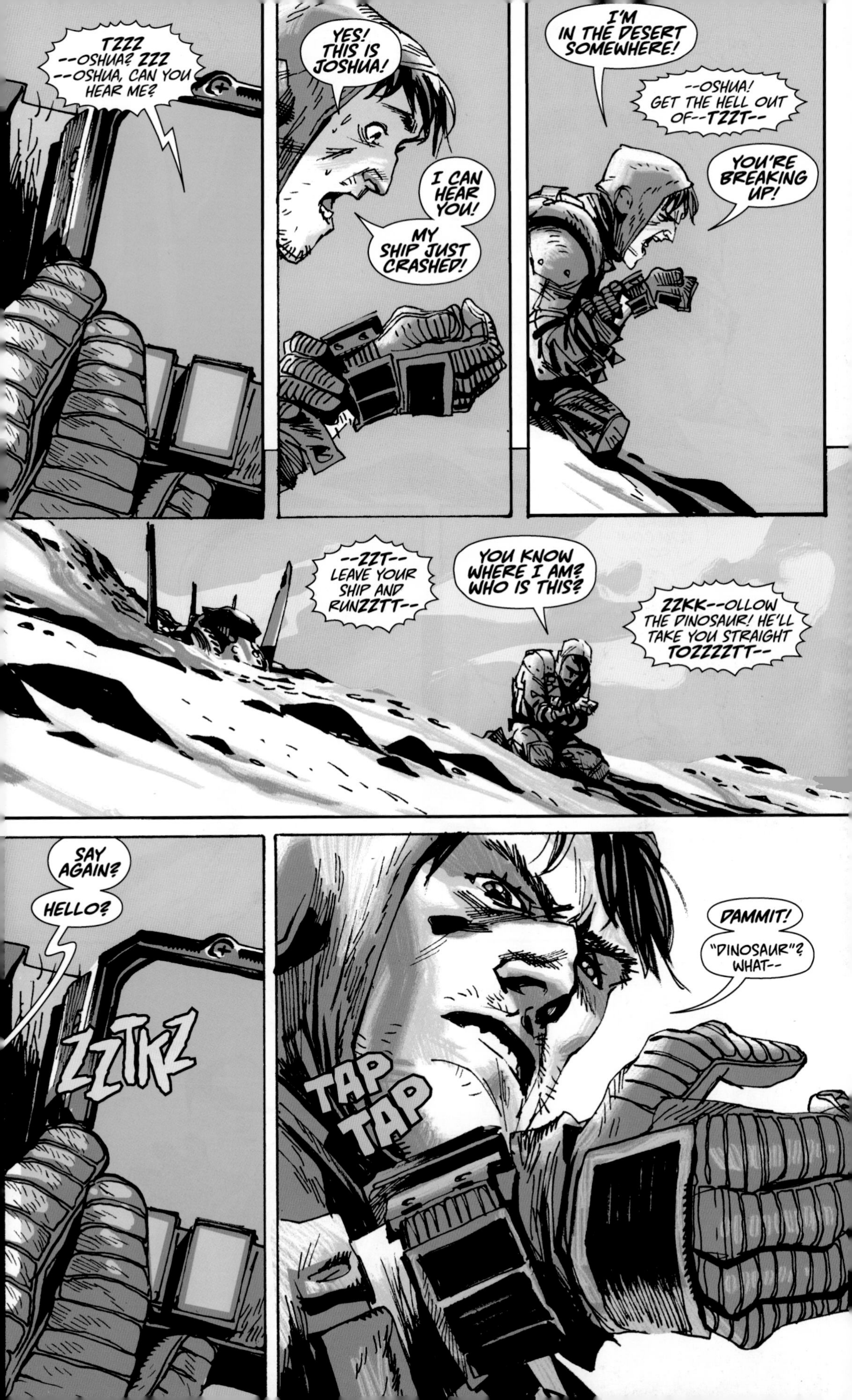
TZZZ --OSHUA? ZZZ --OSHUA, CAN YOU HEAR ME?
YES! THIS IS JOSHUA!
I CAN HEAR YOU!
MY SHIP JUST CRASHED!
I'M IN THE DESERT SOMEWHERE!
--OSHUA! GET THE HELL OUT OF--TZZT--
YOU'RE BREAKING UP!
--ZZT-- LEAVE YOUR SHIP AND RUNZZZTT--
YOU KNOW WHERE I AM? WHO IS THIS?
ZZKK--OLLOW THE DINOSAUR! HE'LL TAKE YOU STRAIGHT TOZZZZZTT--
SAY AGAIN?
HELLO?
ZZTKZ
DAMMIT!
"DINOSAUR"? WHAT--
TAP TAP

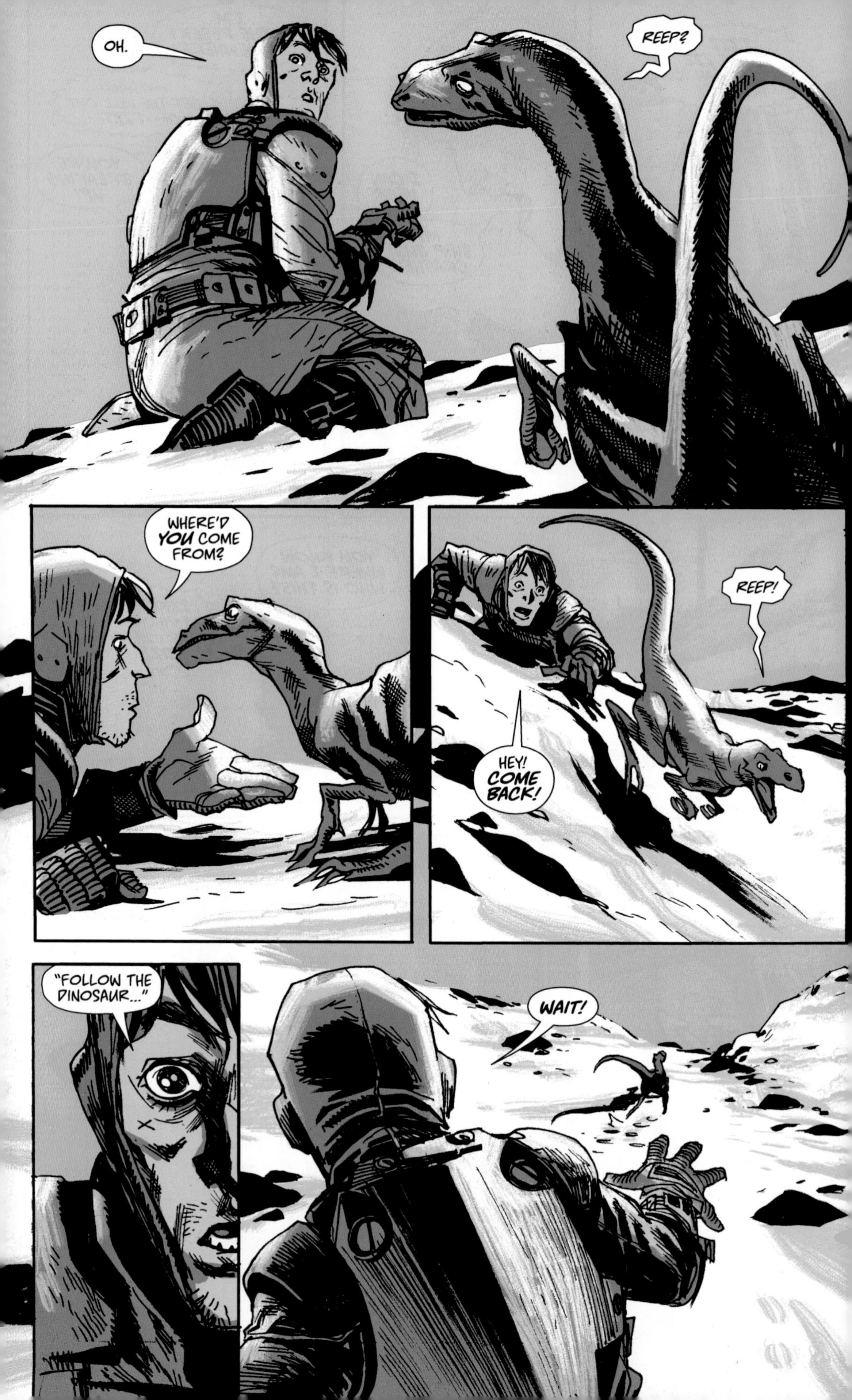
OH.
REEP?
WHERE'D YOU COME FROM?
REEP!
HEY! COME BACK!
"FOLLOW THE DINOSAUR..."
WAIT!

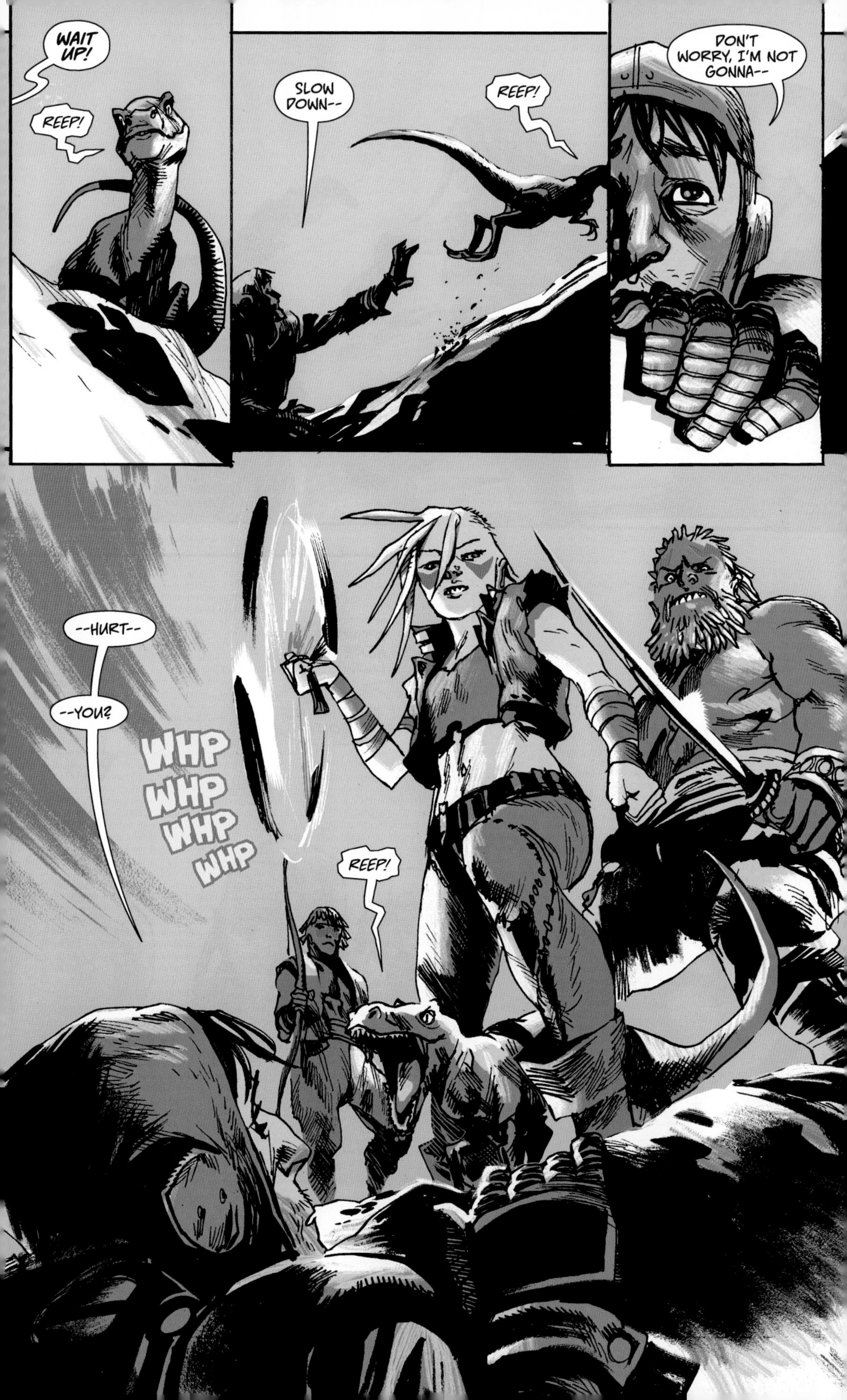
WAIT UP!
REEP!
SLOW DOWN--
REEP!
DON'T WORRY, I'M NOT GONNA--
--HURT--
--YOU?
WHP WHP WHP WHP
REEP!

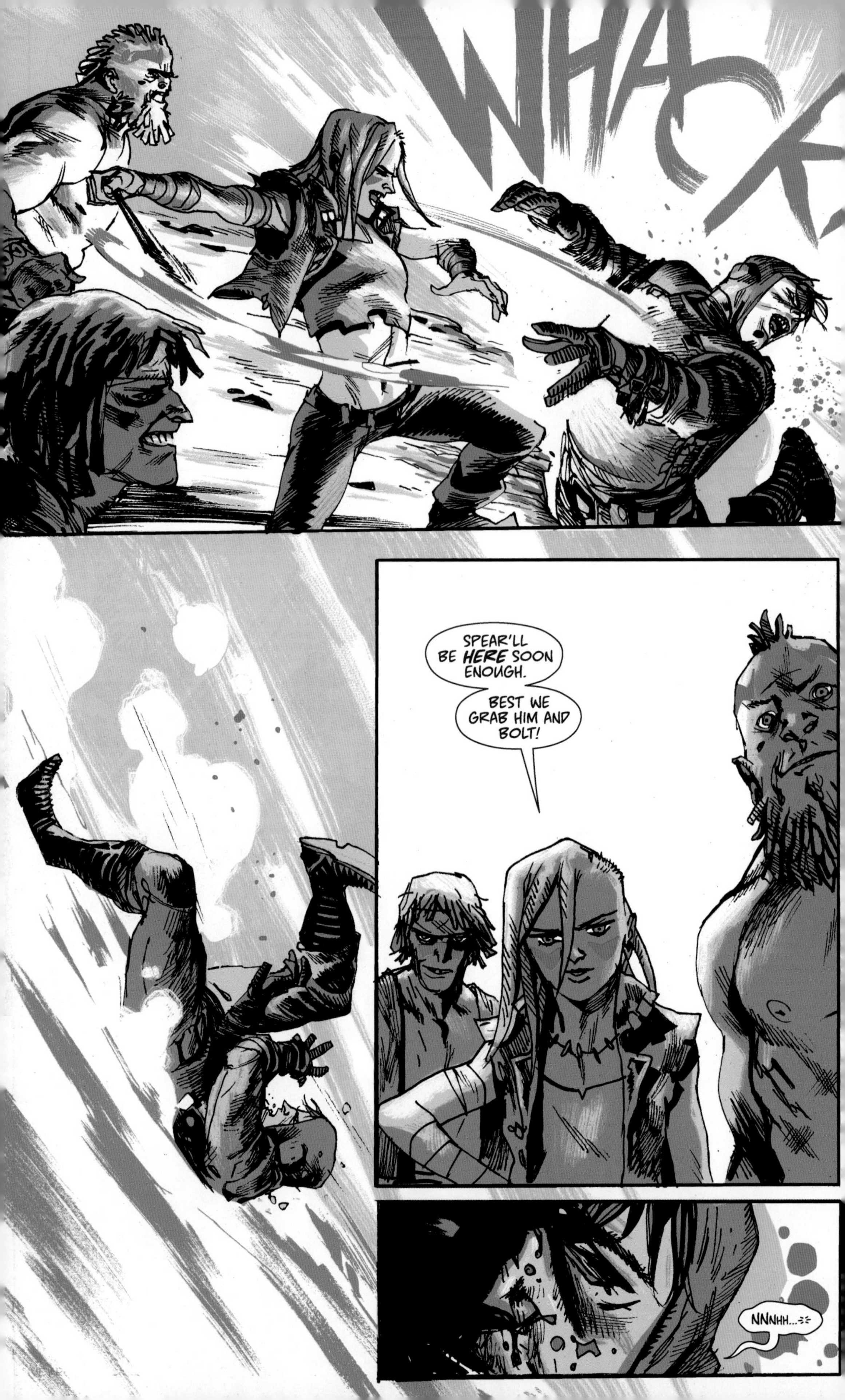
WHACK!
SPEAR'LL BE HERE SOON ENOUGH.
BEST WE GRAB HIM AND BOLT!
NNNHH...

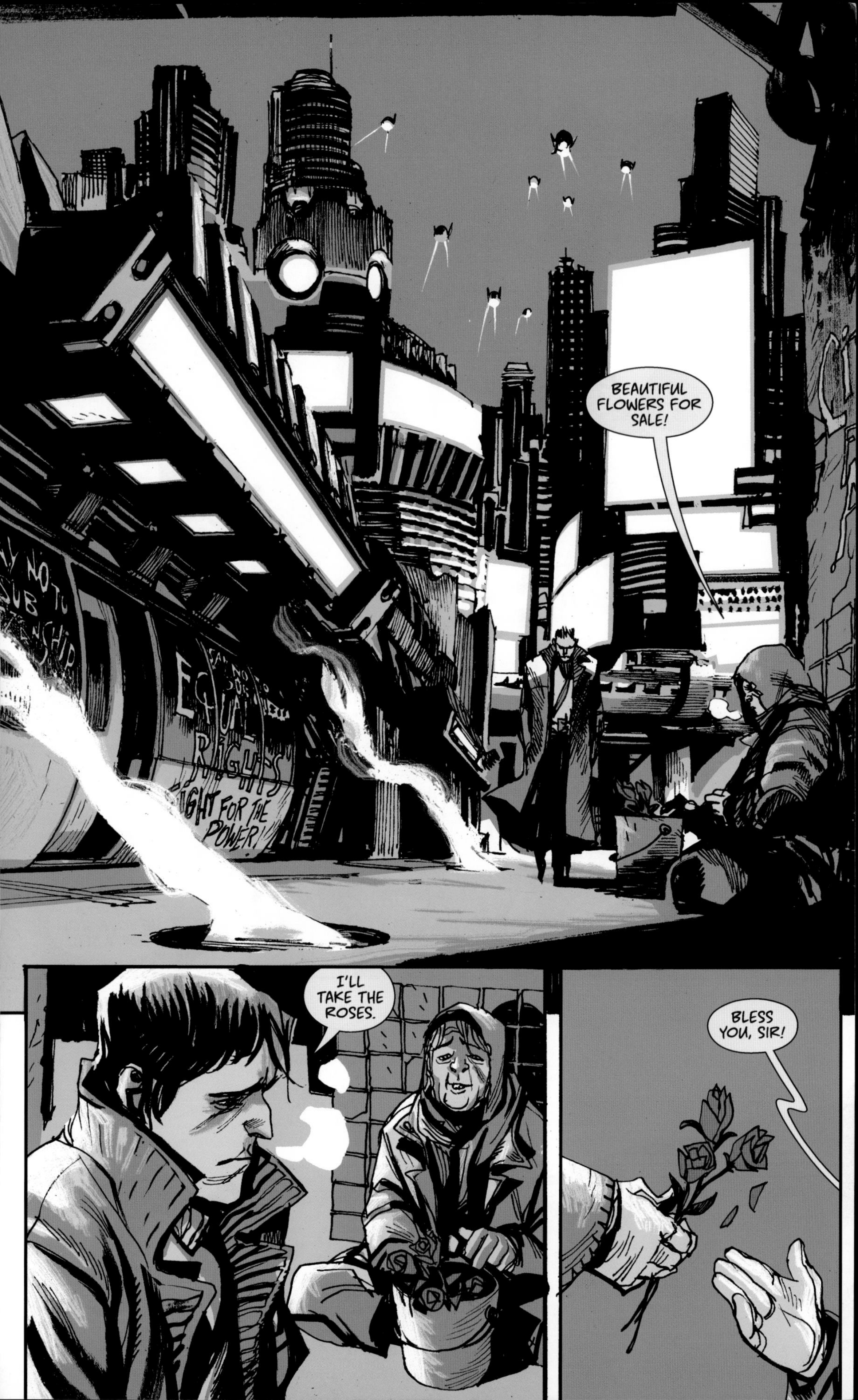
BEAUTIFUL FLOWERS FOR SALE!
EQUAL RIGHTS
I'LL TAKE THE ROSES.
BLESS YOU, SIR!

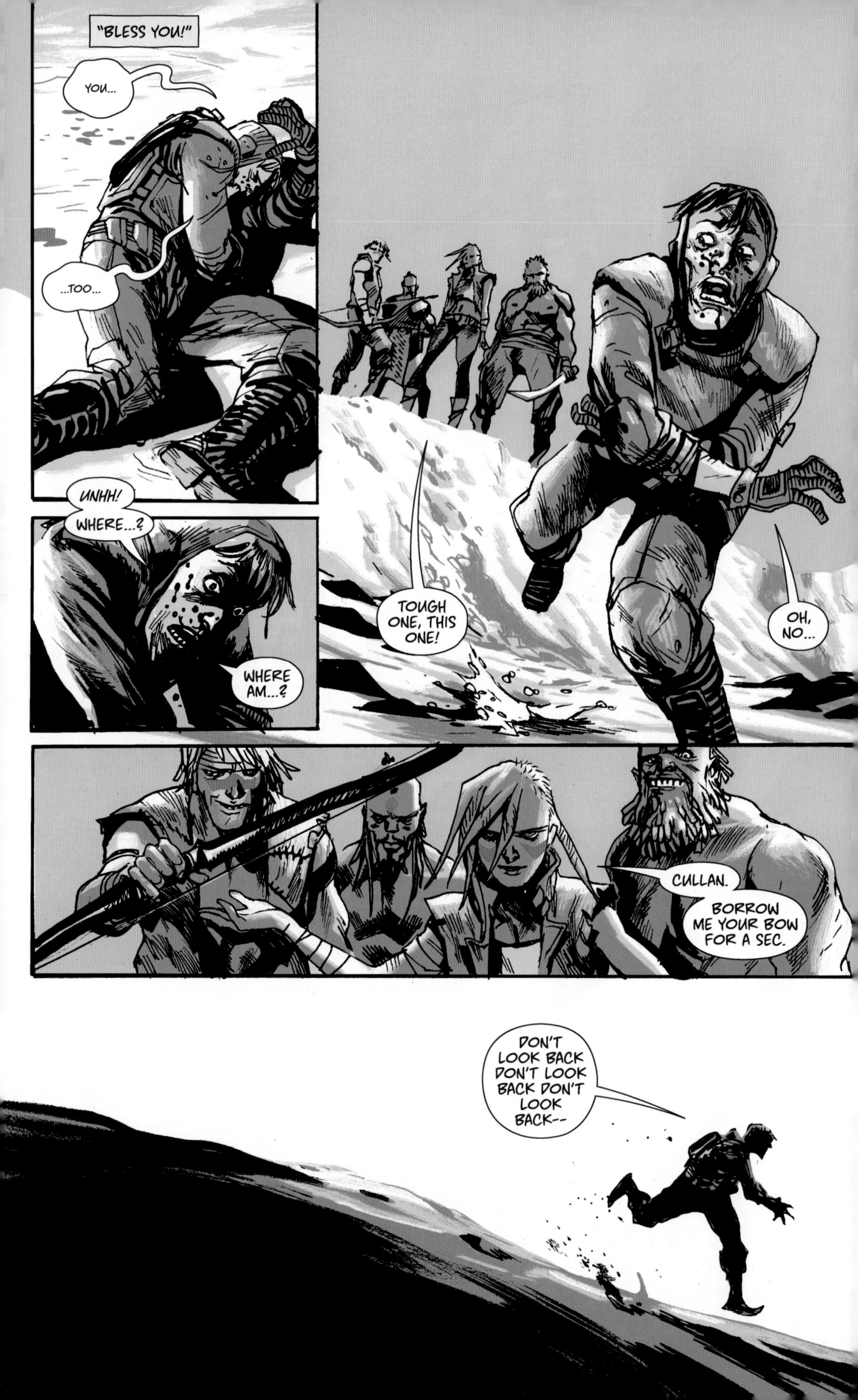
"BLESS YOU!"
YOU...
...TOO...
UNHH!
WHERE...?
WHERE AM...?
TOUGH ONE, THIS ONE!
OH, NO...
CULLAN.
BORROW ME YOUR BOW FOR A SEC.
DON'T LOOK BACK DON'T LOOK BACK DON'T LOOK BACK--

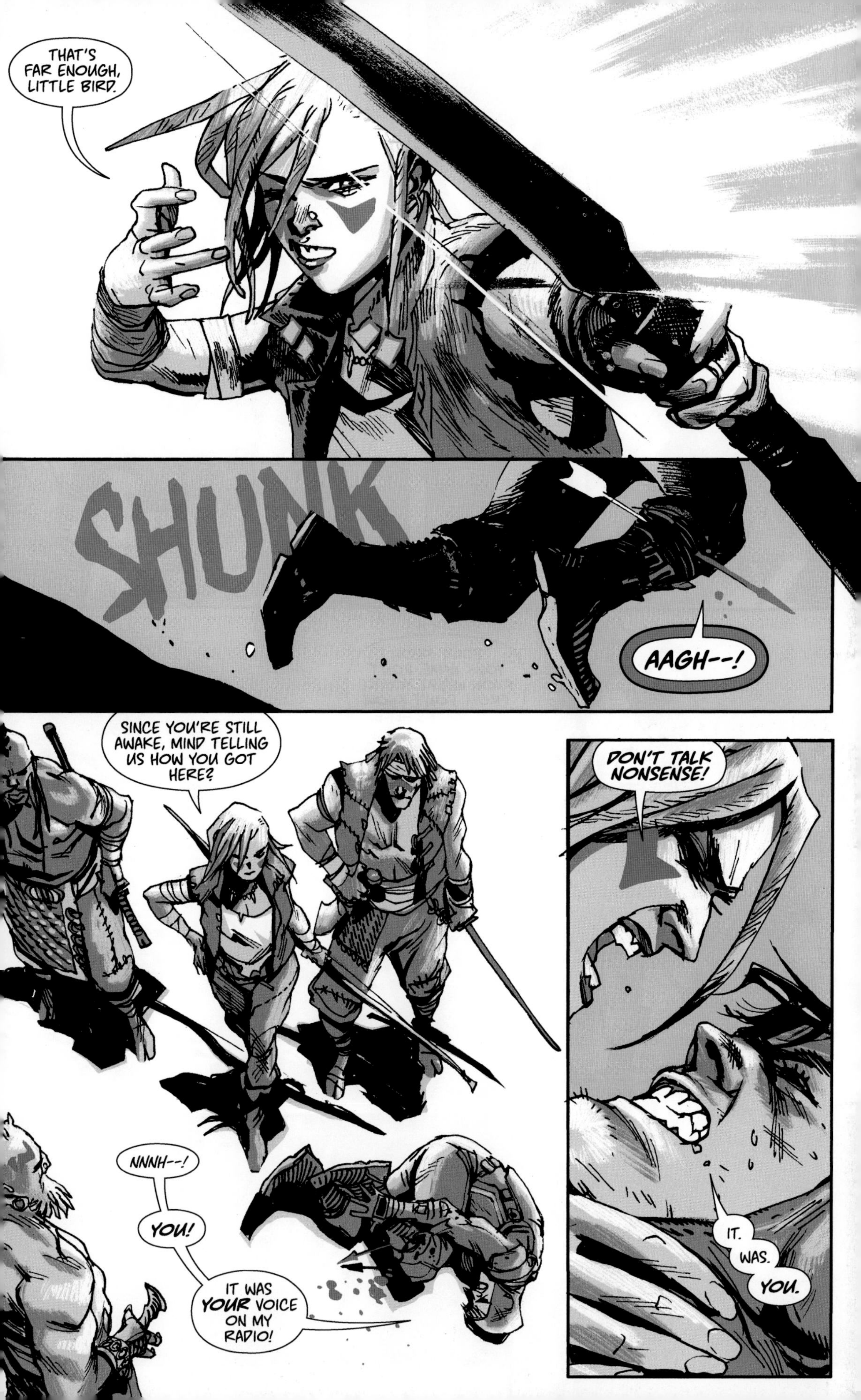
THAT'S FAR ENOUGH, LITTLE BIRD.
SHUNK
AAGH--!
SINCE YOU'RE STILL AWAKE, MIND TELLING US HOW YOU GOT HERE?
NNNH--!
YOU!
IT WAS YOUR VOICE ON MY RADIO!
DON'T TALK NONSENSE!
IT.
WAS.
YOU.

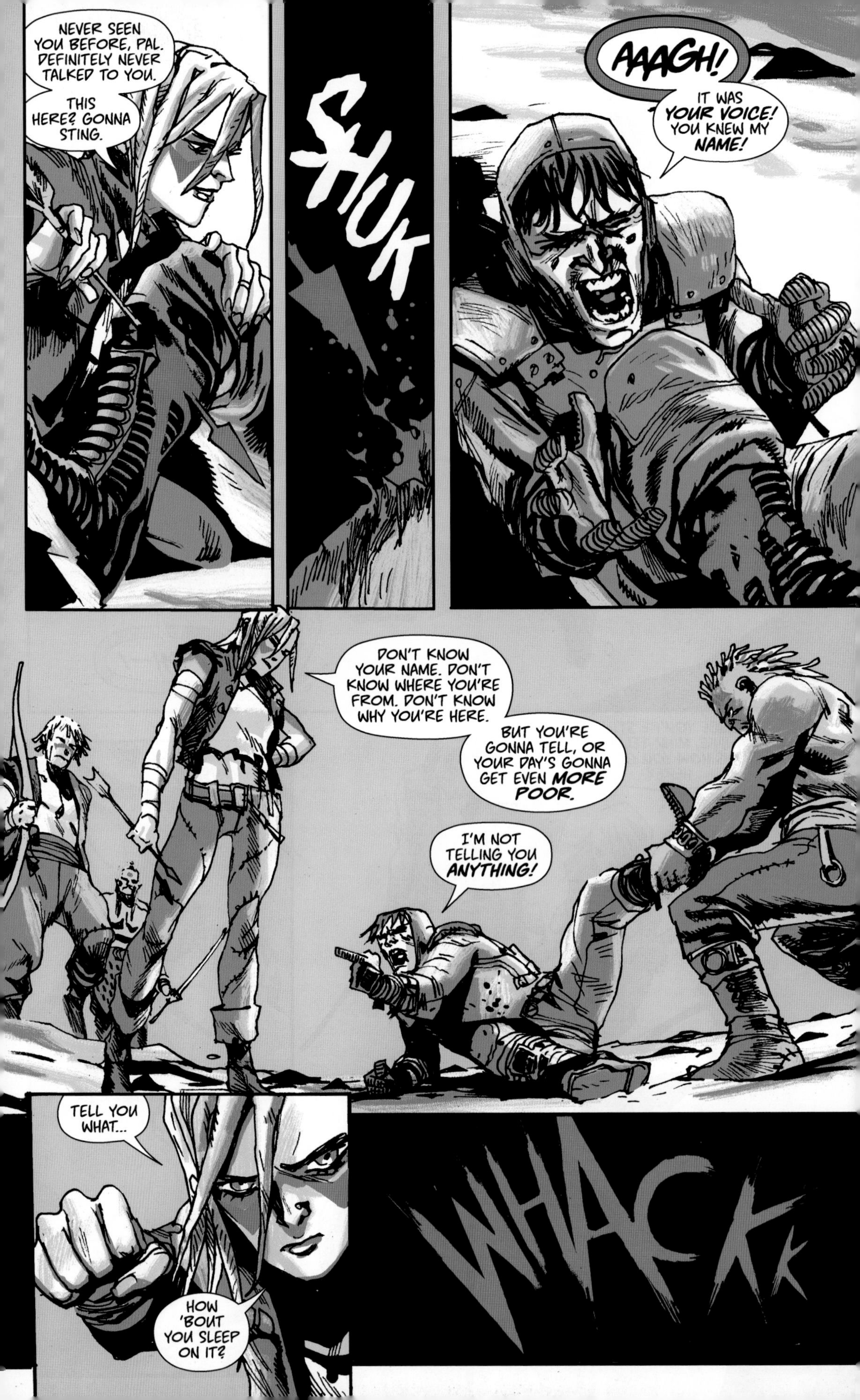
NEVER SEEN YOU BEFORE, PAL. DEFINITELY NEVER TALKED TO YOU.
THIS HERE? GONNA STING.
SHUK
AAAGH!
IT WAS YOUR VOICE! YOU KNEW MY NAME!
DON'T KNOW YOUR NAME. DON'T KNOW WHERE YOU'RE FROM. DON'T KNOW WHY YOU'RE HERE.
BUT YOU'RE GONNA TELL, OR YOUR DAY'S GONNA GET EVEN MORE POOR.
I'M NOT TELLING YOU ANYTHING!
TELL YOU WHAT...
HOW 'BOUT YOU SLEEP ON IT?
WHACK

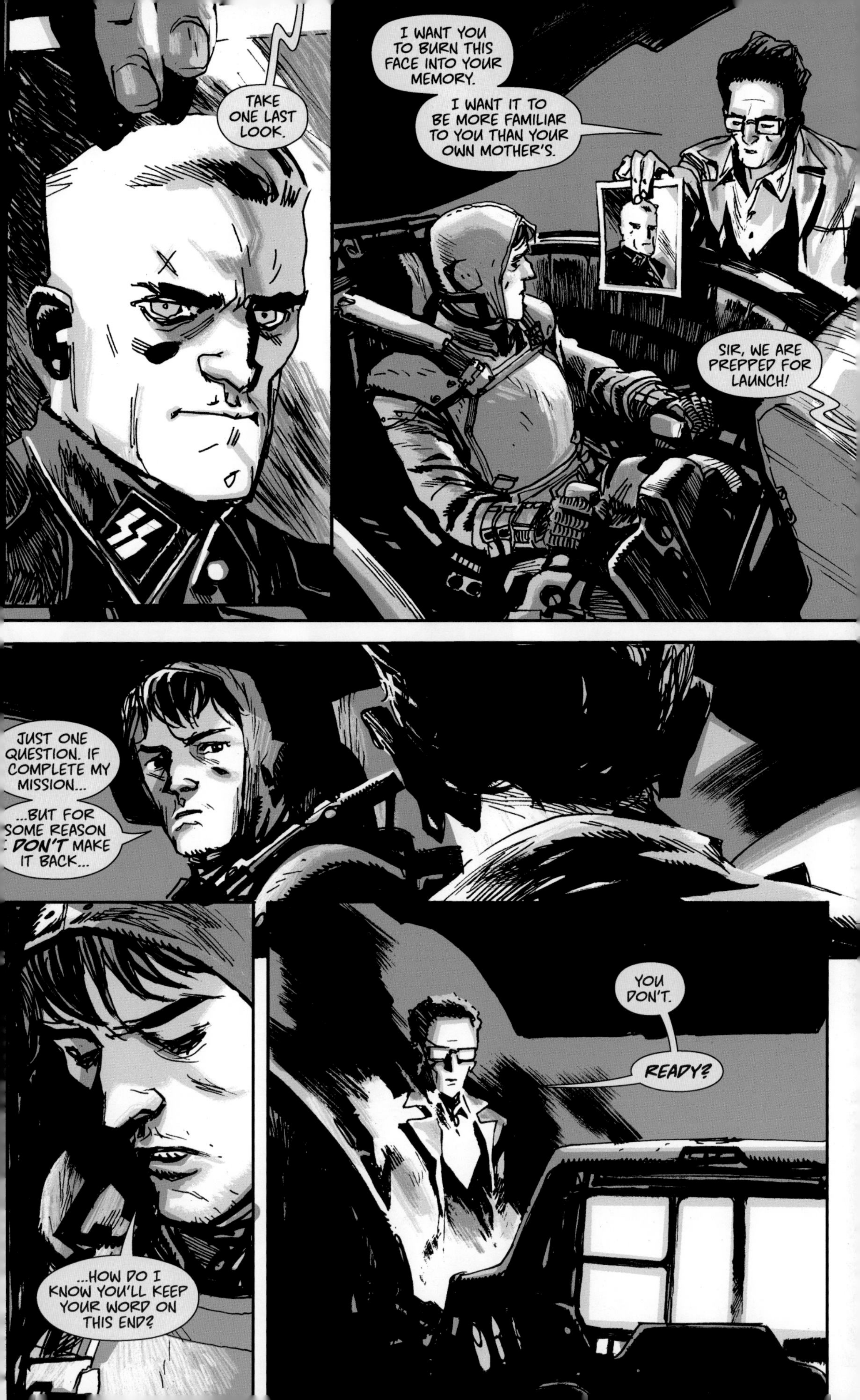
TAKE ONE LAST LOOK.
I WANT YOU TO BURN THIS FACE INTO YOUR MEMORY.
I WANT IT TO BE MORE FAMILIAR TO YOU THAN YOUR OWN MOTHER'S.
SIR, WE ARE PREPPED FOR LAUNCH!
JUST ONE QUESTION. IF COMPLETE MY MISSION...
...BUT FOR SOME REASON DON'T MAKE IT BACK...
...HOW DO I KNOW YOU'LL KEEP YOUR WORD ON THIS END?
YOU DON'T.
READY?

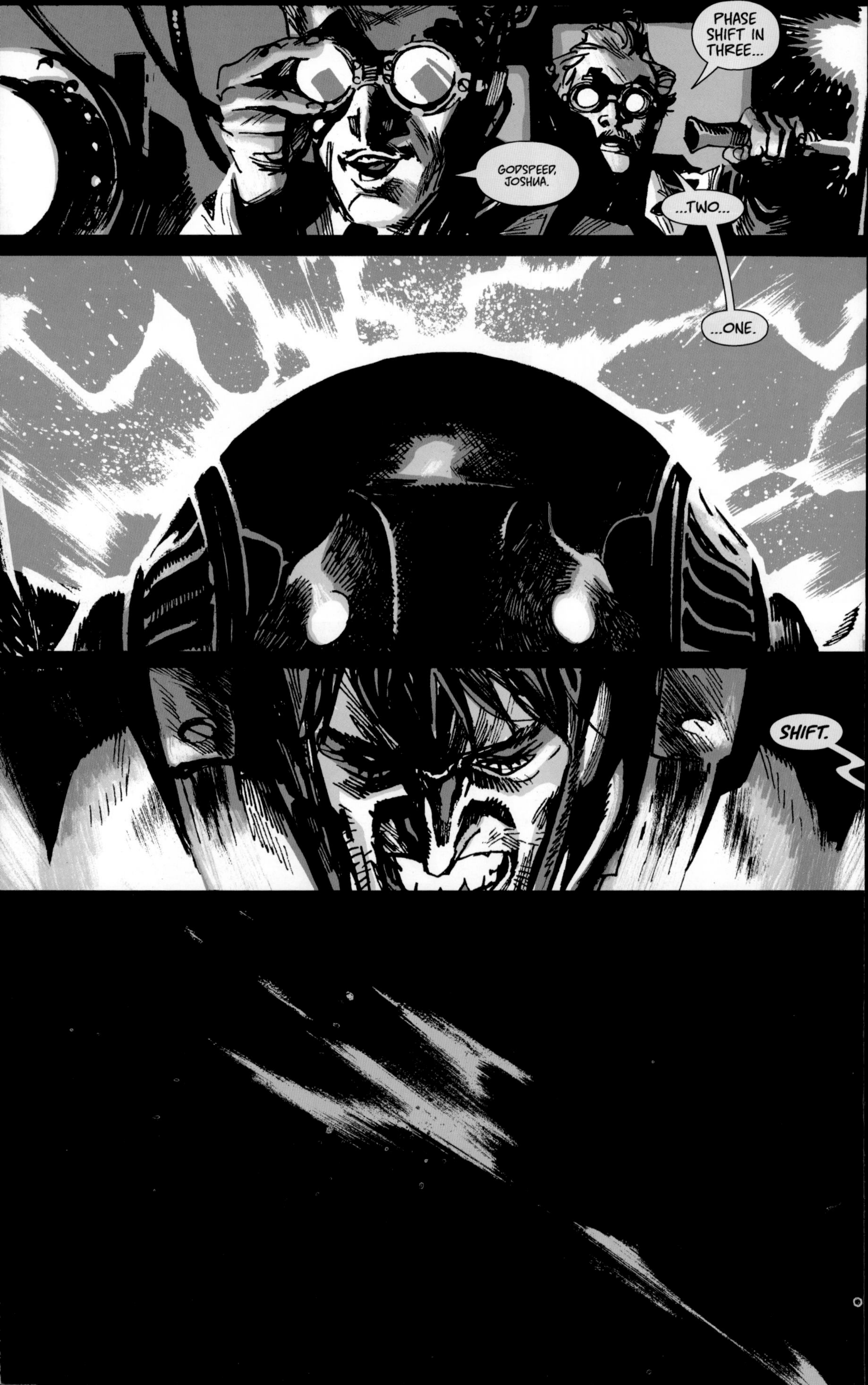
PHASE SHIFT IN THREE...
GODSPEED, JOSHUA.
...TWO...
...ONE.
SHIFT.

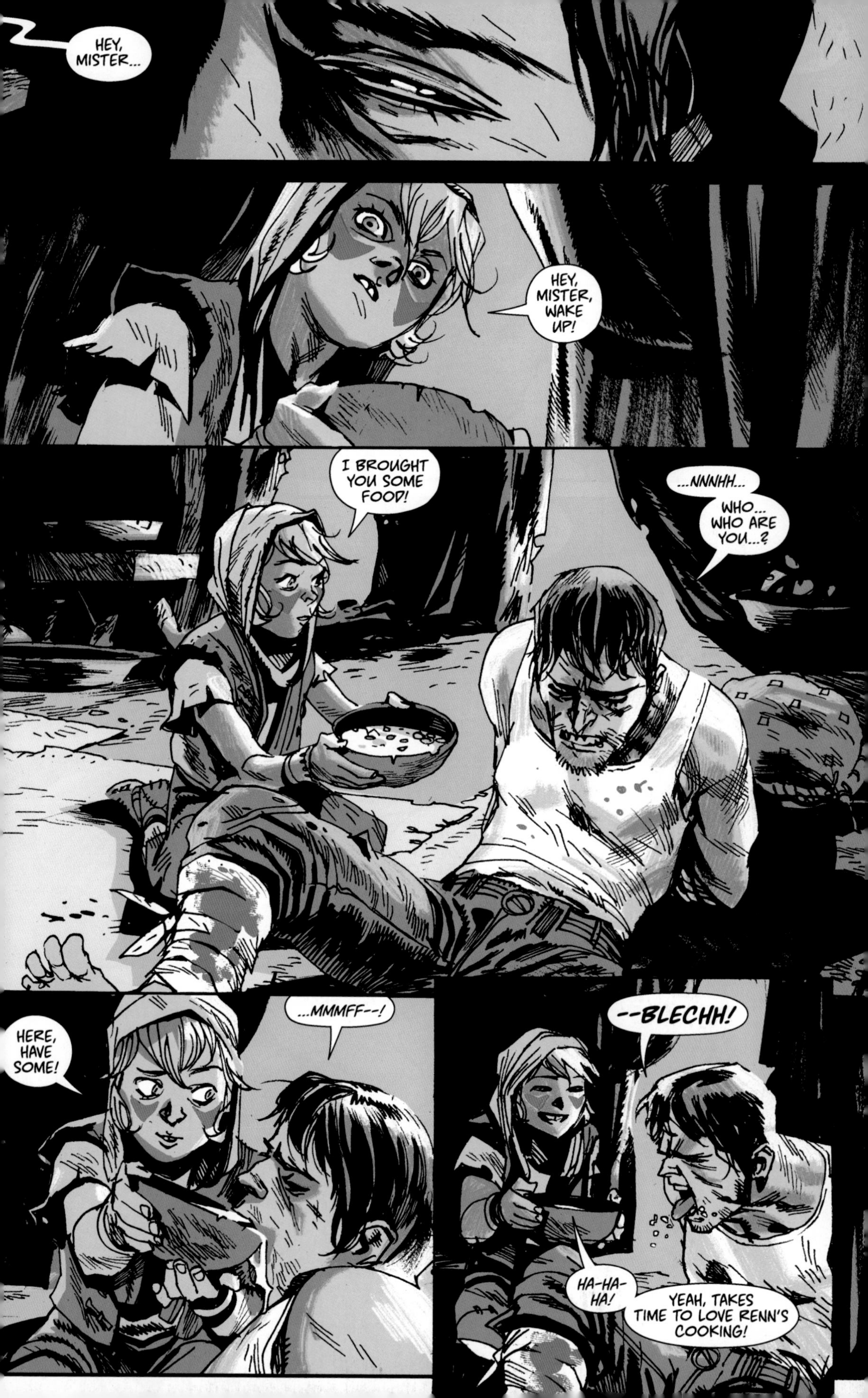
HEY, MISTER...
HEY, MISTER, WAKE UP!
I BROUGHT YOU SOME FOOD!
...NNNHH...
WHO... WHO ARE YOU...?
HERE, HAVE SOME!
...MMMFF--!
--BLECHH!
HA-HA-HA!
YEAH, TAKES TIME TO LOVE RENN'S COOKING!

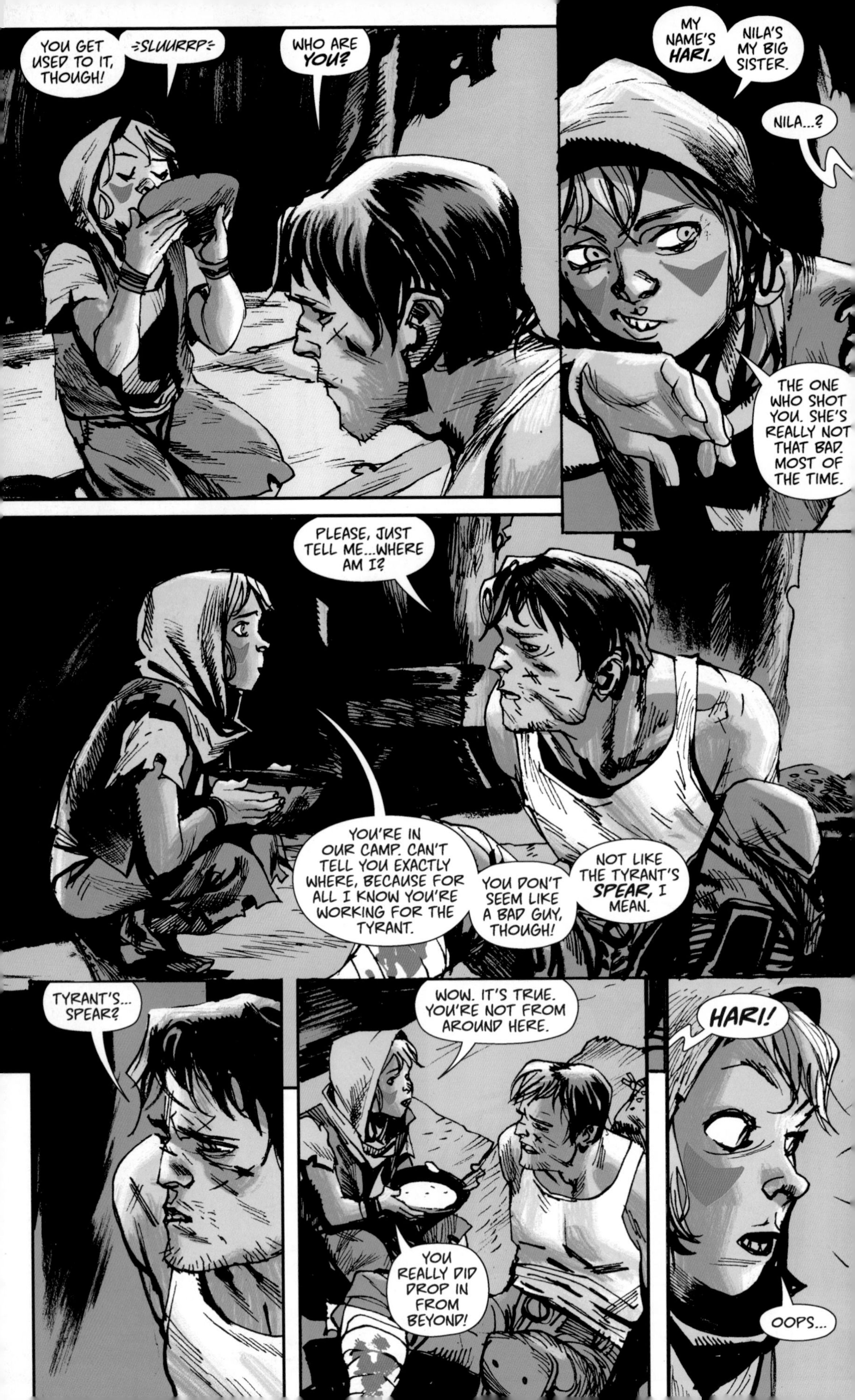
YOU GET USED TO IT, THOUGH!
SLUURRP
WHO ARE YOU?
MY NAME'S HARI.
NILA'S MY BIG SISTER.
NILA...?
THE ONE WHO SHOT YOU. SHE'S REALLY NOT THAT BAD. MOST OF THE TIME.
PLEASE, JUST TELL ME...WHERE AM I?
YOU'RE IN OUR CAMP. CAN'T TELL YOU EXACTLY WHERE, BECAUSE FOR ALL I KNOW YOU'RE WORKING FOR THE TYRANT.
YOU DON'T SEEM LIKE A BAD GUY, THOUGH!
NOT LIKE THE TYRANT'S SPEAR, I MEAN.
TYRANT'S... SPEAR?
WOW. IT'S TRUE. YOU'RE NOT FROM AROUND HERE.
YOU REALLY DID DROP IN FROM BEYOND!
HARI!
OOPS...

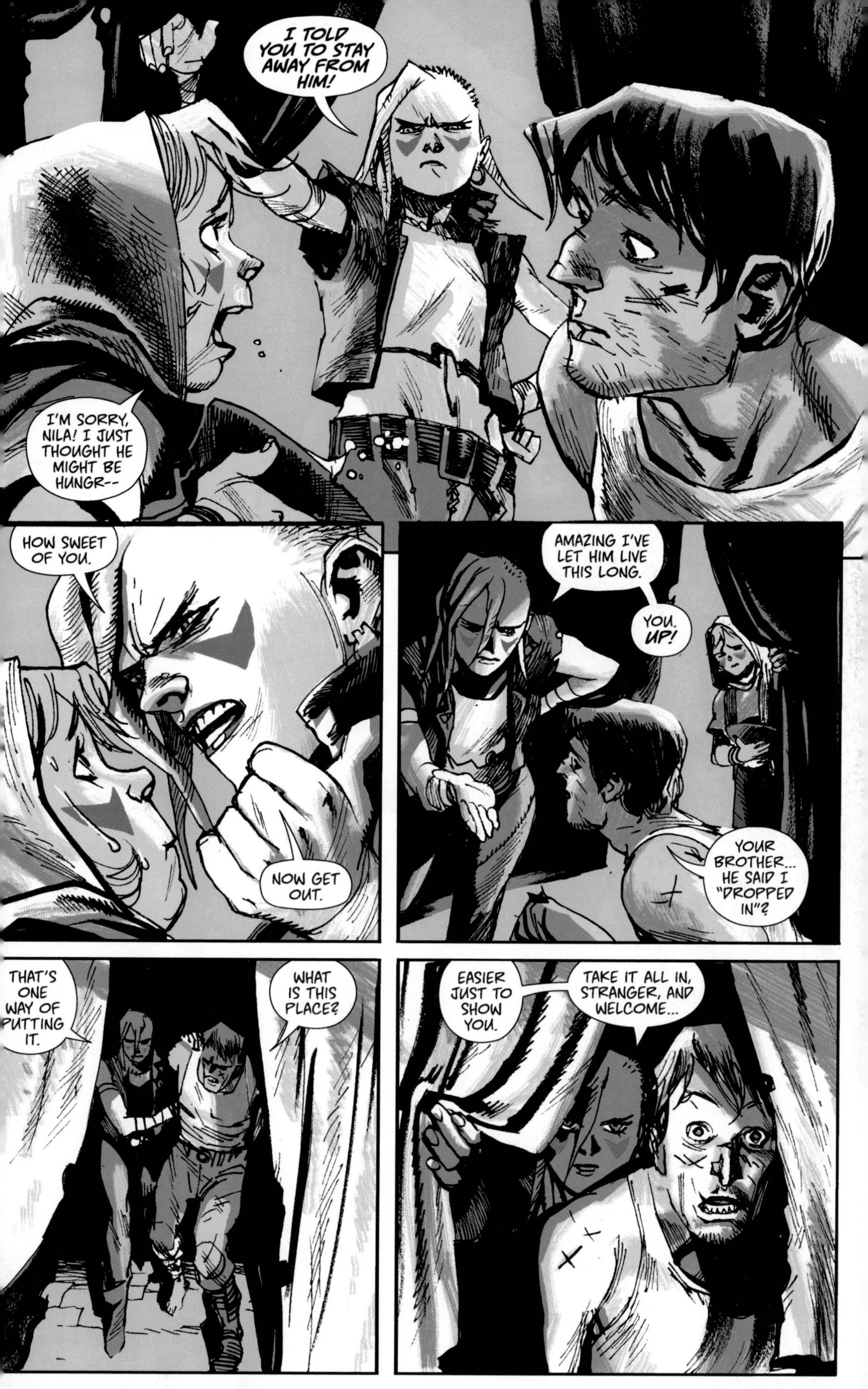
I TOLD YOU TO STAY AWAY FROM HIM!
I'M SORRY, NILA! I JUST THOUGHT HE MIGHT BE HUNGR--
HOW SWEET OF YOU.
NOW GET OUT.
AMAZING I'VE LET HIM LIVE THIS LONG.
YOU. UP!
YOUR BROTHER... HE SAID I "DROPPED IN"?
THAT'S ONE WAY OF PUTTING IT.
WHAT IS THIS PLACE?
EASIER JUST TO SHOW YOU.
TAKE IT ALL IN, STRANGER, AND WELCOME...

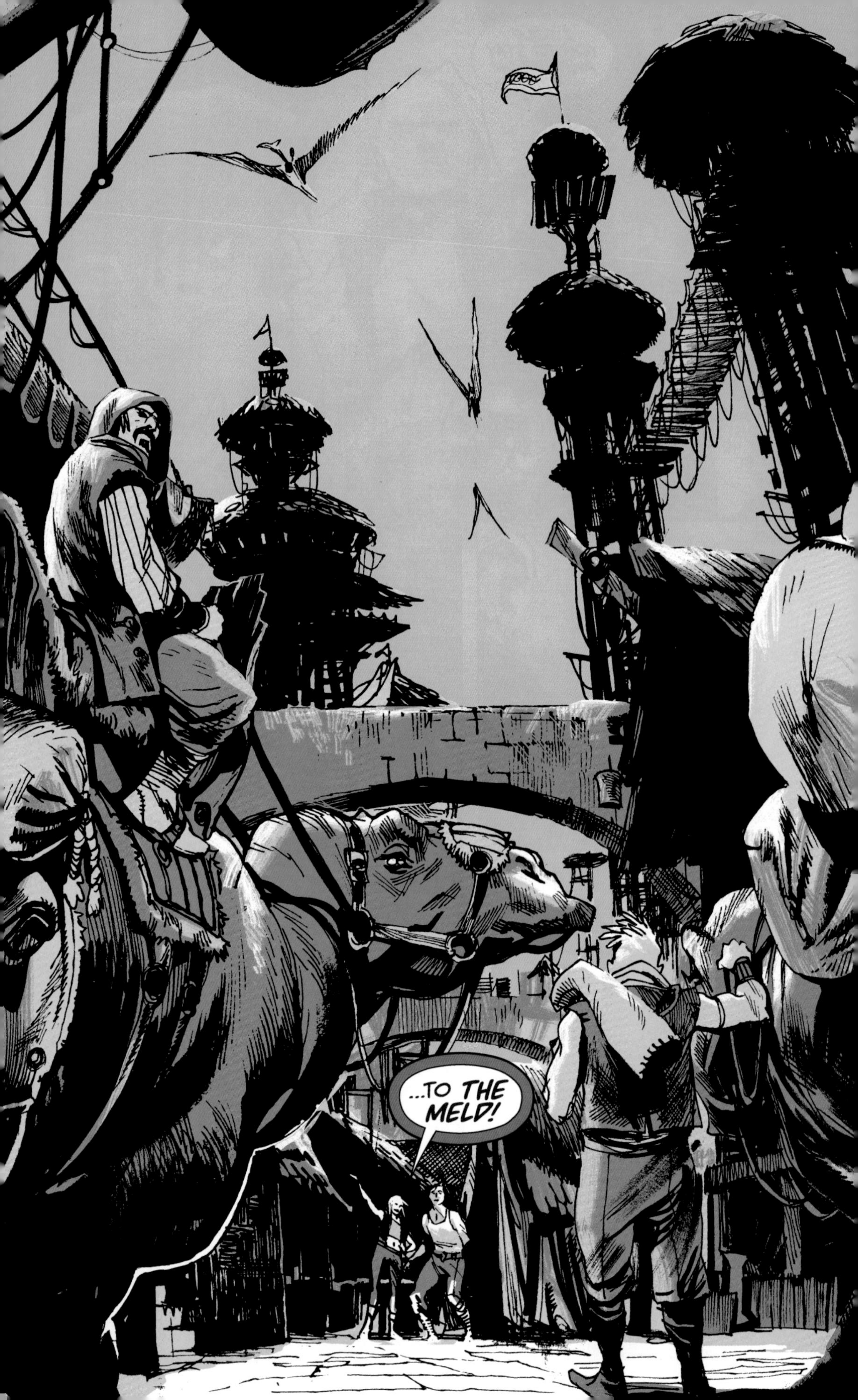
...TO THE MELD!

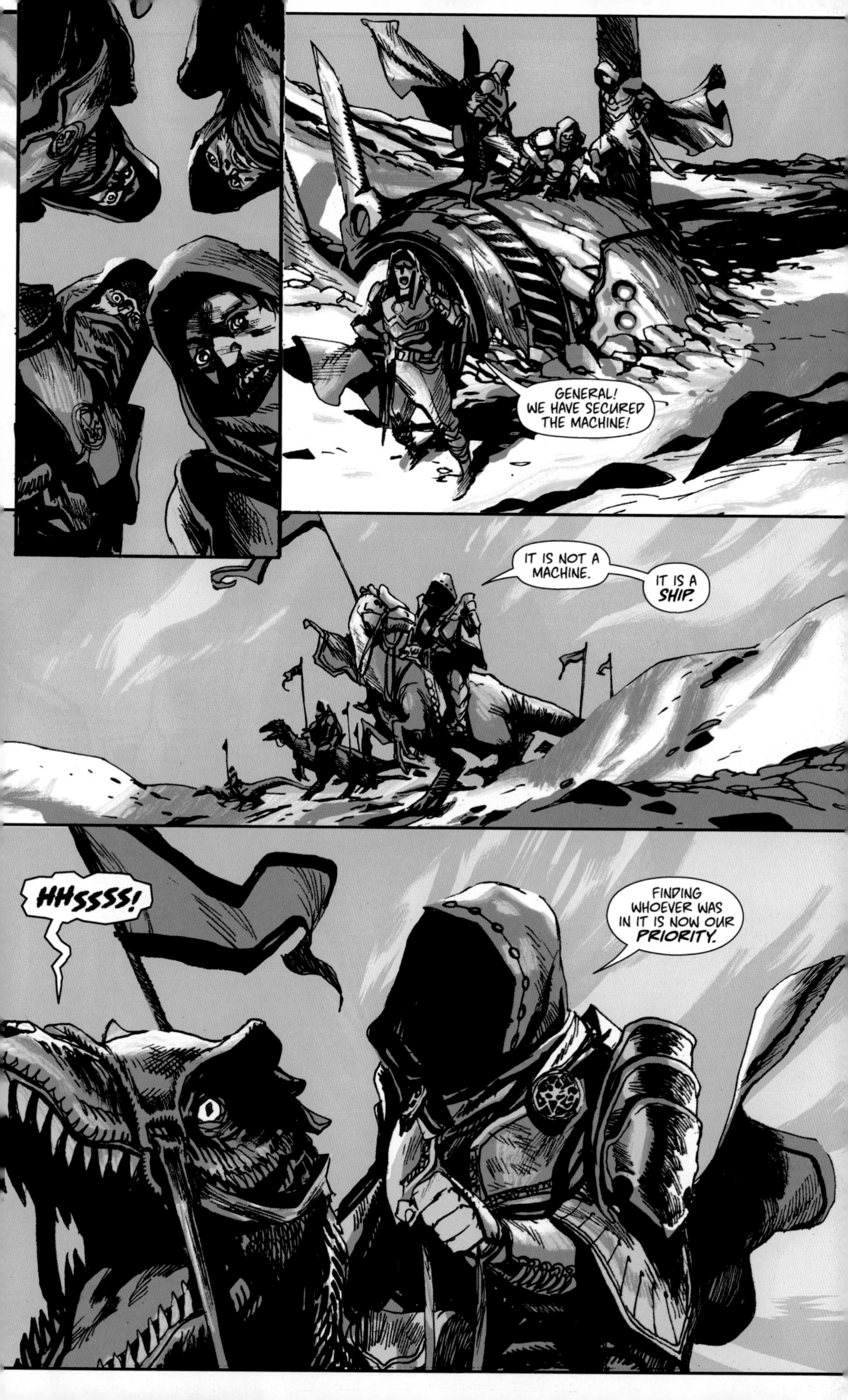
GENERAL! WE HAVE SECURED THE MACHINE!
IT IS NOT A MACHINE.
IT IS A SHIP.
HHSSSS!
FINDING WHOEVER WAS IN IT IS NOW OUR PRIORITY.

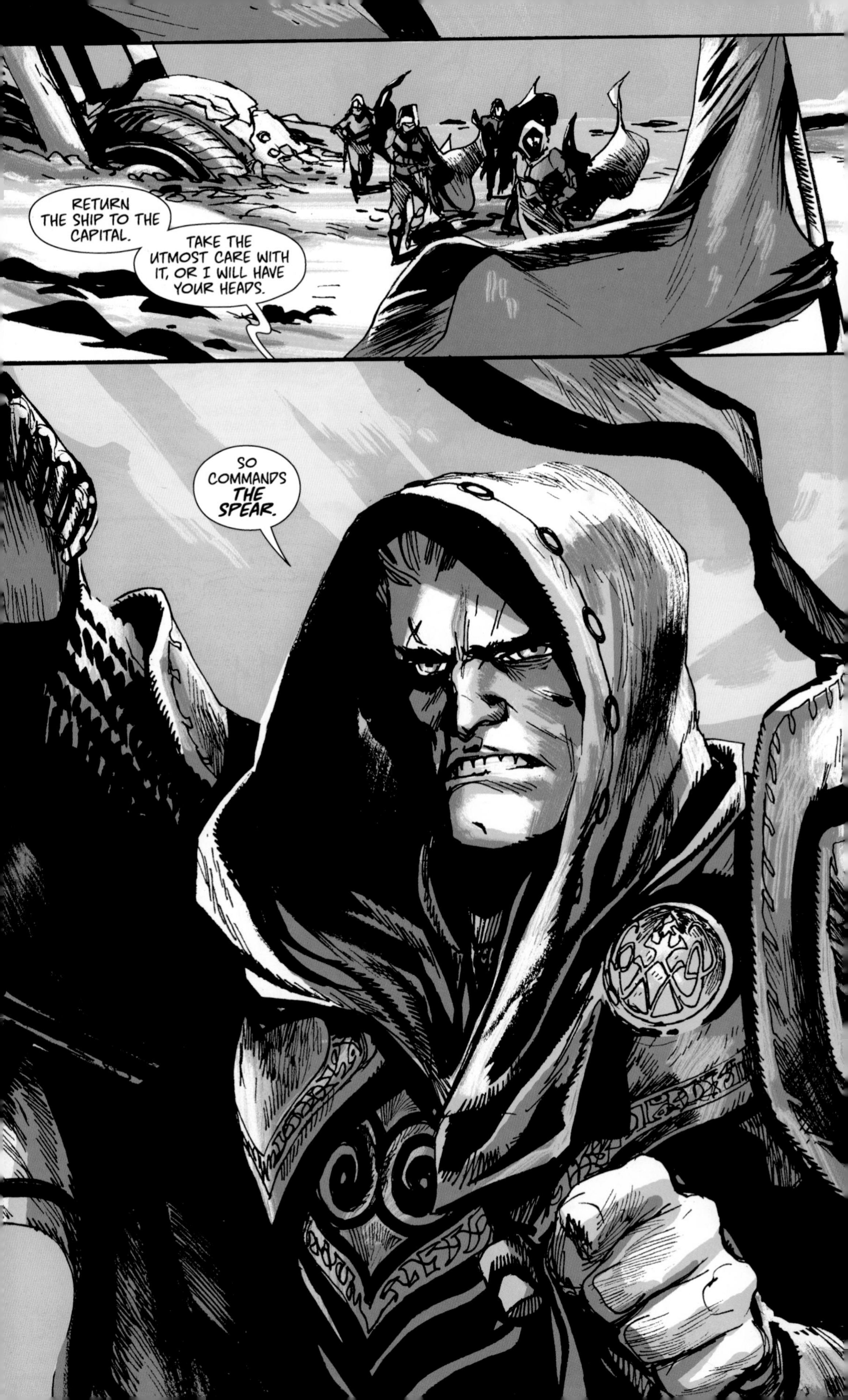
RETURN THE SHIP TO THE CAPITAL.
TAKE THE UTMOST CARE WITH IT, OR I WILL HAVE YOUR HEADS.
SO COMMANDS **THE SPEAR.**

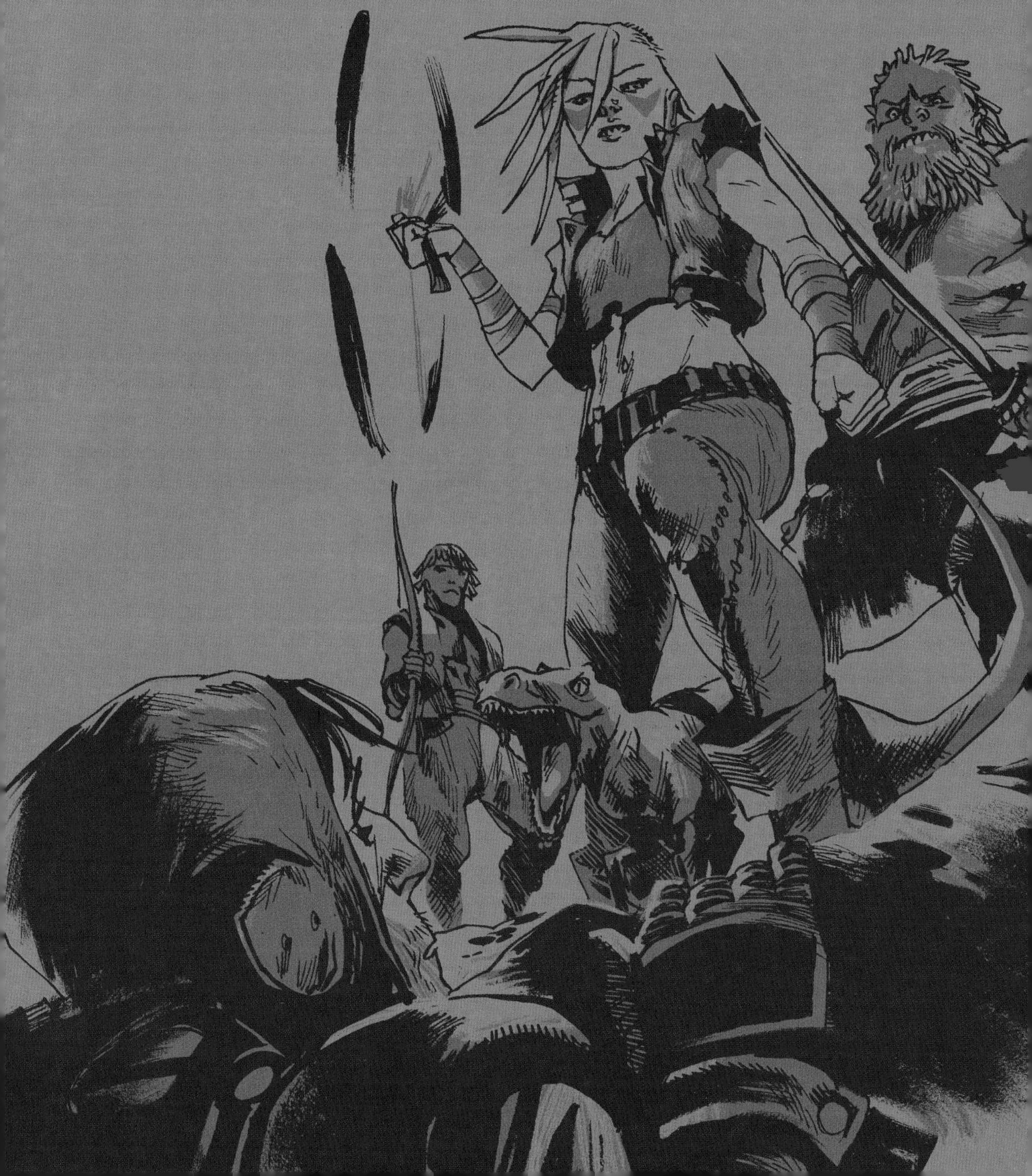

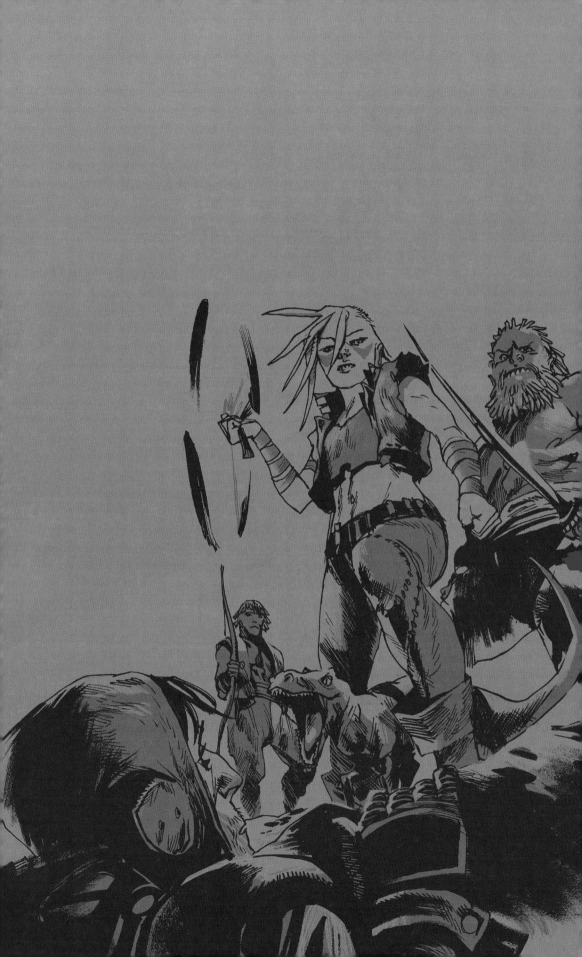

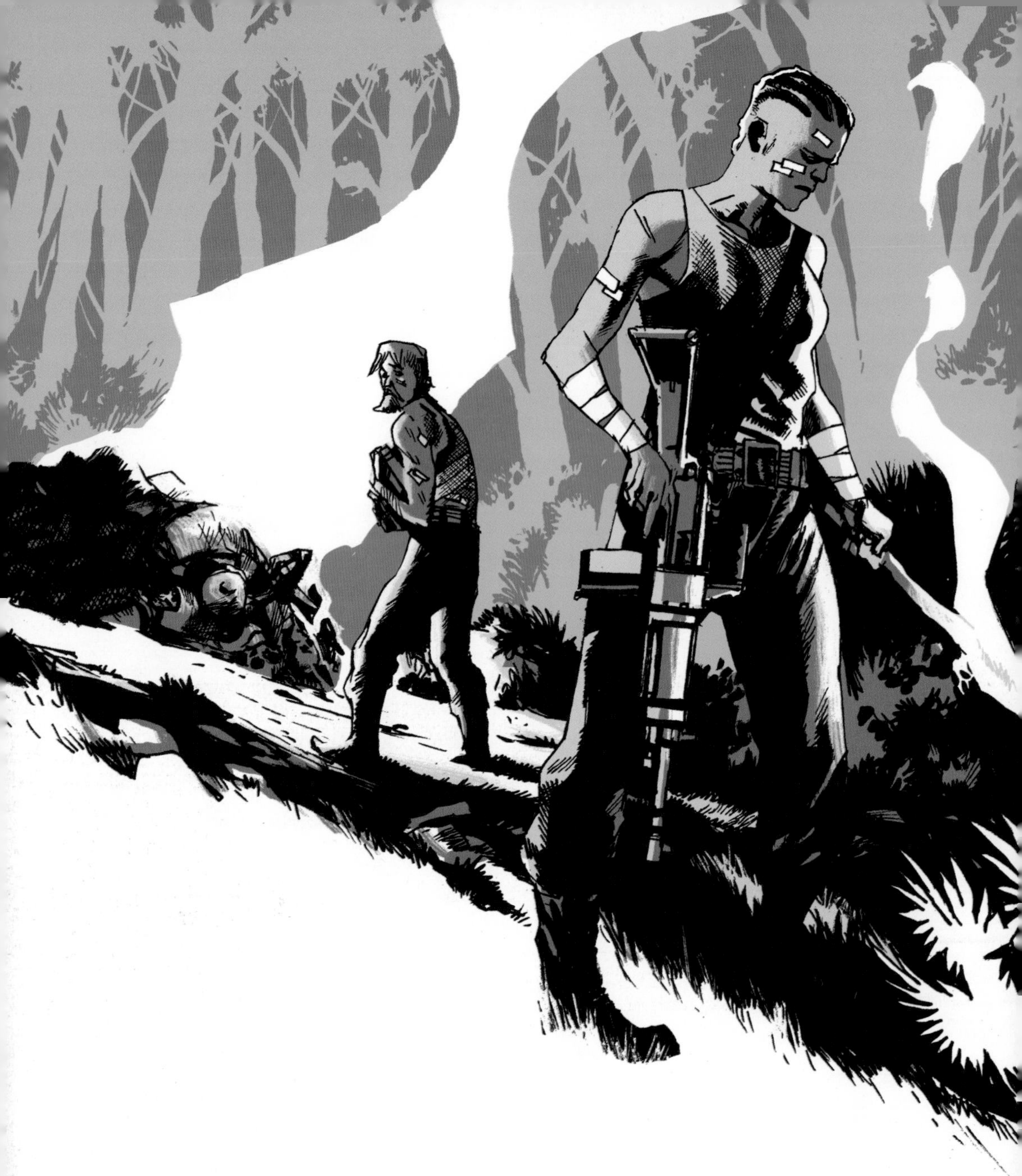

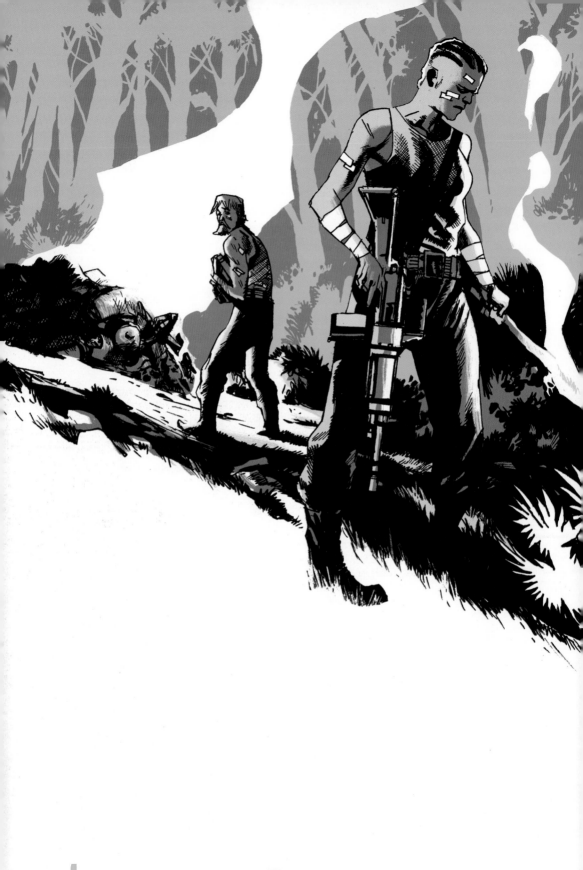

chapter 2

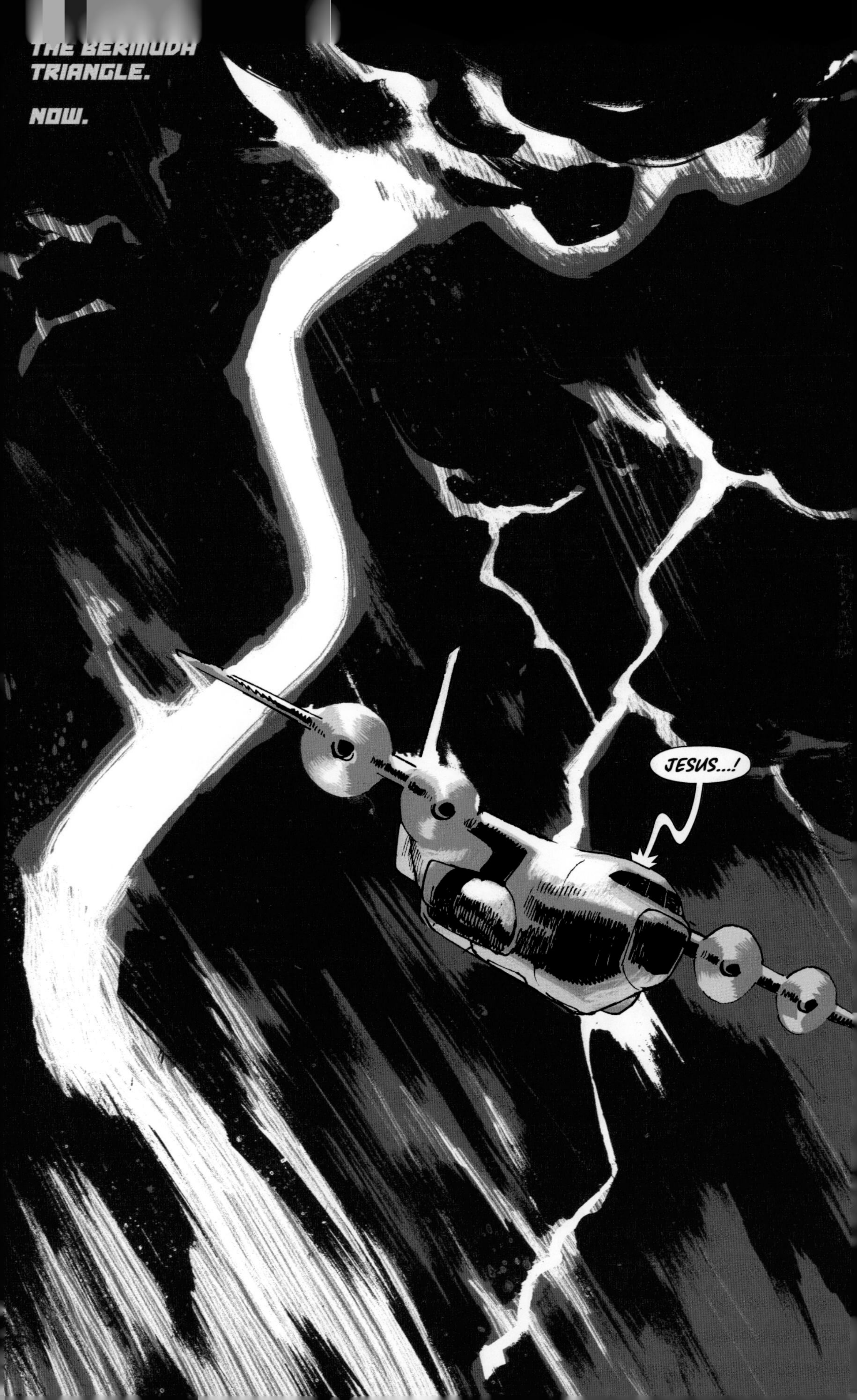
THE BERMUDA TRIANGLE.
NOW.
JESUS...!

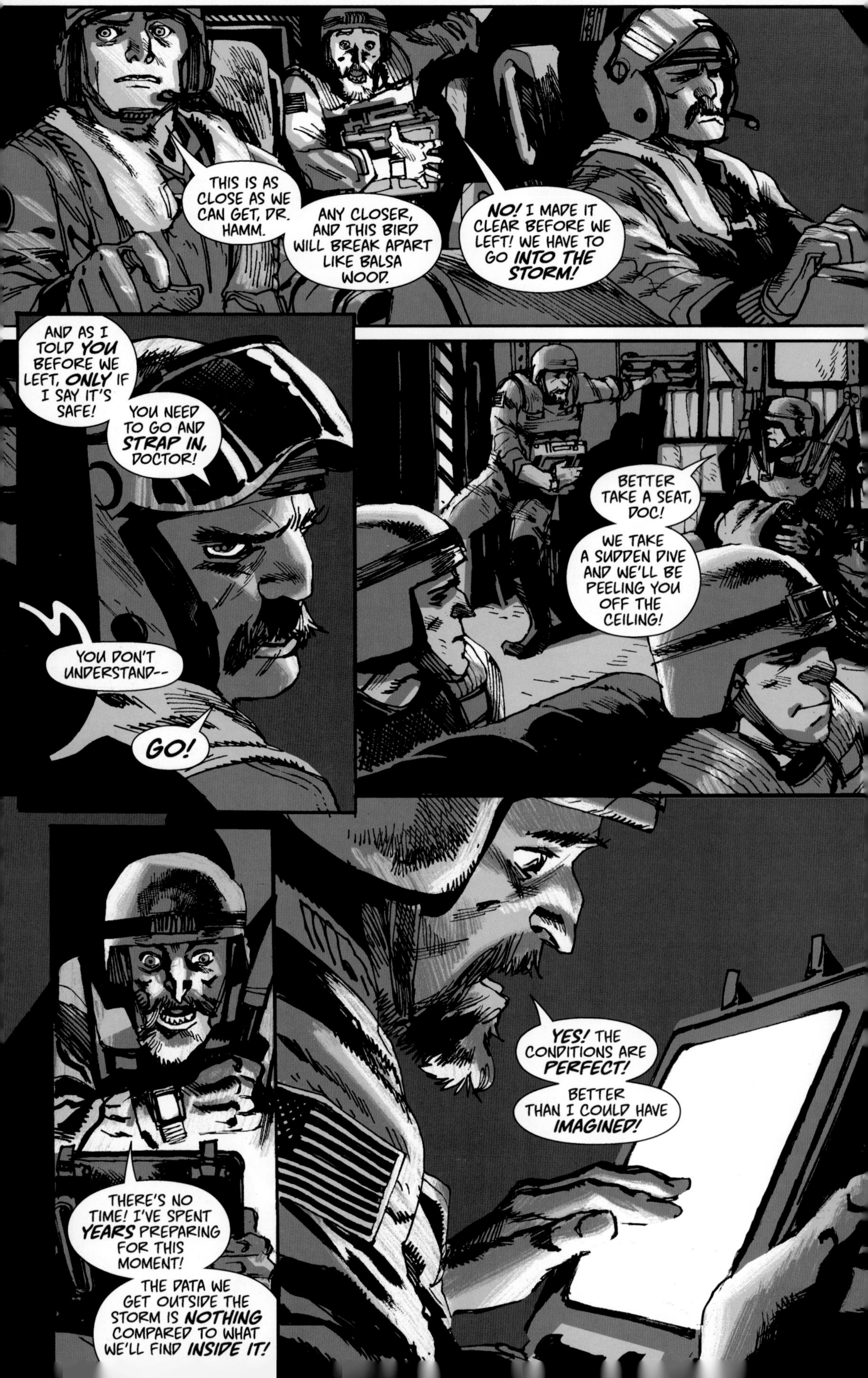
THIS IS AS CLOSE AS WE CAN GET, DR. HAMM.
ANY CLOSER, AND THIS BIRD WILL BREAK APART LIKE BALSA WOOD.
NO! I MADE IT CLEAR BEFORE WE LEFT! WE HAVE TO GO INTO THE STORM!
AND AS I TOLD YOU BEFORE WE LEFT, ONLY IF I SAY IT'S SAFE!
YOU NEED TO GO AND STRAP IN, DOCTOR!
YOU DON'T UNDERSTAND--
GO!
BETTER TAKE A SEAT, DOC!
WE TAKE A SUDDEN DIVE AND WE'LL BE PEELING YOU OFF THE CEILING!
YES! THE CONDITIONS ARE PERFECT!
BETTER THAN I COULD HAVE IMAGINED!
THERE'S NO TIME! I'VE SPENT YEARS PREPARING FOR THIS MOMENT!
THE DATA WE GET OUTSIDE THE STORM IS NOTHING COMPARED TO WHAT WE'LL FIND INSIDE IT!

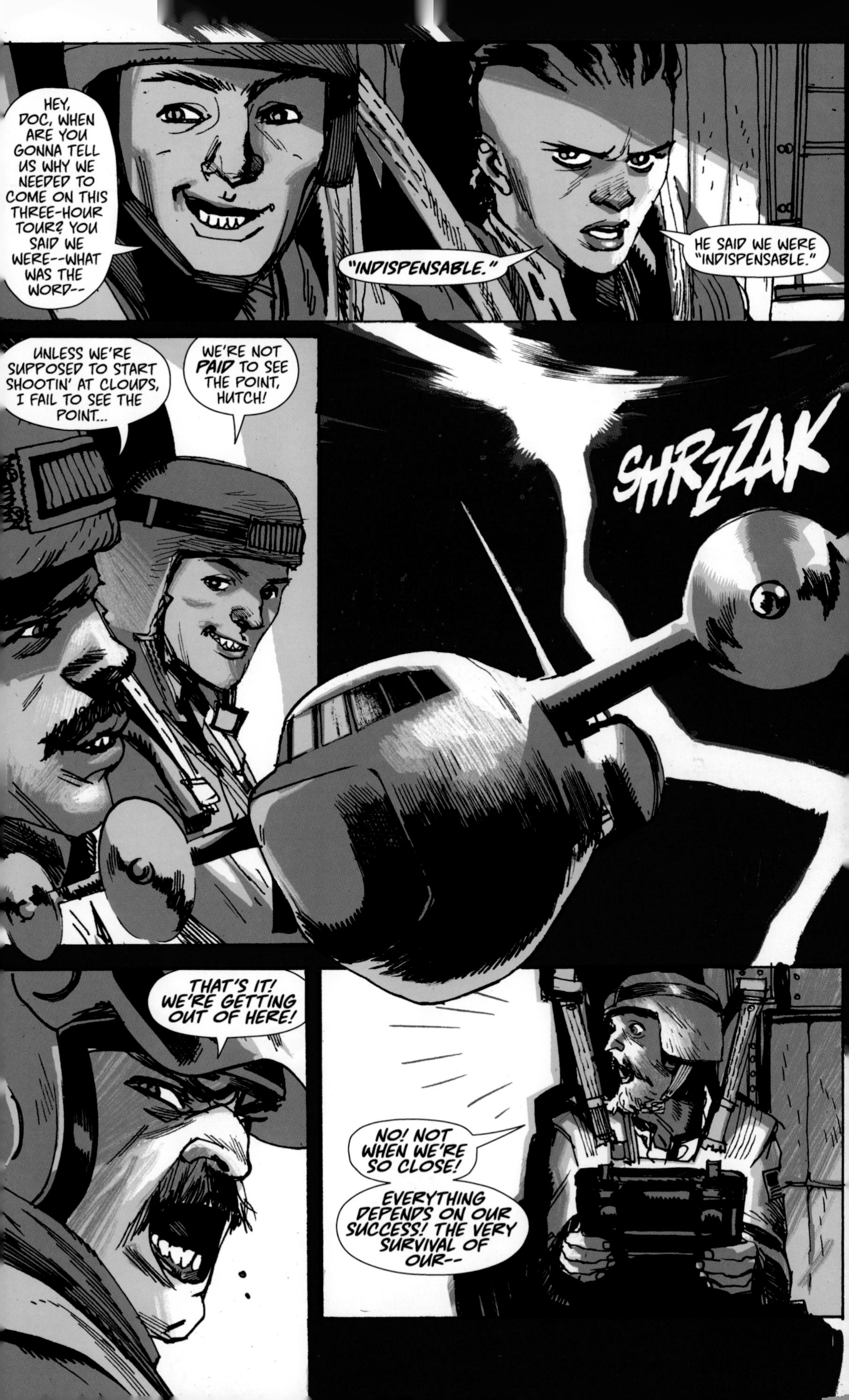
HEY, DOC, WHEN ARE YOU GONNA TELL US WHY WE NEEDED TO COME ON THIS THREE-HOUR TOUR? YOU SAID WE WERE--WHAT WAS THE WORD--
"INDISPENSABLE."
HE SAID WE WERE "INDISPENSABLE."
UNLESS WE'RE SUPPOSED TO START SHOOTIN' AT CLOUDS, I FAIL TO SEE THE POINT...
WE'RE NOT PAID TO SEE THE POINT, HUTCH!
SHRZZAK
THAT'S IT! WE'RE GETTING OUT OF HERE!
NO! NOT WHEN WE'RE SO CLOSE!
EVERYTHING DEPENDS ON OUR SUCCESS! THE VERY SURVIVAL OF OUR--

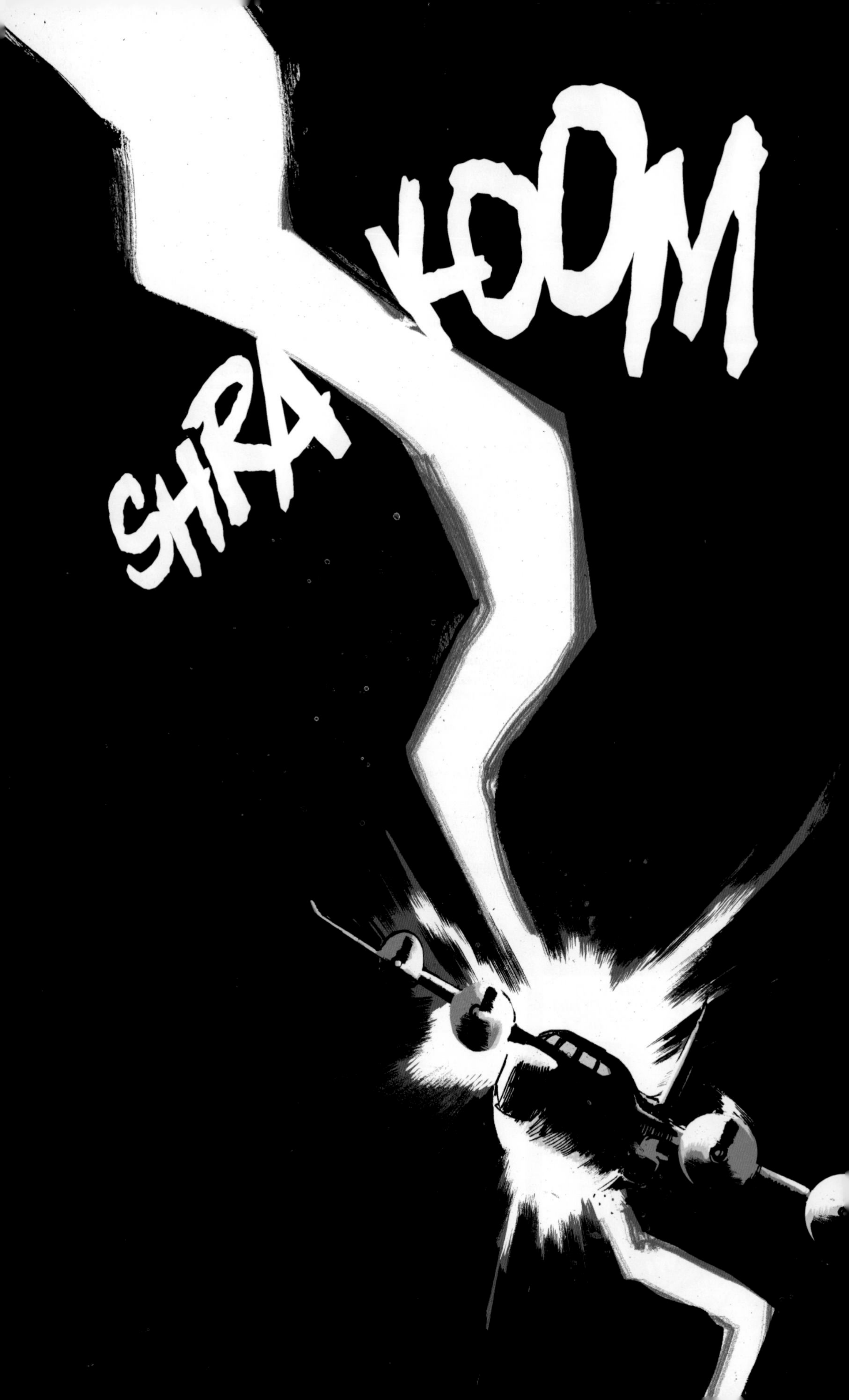
SHRAKOOM

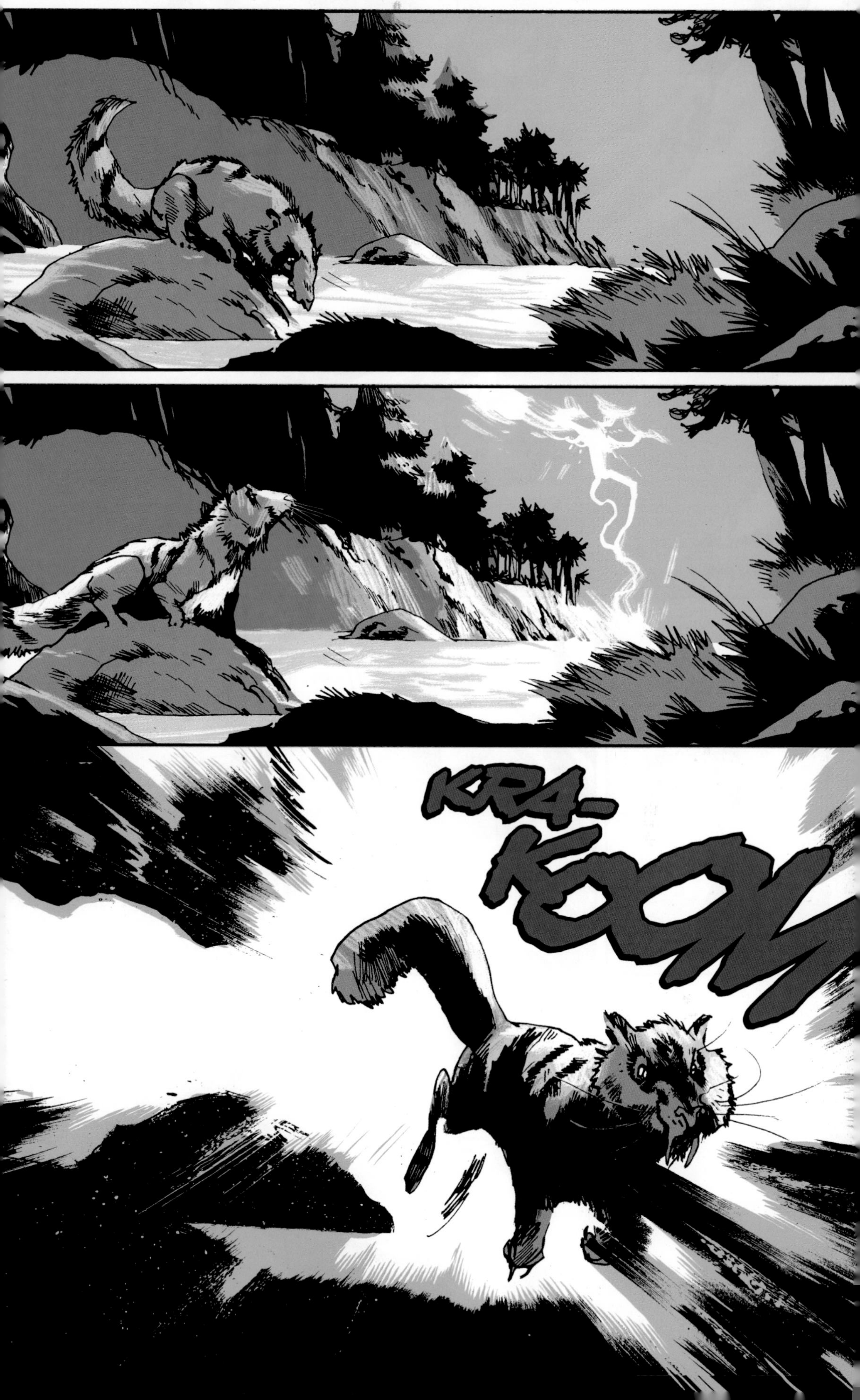
KRA-
KOOM

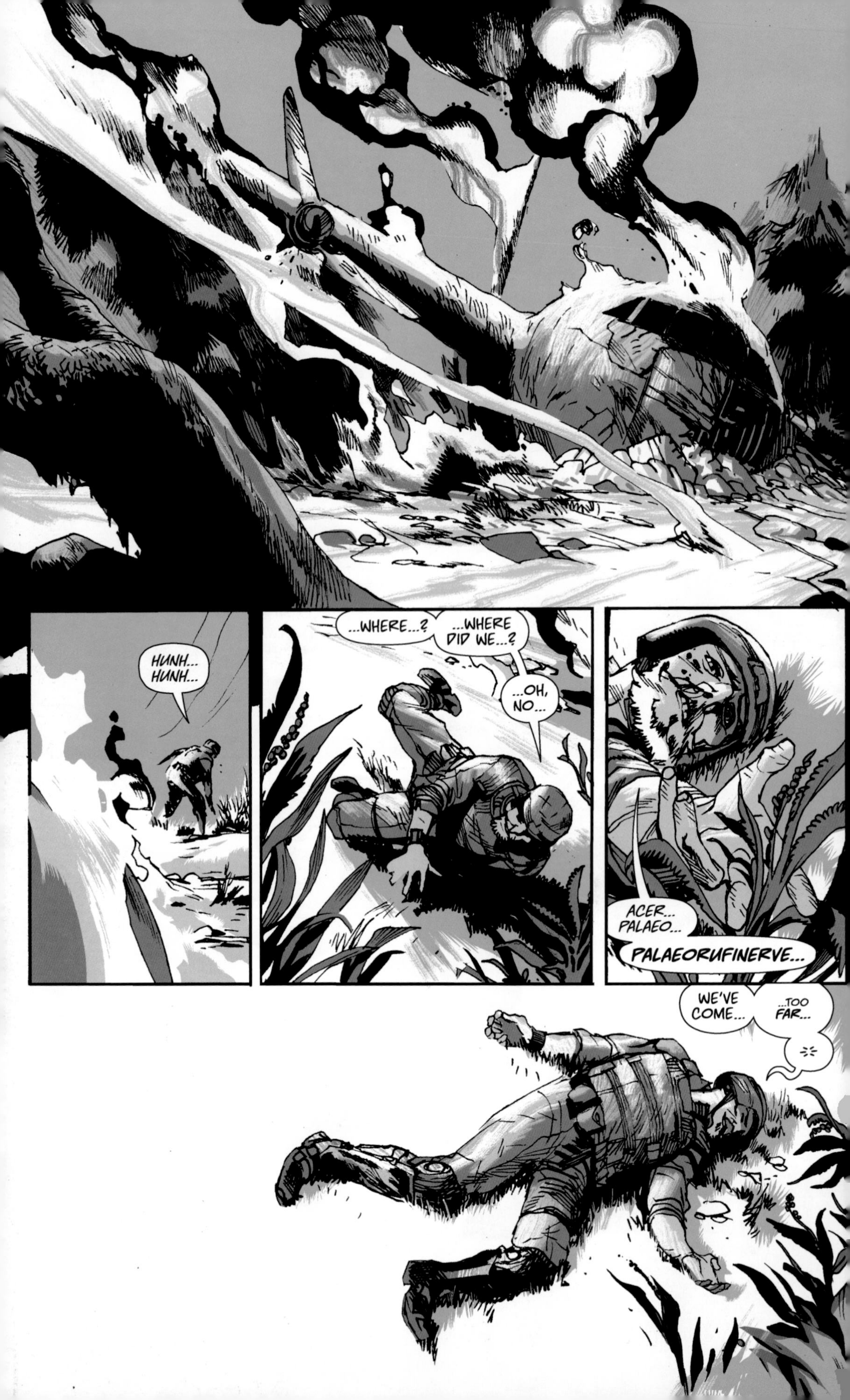
HUNH... HUNH...
...WHERE...?
...WHERE DID WE...?
...OH, NO...
ACER... PALAEO...
PALAEORUFINERVE...
WE'VE COME...
...TOO FAR...

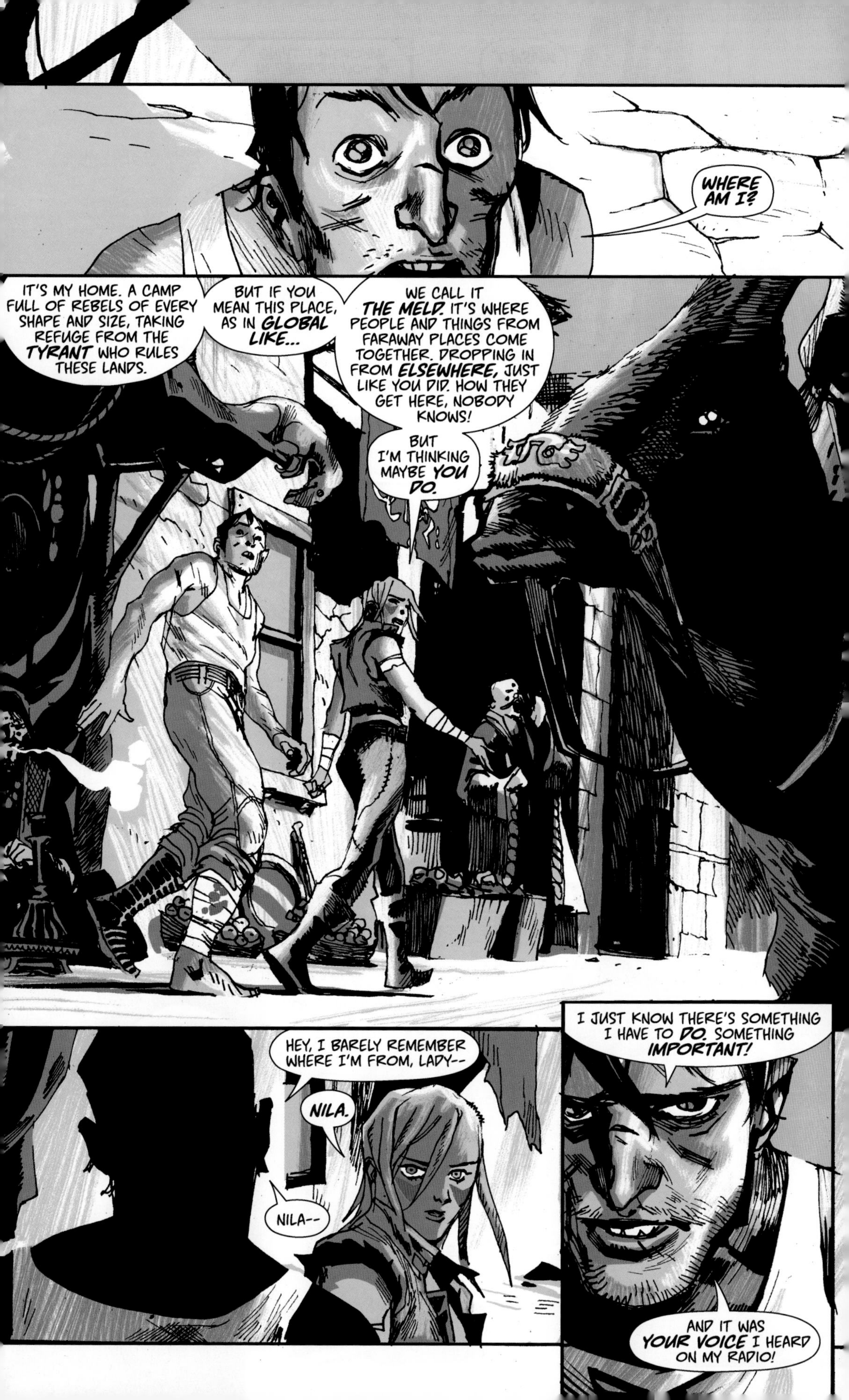
WHERE AM I?
IT'S MY HOME. A CAMP FULL OF REBELS OF EVERY SHAPE AND SIZE, TAKING REFUGE FROM THE TYRANT WHO RULES THESE LANDS.
BUT IF YOU MEAN THIS PLACE, AS IN GLOBAL LIKE...
WE CALL IT THE MELD. IT'S WHERE PEOPLE AND THINGS FROM FARAWAY PLACES COME TOGETHER. DROPPING IN FROM ELSEWHERE, JUST LIKE YOU DID. HOW THEY GET HERE, NOBODY KNOWS!
BUT I'M THINKING MAYBE YOU DO.
HEY, I BARELY REMEMBER WHERE I'M FROM, LADY--
NILA.
NILA--
I JUST KNOW THERE'S SOMETHING I HAVE TO DO. SOMETHING IMPORTANT!
AND IT WAS YOUR VOICE I HEARD ON MY RADIO!

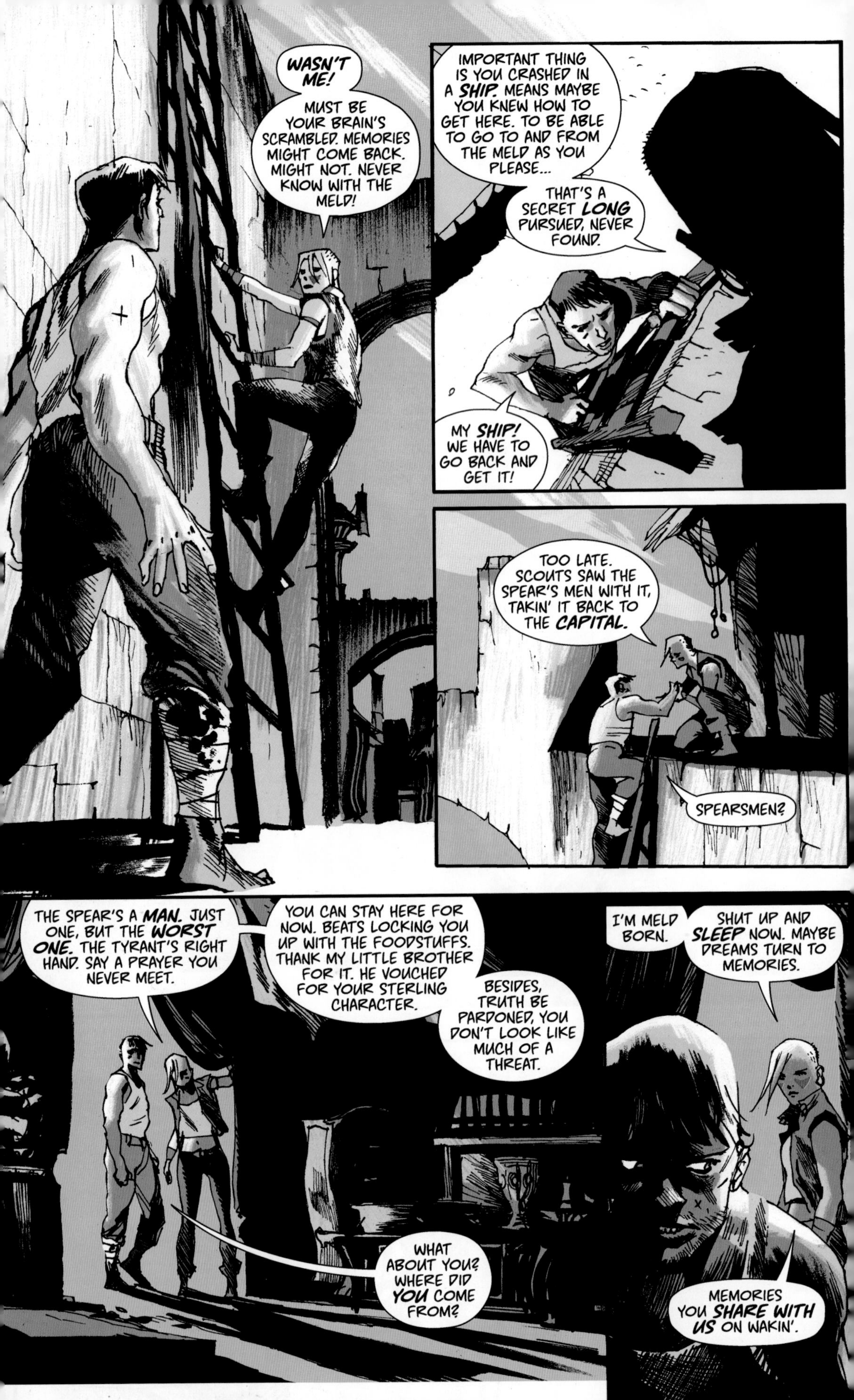
WASN'T ME!
MUST BE YOUR BRAIN'S SCRAMBLED. MEMORIES MIGHT COME BACK. MIGHT NOT. NEVER KNOW WITH THE MELD!
IMPORTANT THING IS YOU CRASHED IN A SHIP. MEANS MAYBE YOU KNEW HOW TO GET HERE. TO BE ABLE TO GO TO AND FROM THE MELD AS YOU PLEASE...
THAT'S A SECRET LONG PURSUED, NEVER FOUND.
MY SHIP! WE HAVE TO GO BACK AND GET IT!
TOO LATE. SCOUTS SAW THE SPEAR'S MEN WITH IT, TAKIN' IT BACK TO THE CAPITAL.
SPEARSMEN?
THE SPEAR'S A MAN. JUST ONE, BUT THE WORST ONE. THE TYRANT'S RIGHT HAND. SAY A PRAYER YOU NEVER MEET.
YOU CAN STAY HERE FOR NOW. BEATS LOCKING YOU UP WITH THE FOODSTUFFS. THANK MY LITTLE BROTHER FOR IT. HE VOUCHED FOR YOUR STERLING CHARACTER.
BESIDES, TRUTH BE PARDONED, YOU DON'T LOOK LIKE MUCH OF A THREAT.
WHAT ABOUT YOU? WHERE DID YOU COME FROM?
I'M MELD BORN.
SHUT UP AND SLEEP NOW. MAYBE DREAMS TURN TO MEMORIES.
MEMORIES YOU SHARE WITH US ON WAKIN'.

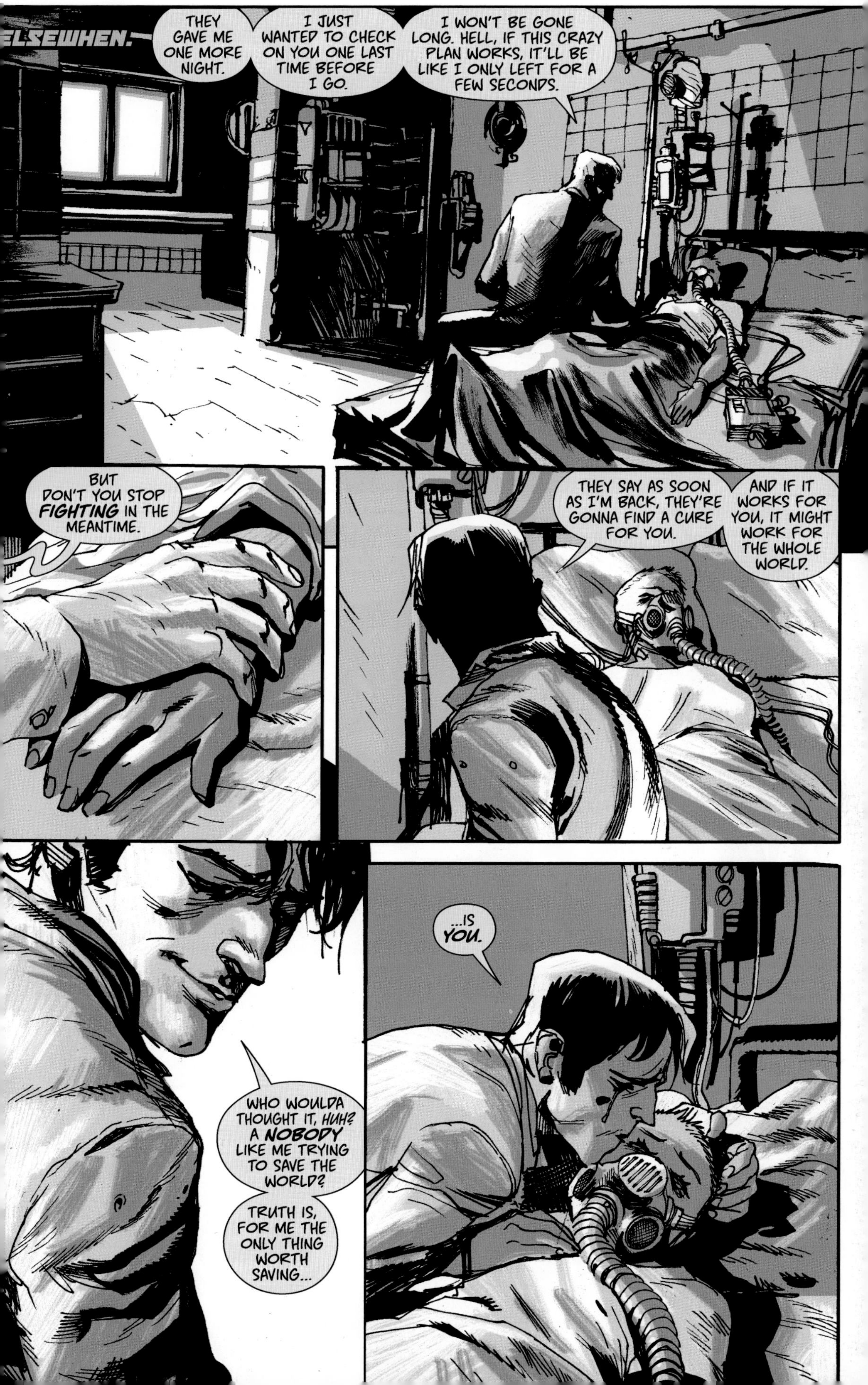
ELSEWHEN.
THEY GAVE ME ONE MORE NIGHT.
I JUST WANTED TO CHECK ON YOU ONE LAST TIME BEFORE I GO.
I WON'T BE GONE LONG. HELL, IF THIS CRAZY PLAN WORKS, IT'LL BE LIKE I ONLY LEFT FOR A FEW SECONDS.
BUT DON'T YOU STOP FIGHTING IN THE MEANTIME.
THEY SAY AS SOON AS I'M BACK, THEY'RE GONNA FIND A CURE FOR YOU.
AND IF IT WORKS FOR YOU, IT MIGHT WORK FOR THE WHOLE WORLD.
WHO WOULDA THOUGHT IT, HUH? A NOBODY LIKE ME TRYING TO SAVE THE WORLD?
TRUTH IS, FOR ME THE ONLY THING WORTH SAVING...
...IS YOU.

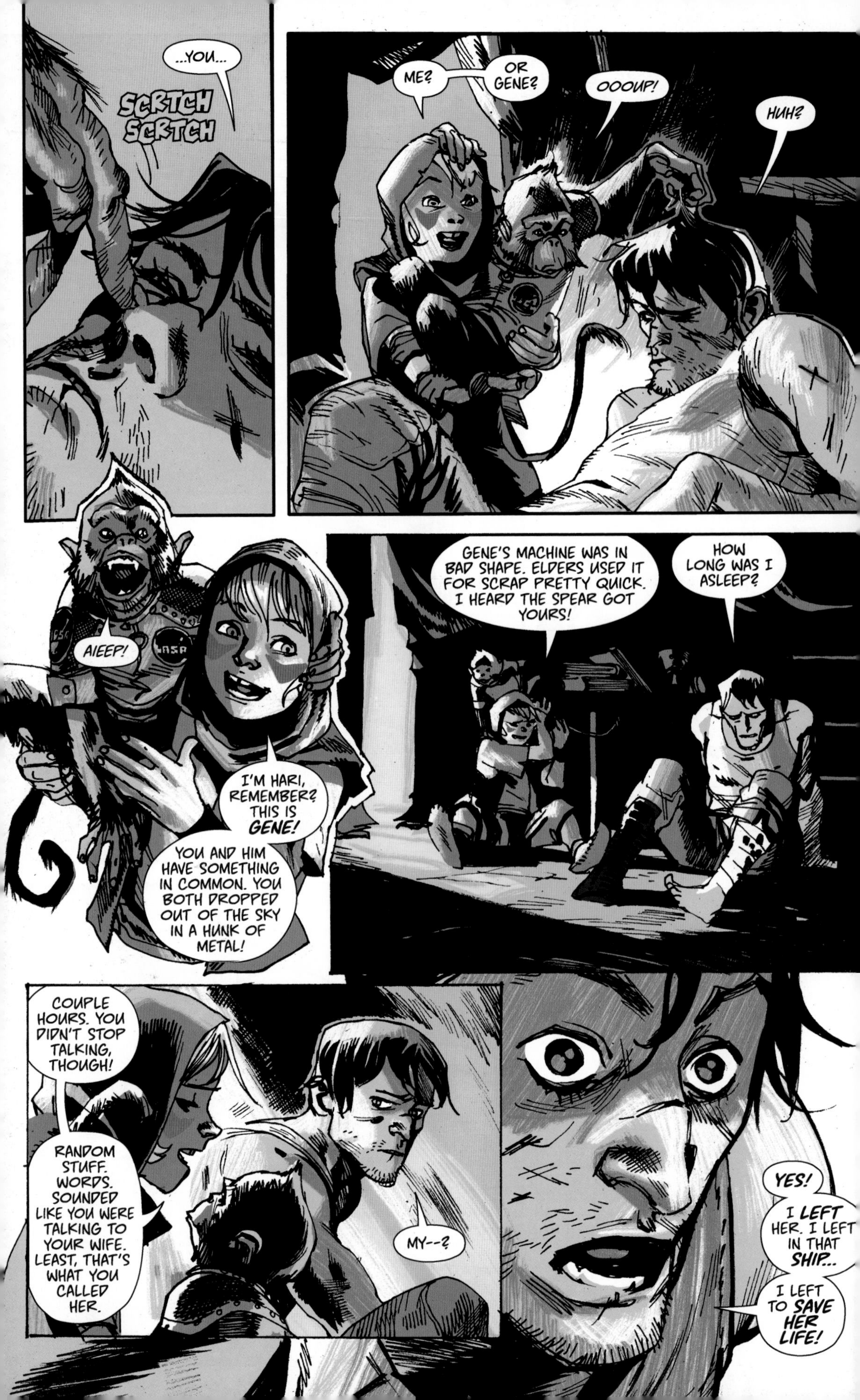
...YOU...
SCRTCH SCRTCH
ME?
OR GENE?
OOOUP!
HUH?
AIEEP!
I'M HARI, REMEMBER? THIS IS **GENE!**
YOU AND HIM HAVE SOMETHING IN COMMON. YOU BOTH DROPPED OUT OF THE SKY IN A HUNK OF METAL!
GENE'S MACHINE WAS IN BAD SHAPE. ELDERS USED IT FOR SCRAP PRETTY QUICK. I HEARD THE SPEAR GOT YOURS!
HOW LONG WAS I ASLEEP?
COUPLE HOURS. YOU DIDN'T STOP TALKING, THOUGH!
RANDOM STUFF. WORDS. SOUNDED LIKE YOU WERE TALKING TO YOUR WIFE. LEAST, THAT'S WHAT YOU CALLED HER.
MY--?
YES!
I **LEFT** HER. I LEFT IN THAT **SHIP...**
I LEFT TO **SAVE HER LIFE!**

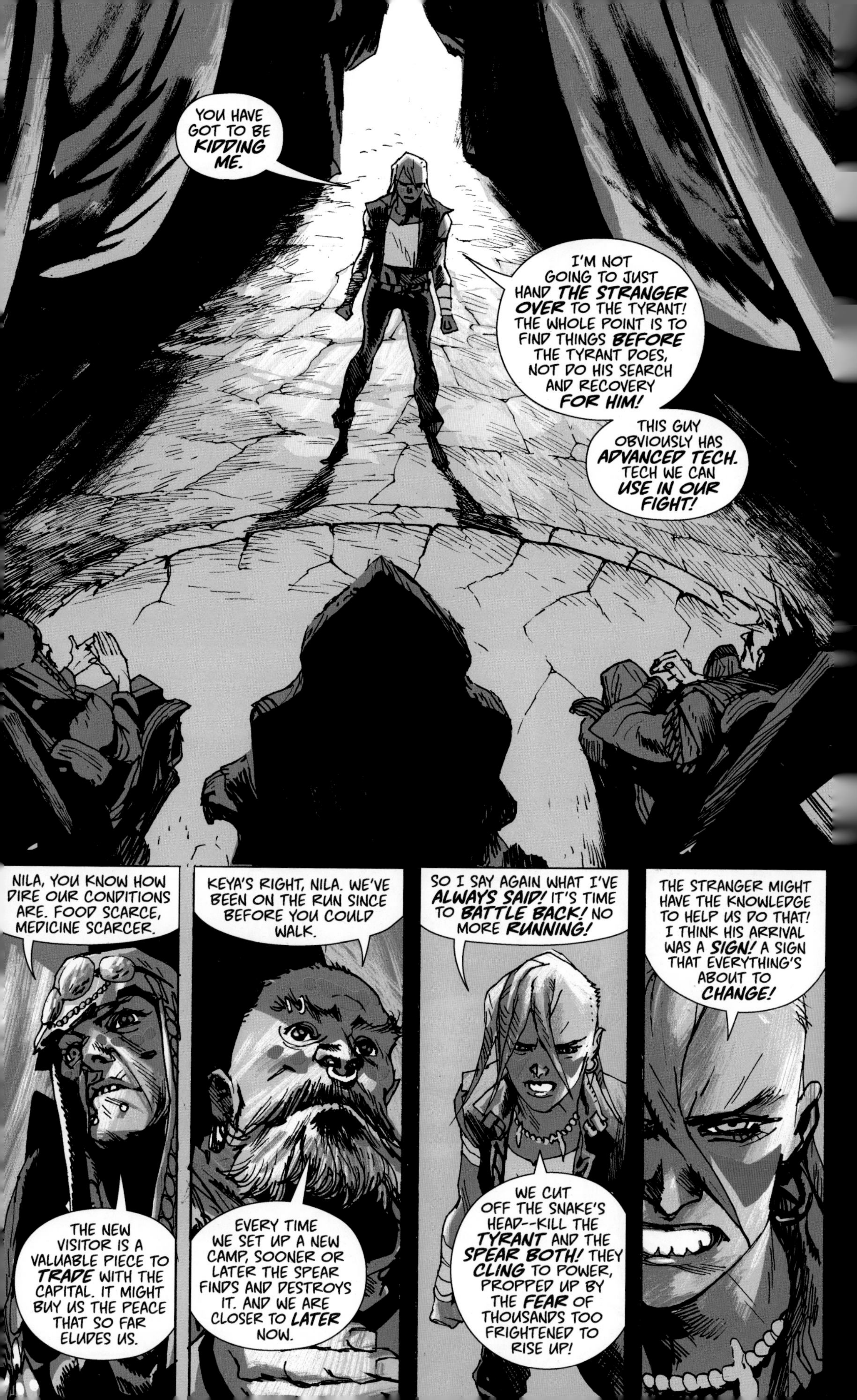
YOU HAVE GOT TO BE KIDDING ME.
I'M NOT GOING TO JUST HAND THE STRANGER OVER TO THE TYRANT! THE WHOLE POINT IS TO FIND THINGS BEFORE THE TYRANT DOES, NOT DO HIS SEARCH AND RECOVERY FOR HIM!
THIS GUY OBVIOUSLY HAS ADVANCED TECH. TECH WE CAN USE IN OUR FIGHT!
NILA, YOU KNOW HOW DIRE OUR CONDITIONS ARE. FOOD SCARCE, MEDICINE SCARCER.
THE NEW VISITOR IS A VALUABLE PIECE TO TRADE WITH THE CAPITAL. IT MIGHT BUY US THE PEACE THAT SO FAR ELUDES US.
KEYA'S RIGHT, NILA. WE'VE BEEN ON THE RUN SINCE BEFORE YOU COULD WALK.
EVERY TIME WE SET UP A NEW CAMP, SOONER OR LATER THE SPEAR FINDS AND DESTROYS IT. AND WE ARE CLOSER TO LATER NOW.
SO I SAY AGAIN WHAT I'VE ALWAYS SAID! IT'S TIME TO BATTLE BACK! NO MORE RUNNING!
WE CUT OFF THE SNAKE'S HEAD--KILL THE TYRANT AND THE SPEAR BOTH! THEY CLING TO POWER, PROPPED UP BY THE FEAR OF THOUSANDS TOO FRIGHTENED TO RISE UP!
THE STRANGER MIGHT HAVE THE KNOWLEDGE TO HELP US DO THAT! I THINK HIS ARRIVAL WAS A SIGN! A SIGN THAT EVERYTHING'S ABOUT TO CHANGE!

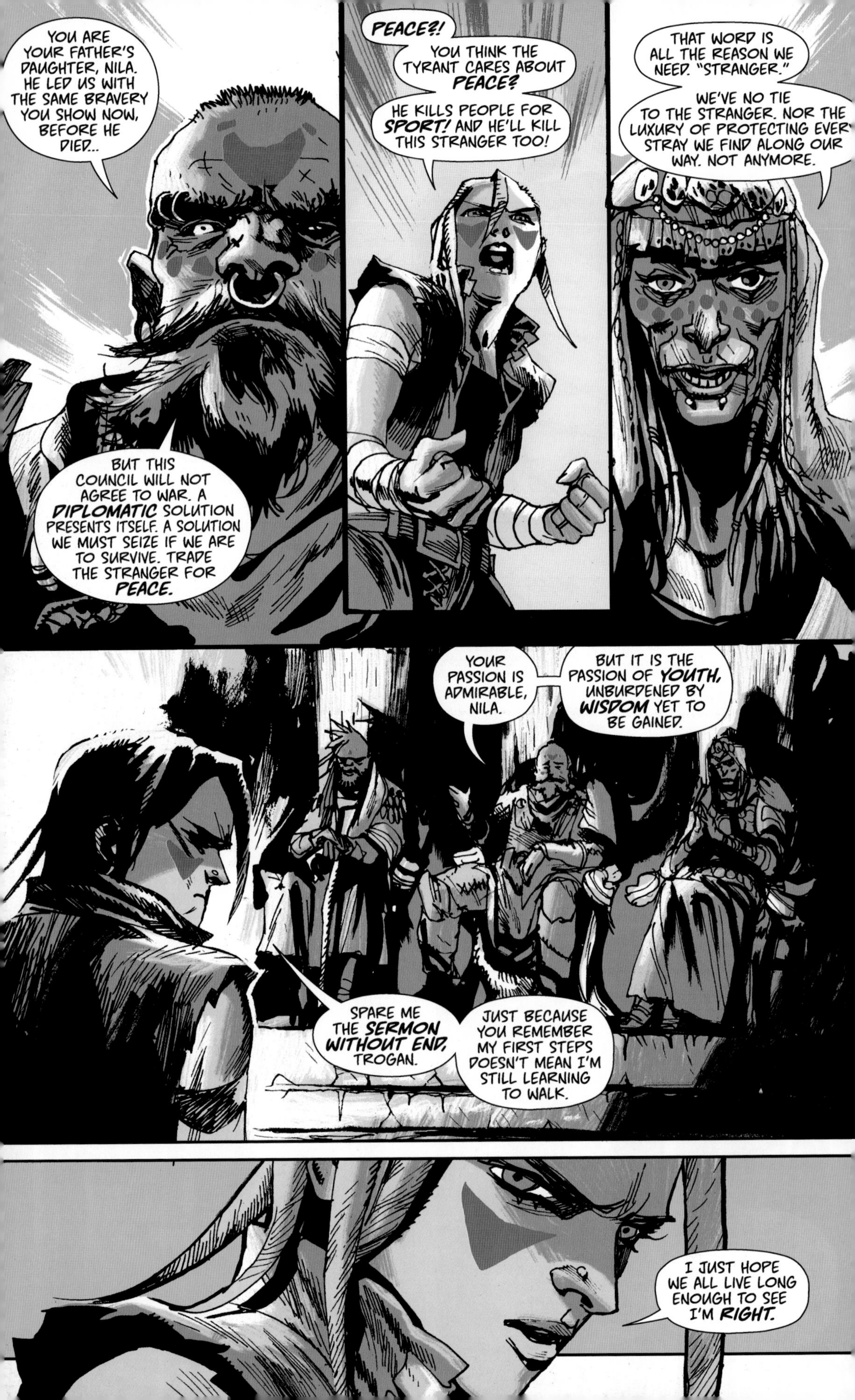

YOU ARE YOUR FATHER'S DAUGHTER, NILA. HE LED US WITH THE SAME BRAVERY YOU SHOW NOW, BEFORE HE DIED...
BUT THIS COUNCIL WILL NOT AGREE TO WAR. A DIPLOMATIC SOLUTION PRESENTS ITSELF. A SOLUTION WE MUST SEIZE IF WE ARE TO SURVIVE. TRADE THE STRANGER FOR PEACE.
PEACE?!
YOU THINK THE TYRANT CARES ABOUT PEACE?
HE KILLS PEOPLE FOR SPORT! AND HE'LL KILL THIS STRANGER TOO!
THAT WORD IS ALL THE REASON WE NEED. "STRANGER."
WE'VE NO TIE TO THE STRANGER. NOR THE LUXURY OF PROTECTING EVERY STRAY WE FIND ALONG OUR WAY. NOT ANYMORE.
YOUR PASSION IS ADMIRABLE, NILA.
BUT IT IS THE PASSION OF YOUTH, UNBURDENED BY WISDOM YET TO BE GAINED.
SPARE ME THE SERMON WITHOUT END, TROGAN.
JUST BECAUSE YOU REMEMBER MY FIRST STEPS DOESN'T MEAN I'M STILL LEARNING TO WALK.
I JUST HOPE WE ALL LIVE LONG ENOUGH TO SEE I'M RIGHT.

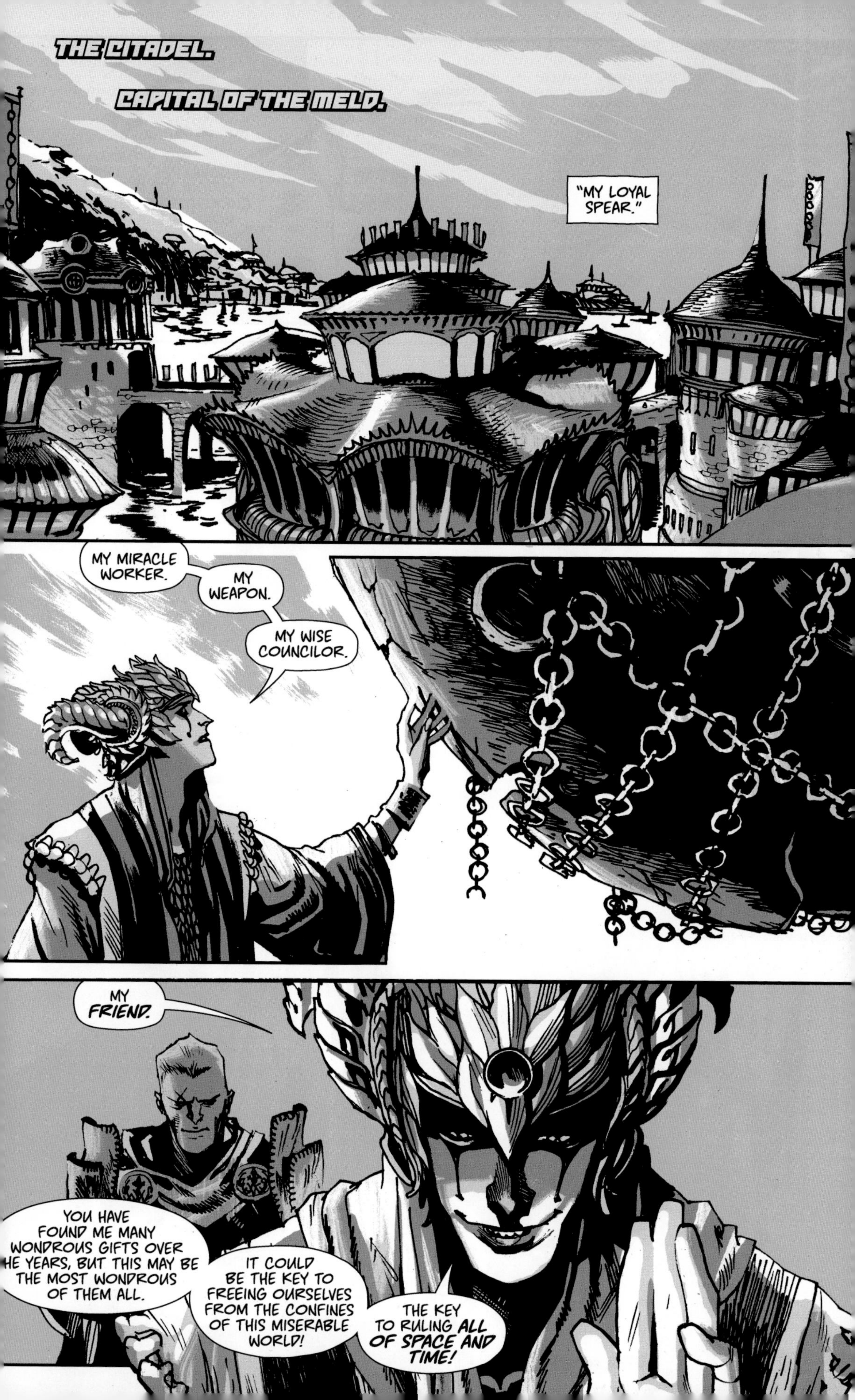
THE CITADEL.
CAPITAL OF THE MELD.
"MY LOYAL SPEAR."
MY MIRACLE WORKER.
MY WEAPON.
MY WISE COUNCILOR.
MY FRIEND.
YOU HAVE FOUND ME MANY WONDROUS GIFTS OVER HE YEARS, BUT THIS MAY BE THE MOST WONDROUS OF THEM ALL.
IT COULD BE THE KEY TO FREEING OURSELVES FROM THE CONFINES OF THIS MISERABLE WORLD!
THE KEY TO RULING ALL OF SPACE AND TIME!

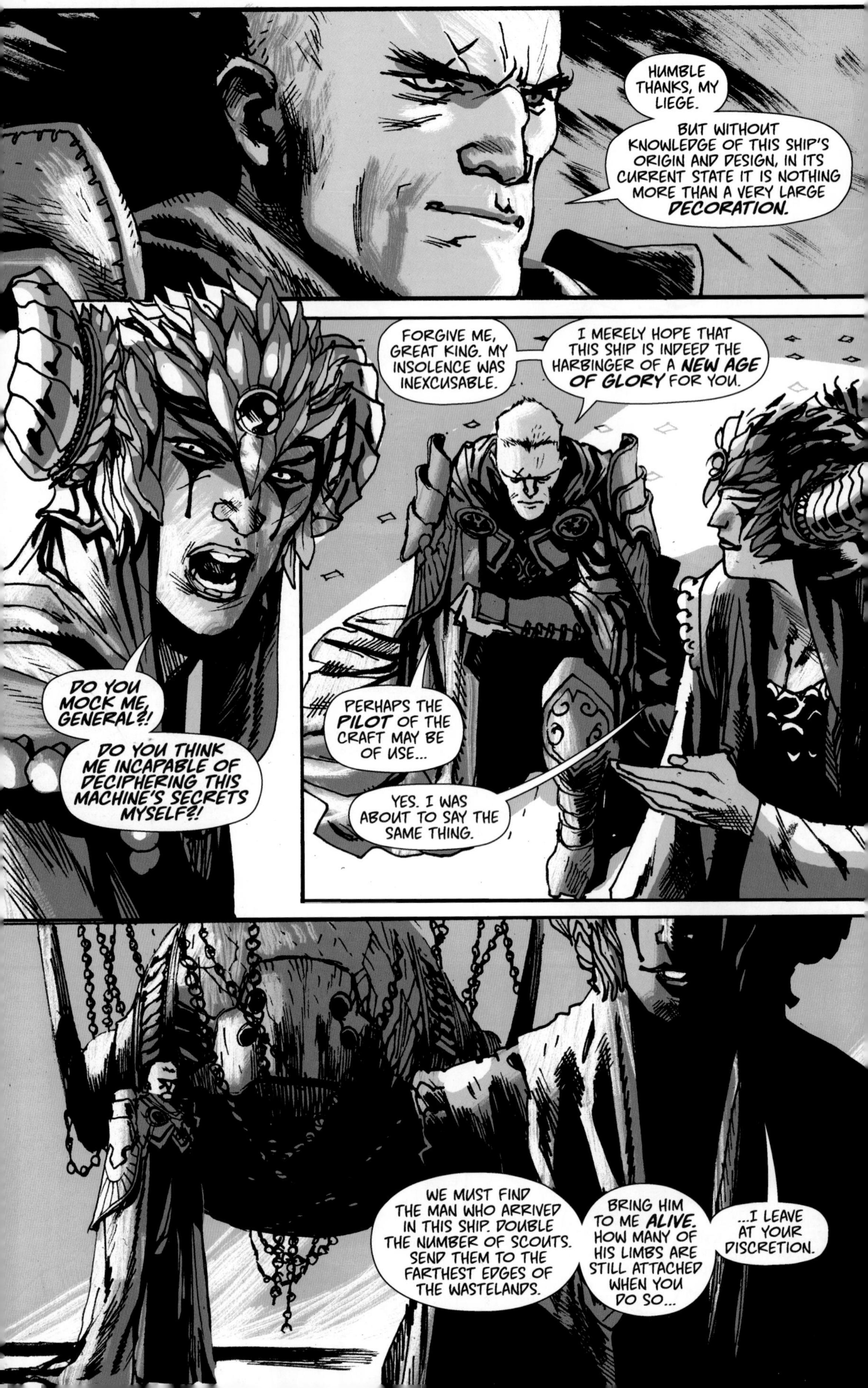
HUMBLE THANKS, MY LIEGE.
BUT WITHOUT KNOWLEDGE OF THIS SHIP'S ORIGIN AND DESIGN, IN ITS CURRENT STATE IT IS NOTHING MORE THAN A VERY LARGE DECORATION.
DO YOU MOCK ME, GENERAL?!
DO YOU THINK ME INCAPABLE OF DECIPHERING THIS MACHINE'S SECRETS MYSELF?!
FORGIVE ME, GREAT KING. MY INSOLENCE WAS INEXCUSABLE.
I MERELY HOPE THAT THIS SHIP IS INDEED THE HARBINGER OF A NEW AGE OF GLORY FOR YOU.
PERHAPS THE PILOT OF THE CRAFT MAY BE OF USE...
YES. I WAS ABOUT TO SAY THE SAME THING.
WE MUST FIND THE MAN WHO ARRIVED IN THIS SHIP. DOUBLE THE NUMBER OF SCOUTS. SEND THEM TO THE FARTHEST EDGES OF THE WASTELANDS.
BRING HIM TO ME ALIVE. HOW MANY OF HIS LIMBS ARE STILL ATTACHED WHEN YOU DO SO...
...I LEAVE AT YOUR DISCRETION.

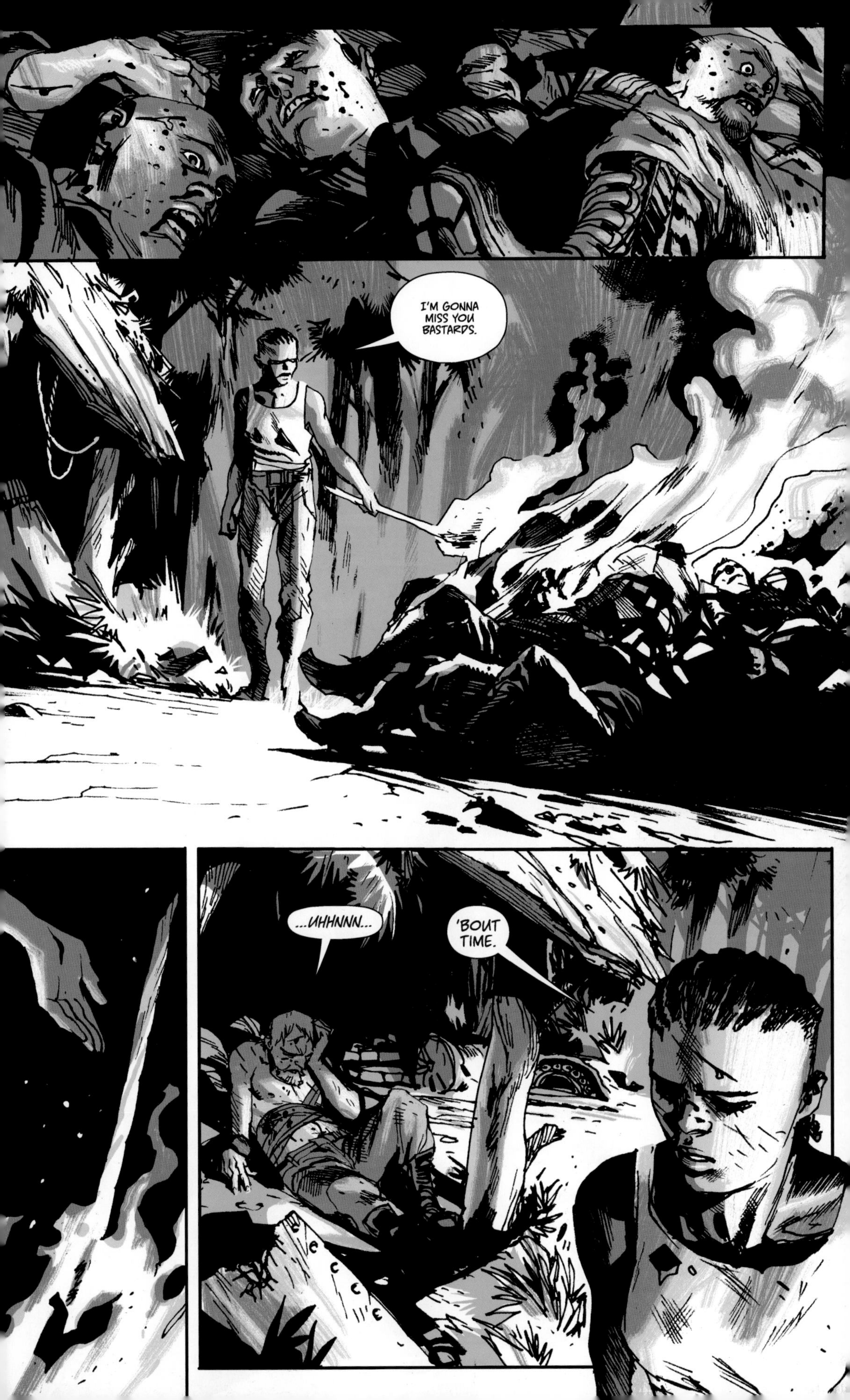
I'M GONNA MISS YOU BASTARDS.
...UHHNNN...
'BOUT TIME.

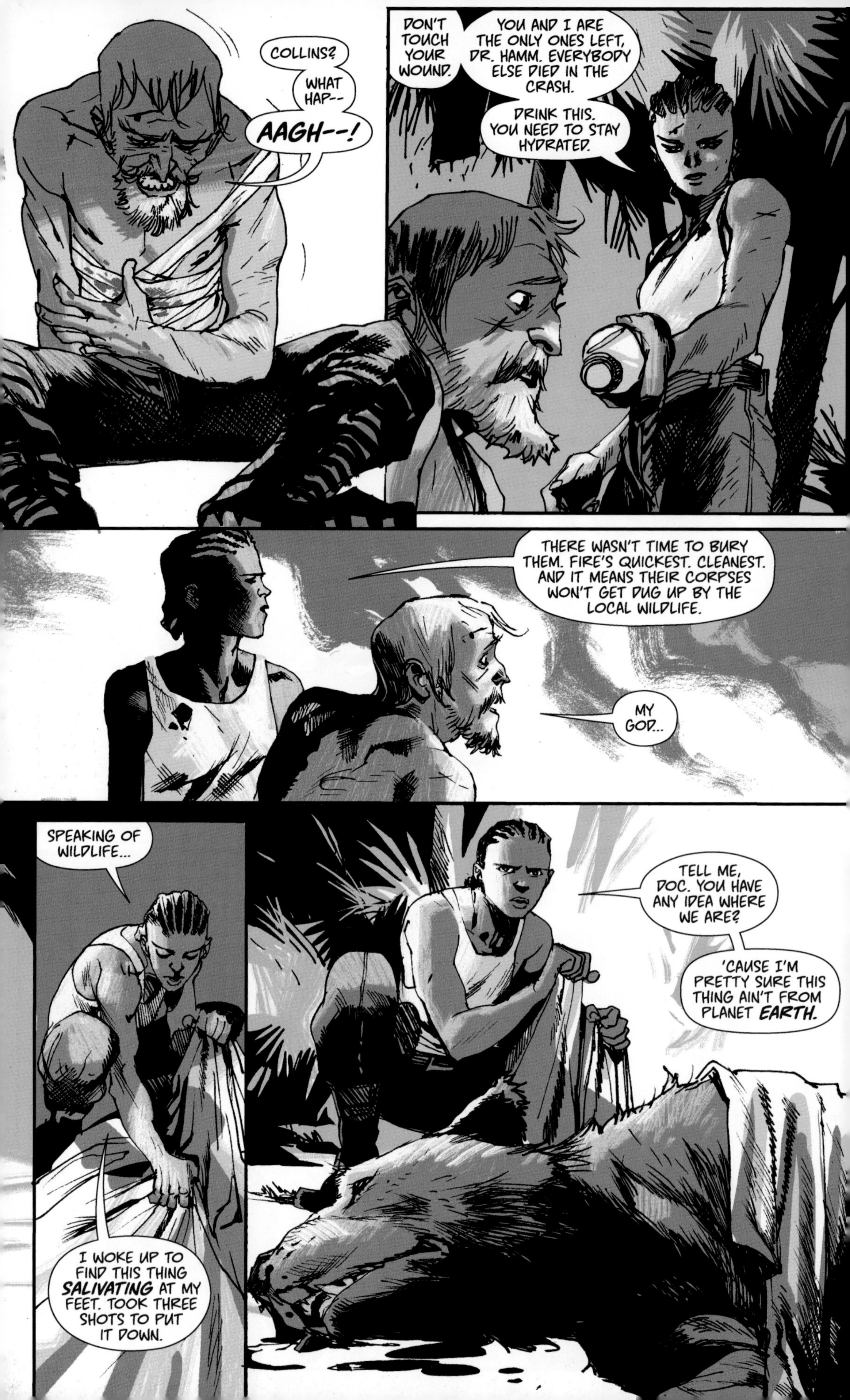

COLLINS?
WHAT HAP--
AAGH--!
DON'T TOUCH YOUR WOUND.
YOU AND I ARE THE ONLY ONES LEFT, DR. HAMM. EVERYBODY ELSE DIED IN THE CRASH.
DRINK THIS. YOU NEED TO STAY HYDRATED.
THERE WASN'T TIME TO BURY THEM. FIRE'S QUICKEST. CLEANEST. AND IT MEANS THEIR CORPSES WON'T GET DUG UP BY THE LOCAL WILDLIFE.
MY GOD...
SPEAKING OF WILDLIFE...
I WOKE UP TO FIND THIS THING SALIVATING AT MY FEET. TOOK THREE SHOTS TO PUT IT DOWN.
TELL ME, DOC. YOU HAVE ANY IDEA WHERE WE ARE?
'CAUSE I'M PRETTY SURE THIS THING AIN'T FROM PLANET EARTH.

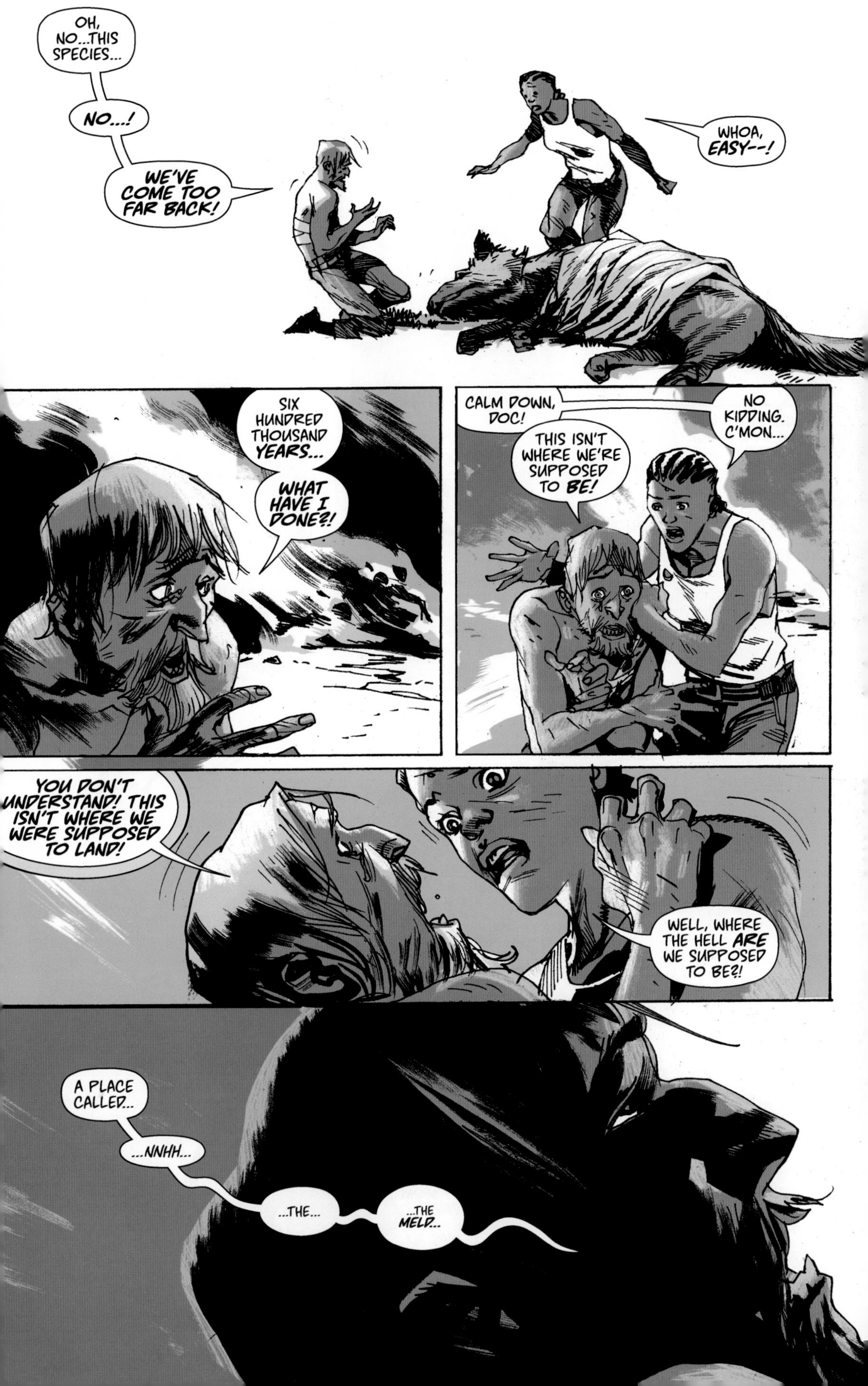
OH, NO...THIS SPECIES...
NO...!
WE'VE COME TOO FAR BACK!
WHOA, EASY--!
SIX HUNDRED THOUSAND YEARS...
WHAT HAVE I DONE?!
CALM DOWN, DOC!
NO KIDDING. C'MON...
THIS ISN'T WHERE WE'RE SUPPOSED TO BE!
YOU DON'T UNDERSTAND! THIS ISN'T WHERE WE WERE SUPPOSED TO LAND!
WELL, WHERE THE HELL ARE WE SUPPOSED TO BE?!
A PLACE CALLED...
...NNHH...
...THE...
...THE MELD...

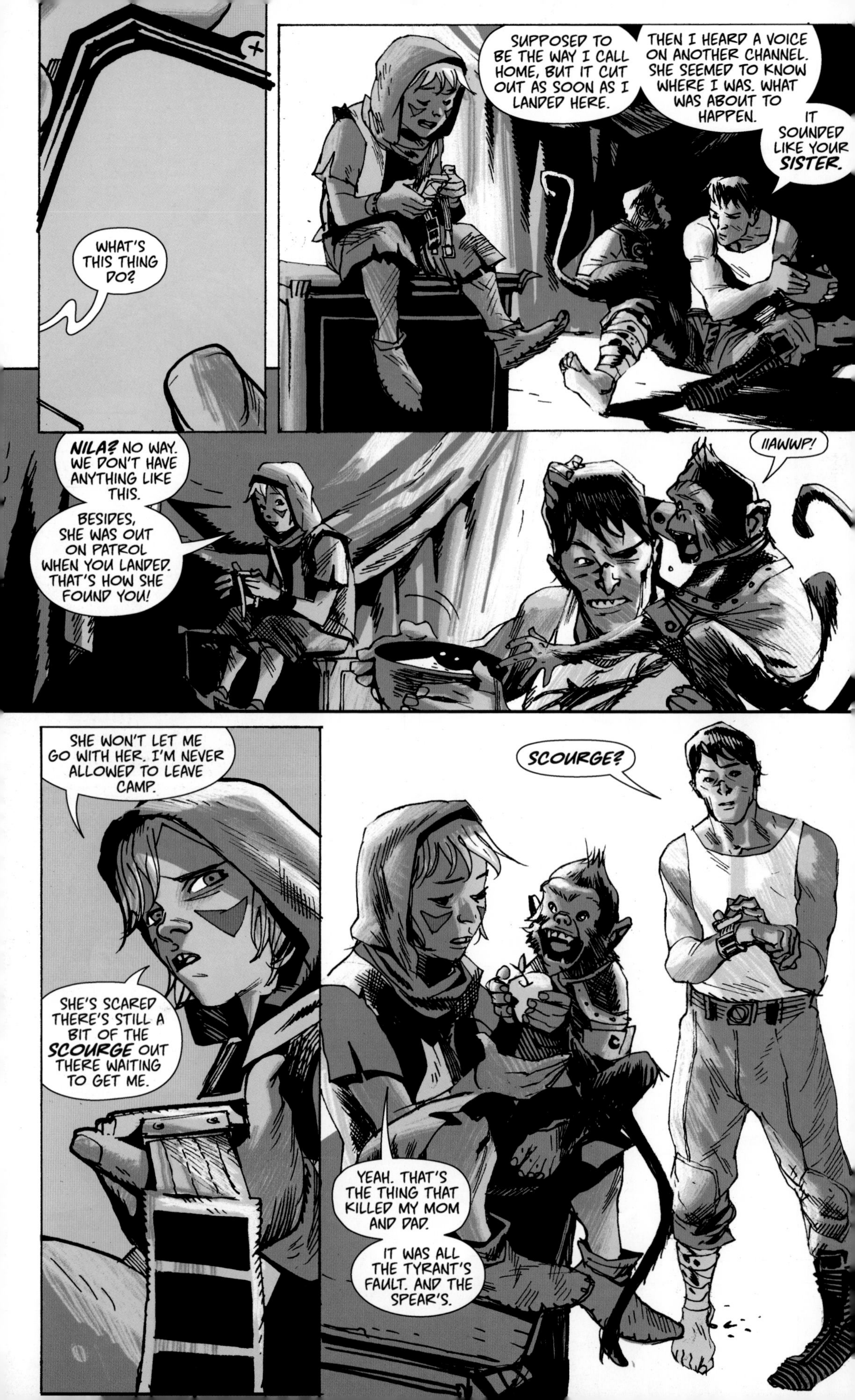
WHAT'S THIS THING DO?
SUPPOSED TO BE THE WAY I CALL HOME, BUT IT CUT OUT AS SOON AS I LANDED HERE.
THEN I HEARD A VOICE ON ANOTHER CHANNEL. SHE SEEMED TO KNOW WHERE I WAS. WHAT WAS ABOUT TO HAPPEN.
IT SOUNDED LIKE YOUR SISTER.
NILA? NO WAY. WE DON'T HAVE ANYTHING LIKE THIS.
BESIDES, SHE WAS OUT ON PATROL WHEN YOU LANDED. THAT'S HOW SHE FOUND YOU!
IIAWWP!
SHE WON'T LET ME GO WITH HER. I'M NEVER ALLOWED TO LEAVE CAMP.
SHE'S SCARED THERE'S STILL A BIT OF THE SCOURGE OUT THERE WAITING TO GET ME.
SCOURGE?
YEAH. THAT'S THE THING THAT KILLED MY MOM AND DAD.
IT WAS ALL THE TYRANT'S FAULT. AND THE SPEAR'S.

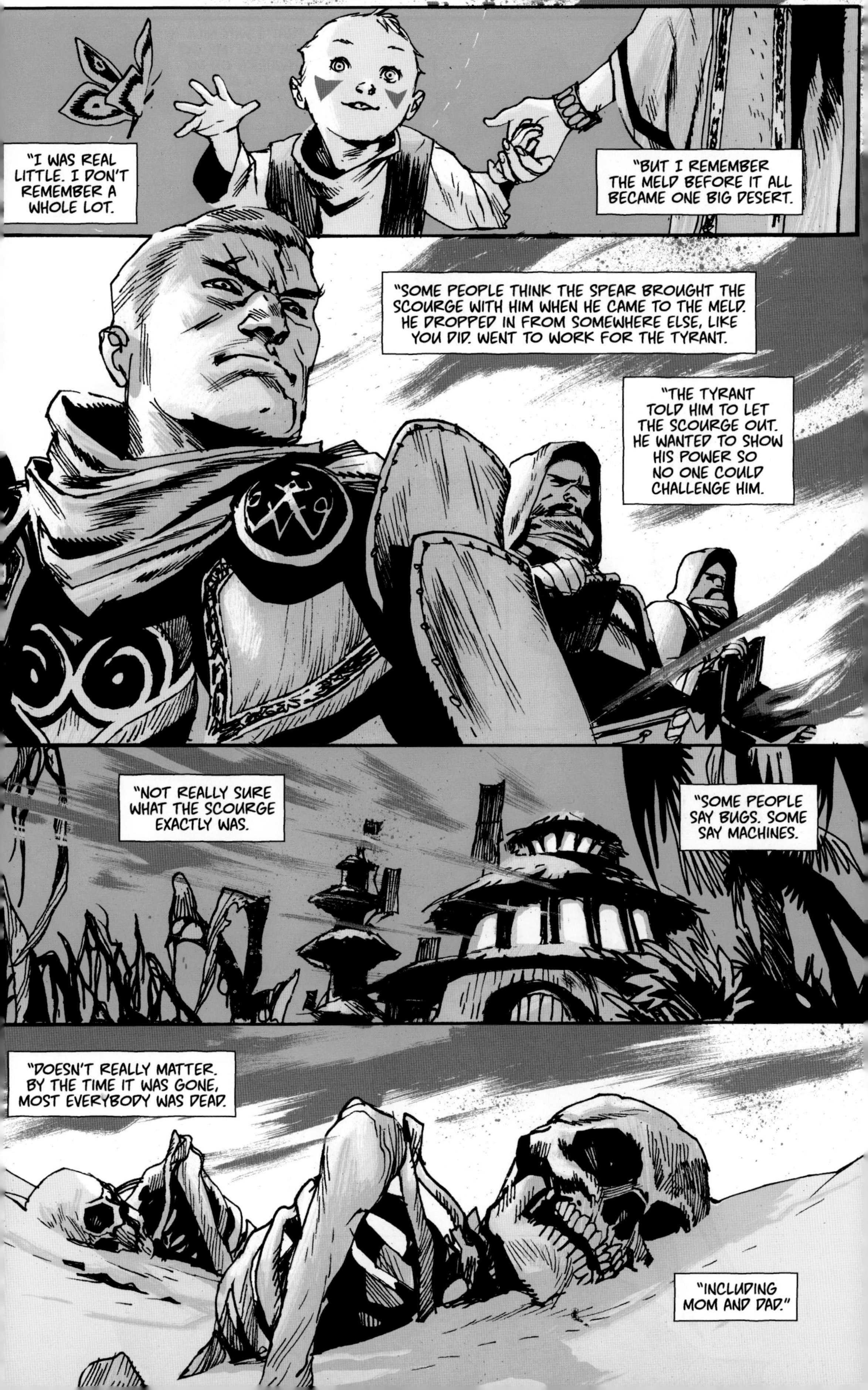
"I WAS REAL LITTLE. I DON'T REMEMBER A WHOLE LOT.
"BUT I REMEMBER THE MELD BEFORE IT ALL BECAME ONE BIG DESERT.
"SOME PEOPLE THINK THE SPEAR BROUGHT THE SCOURGE WITH HIM WHEN HE CAME TO THE MELD. HE DROPPED IN FROM SOMEWHERE ELSE, LIKE YOU DID. WENT TO WORK FOR THE TYRANT.
"THE TYRANT TOLD HIM TO LET THE SCOURGE OUT. HE WANTED TO SHOW HIS POWER SO NO ONE COULD CHALLENGE HIM.
"NOT REALLY SURE WHAT THE SCOURGE EXACTLY WAS.
"SOME PEOPLE SAY BUGS. SOME SAY MACHINES.
"DOESN'T REALLY MATTER. BY THE TIME IT WAS GONE, MOST EVERYBODY WAS DEAD.
"INCLUDING MOM AND DAD."

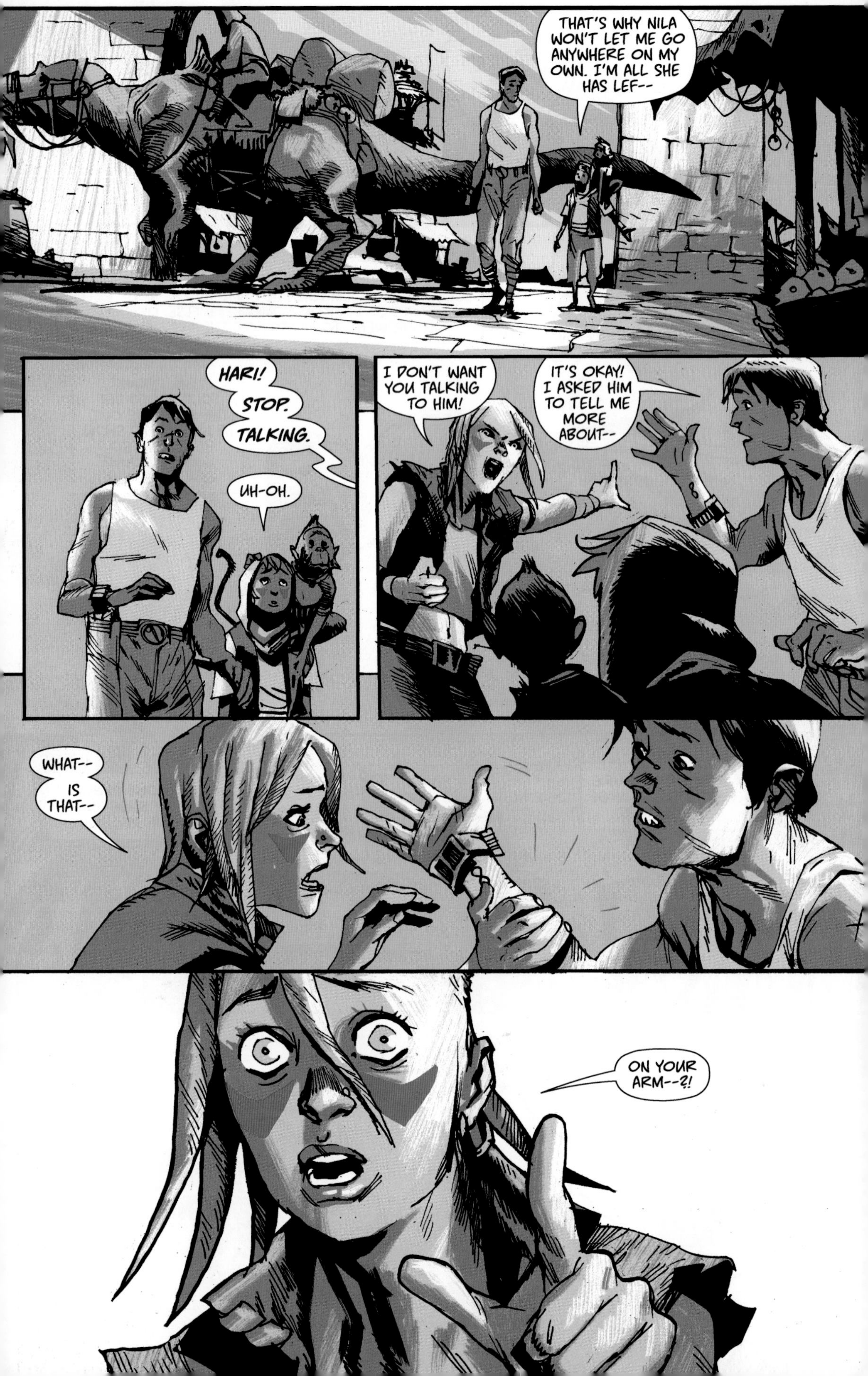
THAT'S WHY NILA WON'T LET ME GO ANYWHERE ON MY OWN. I'M ALL SHE HAS LEF--
HARI!
STOP.
TALKING.
UH-OH.
I DON'T WANT YOU TALKING TO HIM!
IT'S OKAY! I ASKED HIM TO TELL ME MORE ABOUT--
WHAT--
IS THAT--
ON YOUR ARM--?!

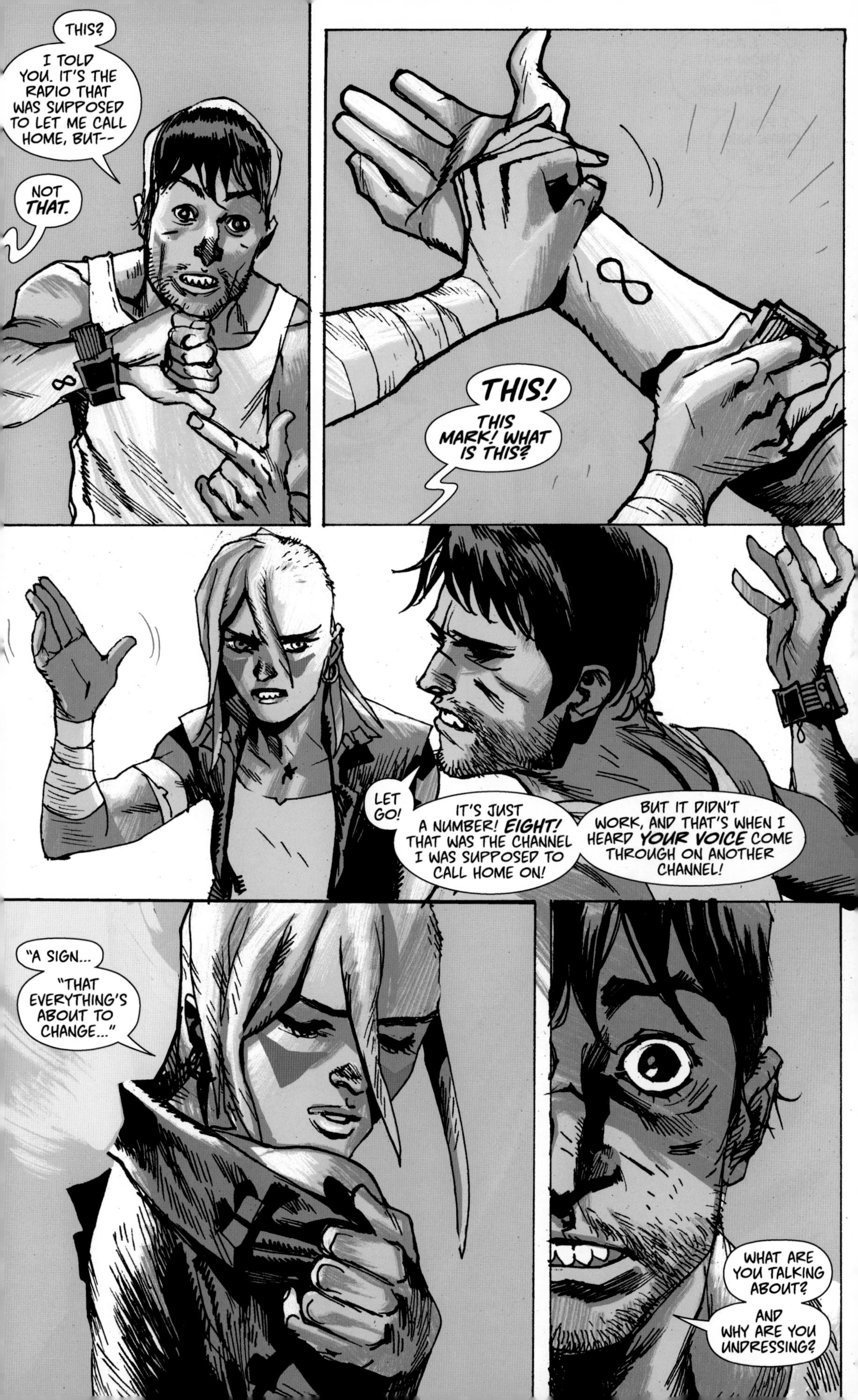
THIS?
I TOLD YOU. IT'S THE RADIO THAT WAS SUPPOSED TO LET ME CALL HOME, BUT--
NOT THAT.
THIS!
THIS MARK! WHAT IS THIS?
LET GO!
IT'S JUST A NUMBER! EIGHT! THAT WAS THE CHANNEL I WAS SUPPOSED TO CALL HOME ON!
BUT IT DIDN'T WORK, AND THAT'S WHEN I HEARD YOUR VOICE COME THROUGH ON ANOTHER CHANNEL!
"A SIGN...
"THAT EVERYTHING'S ABOUT TO CHANGE..."
WHAT ARE YOU TALKING ABOUT?
AND WHY ARE YOU UNDRESSING?

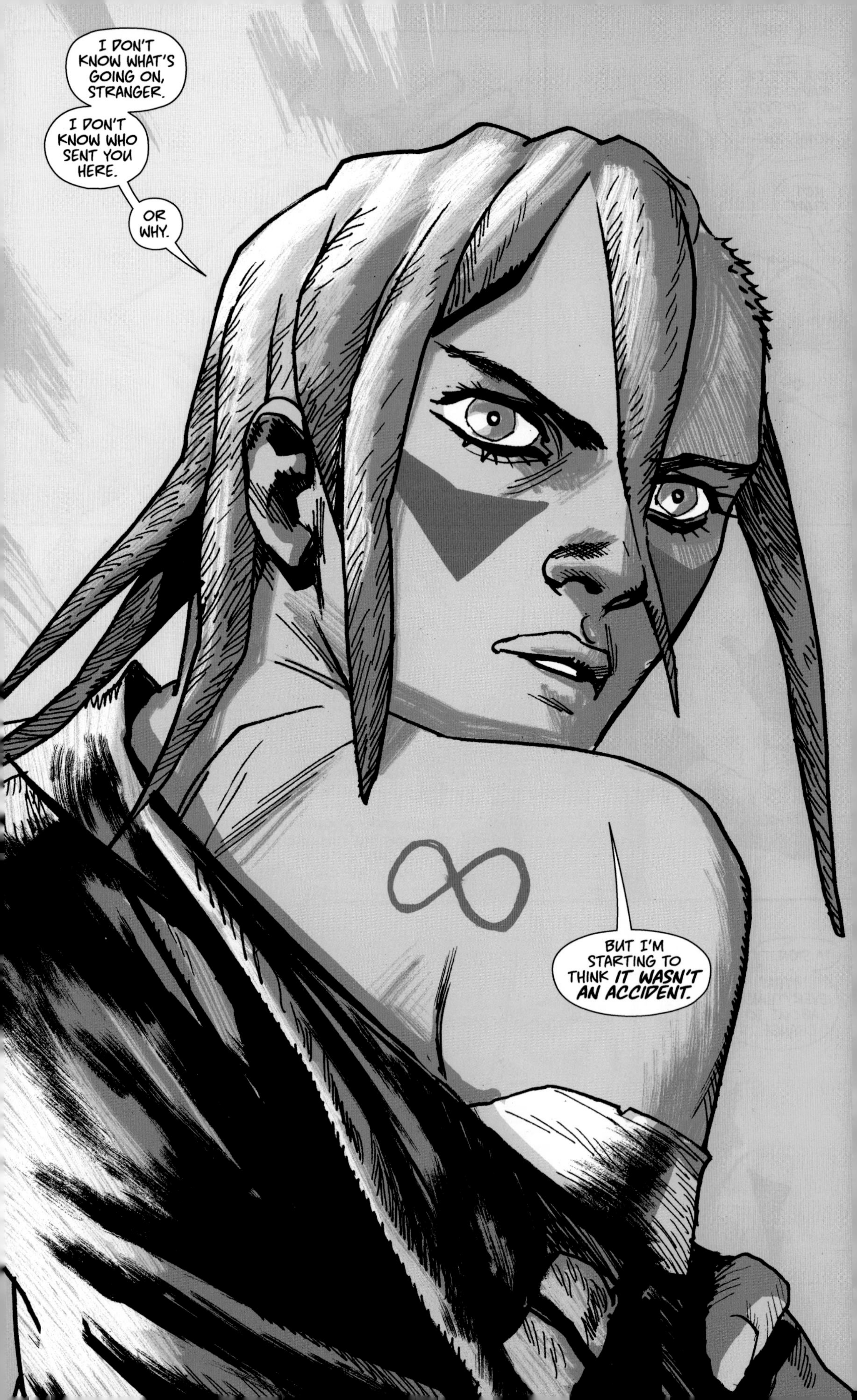
I DON'T KNOW WHAT'S GOING ON, STRANGER.
I DON'T KNOW WHO SENT YOU HERE.
OR WHY.
BUT I'M STARTING TO THINK *IT WASN'T AN ACCIDENT.*

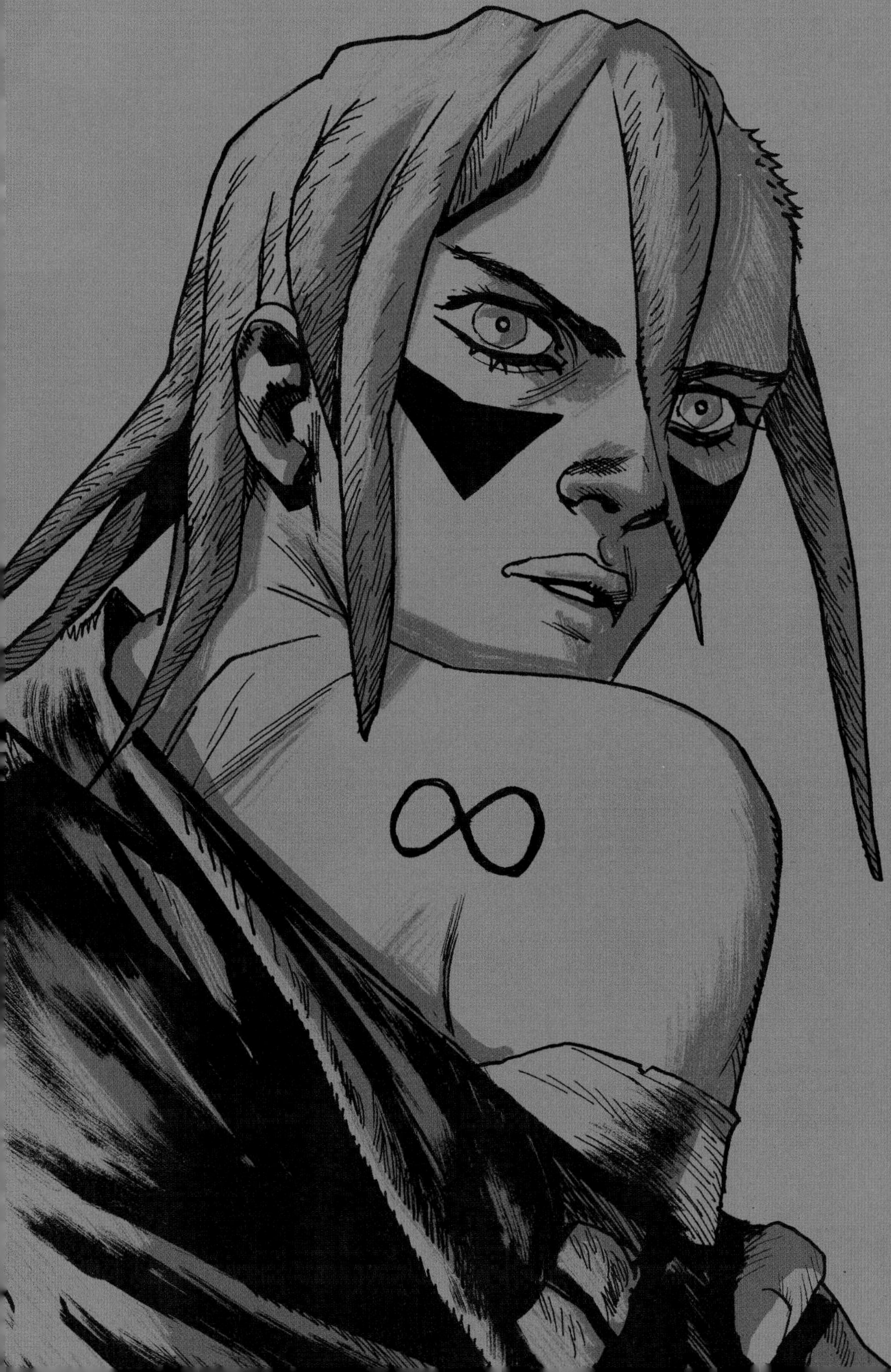

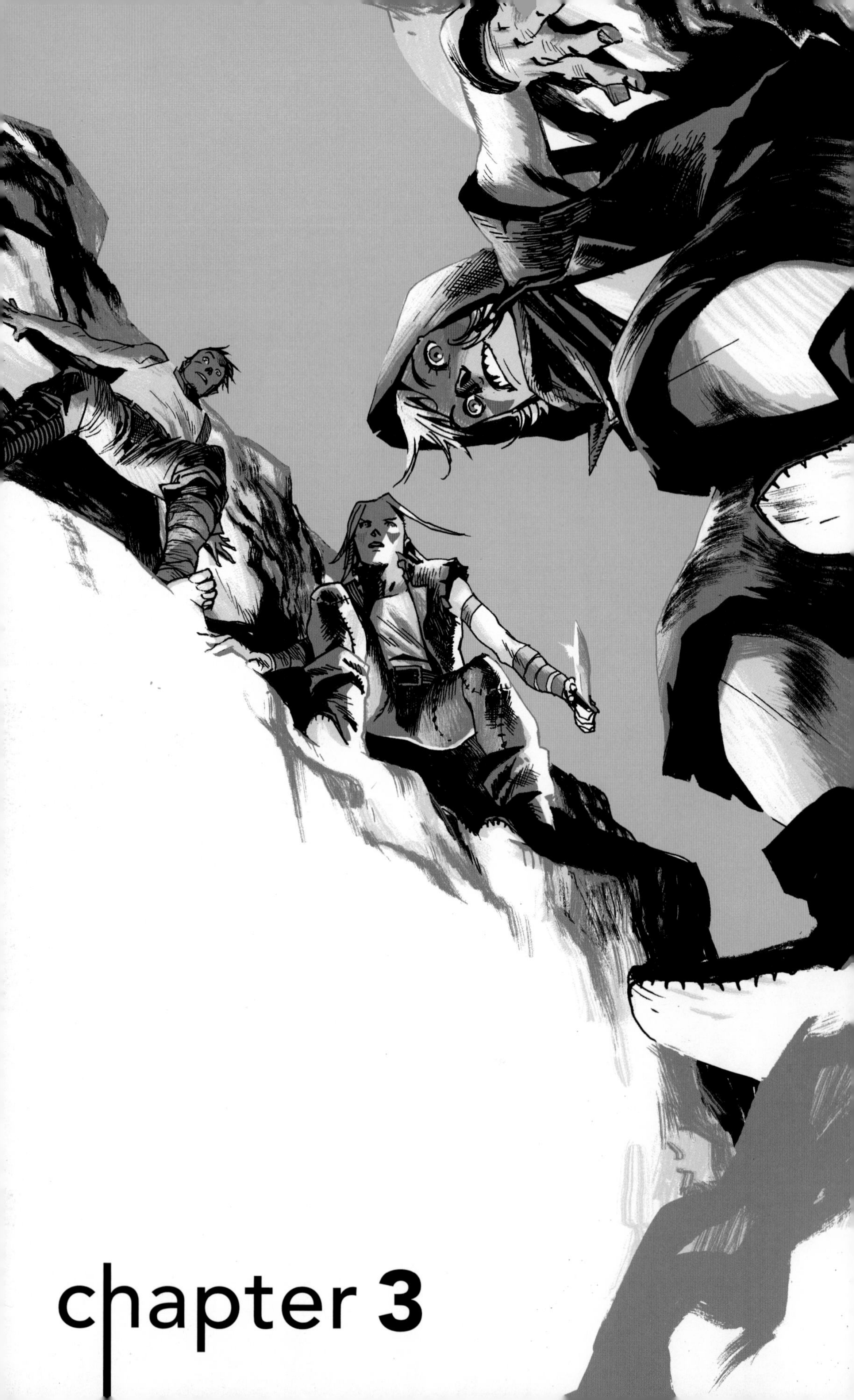

chapter 3

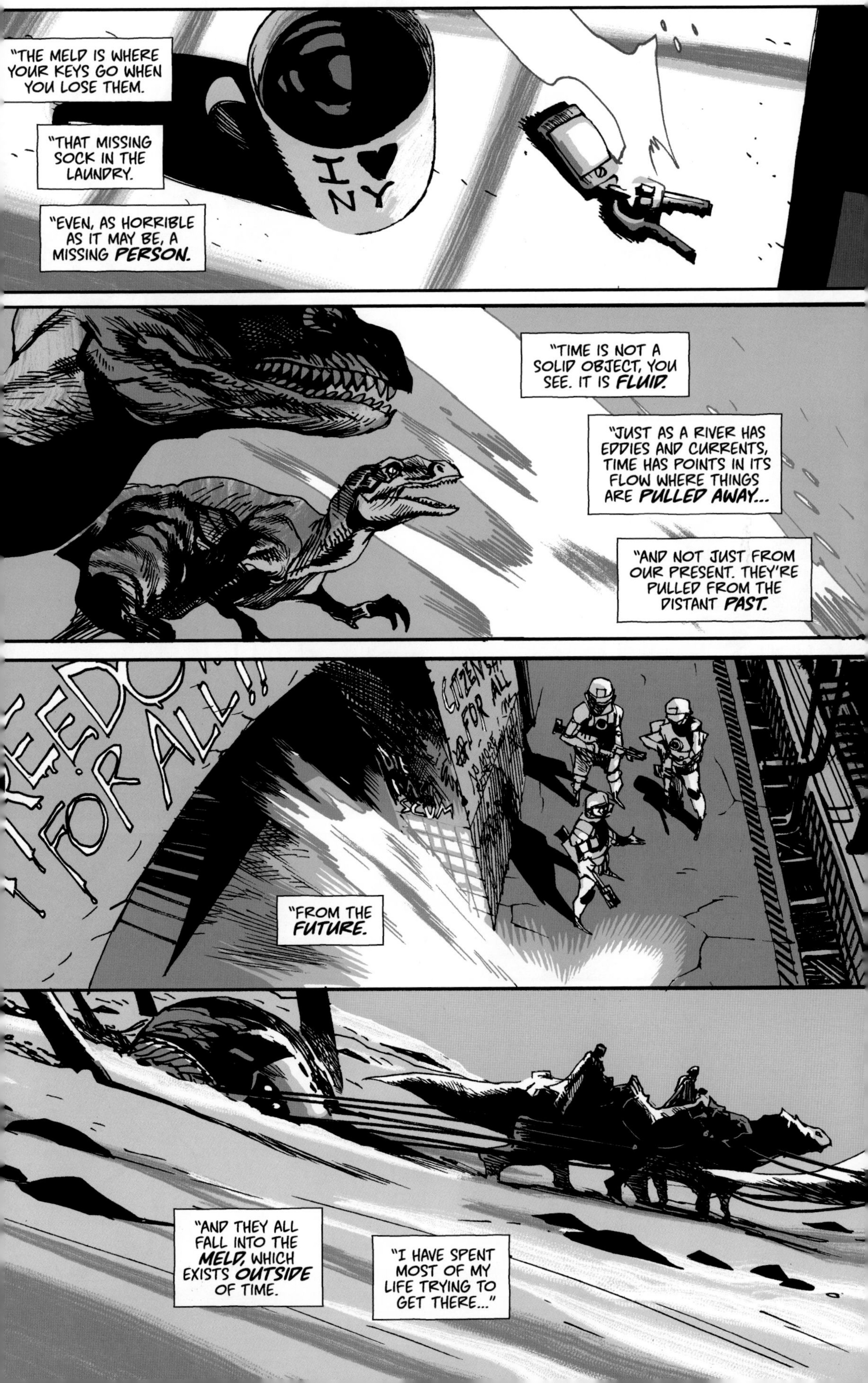
"THE MELD IS WHERE YOUR KEYS GO WHEN YOU LOSE THEM.
I ♥ NY
"THAT MISSING SOCK IN THE LAUNDRY.
"EVEN, AS HORRIBLE AS IT MAY BE, A MISSING *PERSON.*
"TIME IS NOT A SOLID OBJECT, YOU SEE. IT IS *FLUID.*
"JUST AS A RIVER HAS EDDIES AND CURRENTS, TIME HAS POINTS IN ITS FLOW WHERE THINGS ARE *PULLED AWAY...*
"AND NOT JUST FROM OUR PRESENT. THEY'RE PULLED FROM THE DISTANT *PAST.*
FOR ALL!!
FOR ALL
SCUM
"FROM THE *FUTURE.*
"AND THEY ALL FALL INTO THE *MELD,* WHICH EXISTS *OUTSIDE* OF TIME.
"I HAVE SPENT MOST OF MY LIFE TRYING TO GET THERE..."

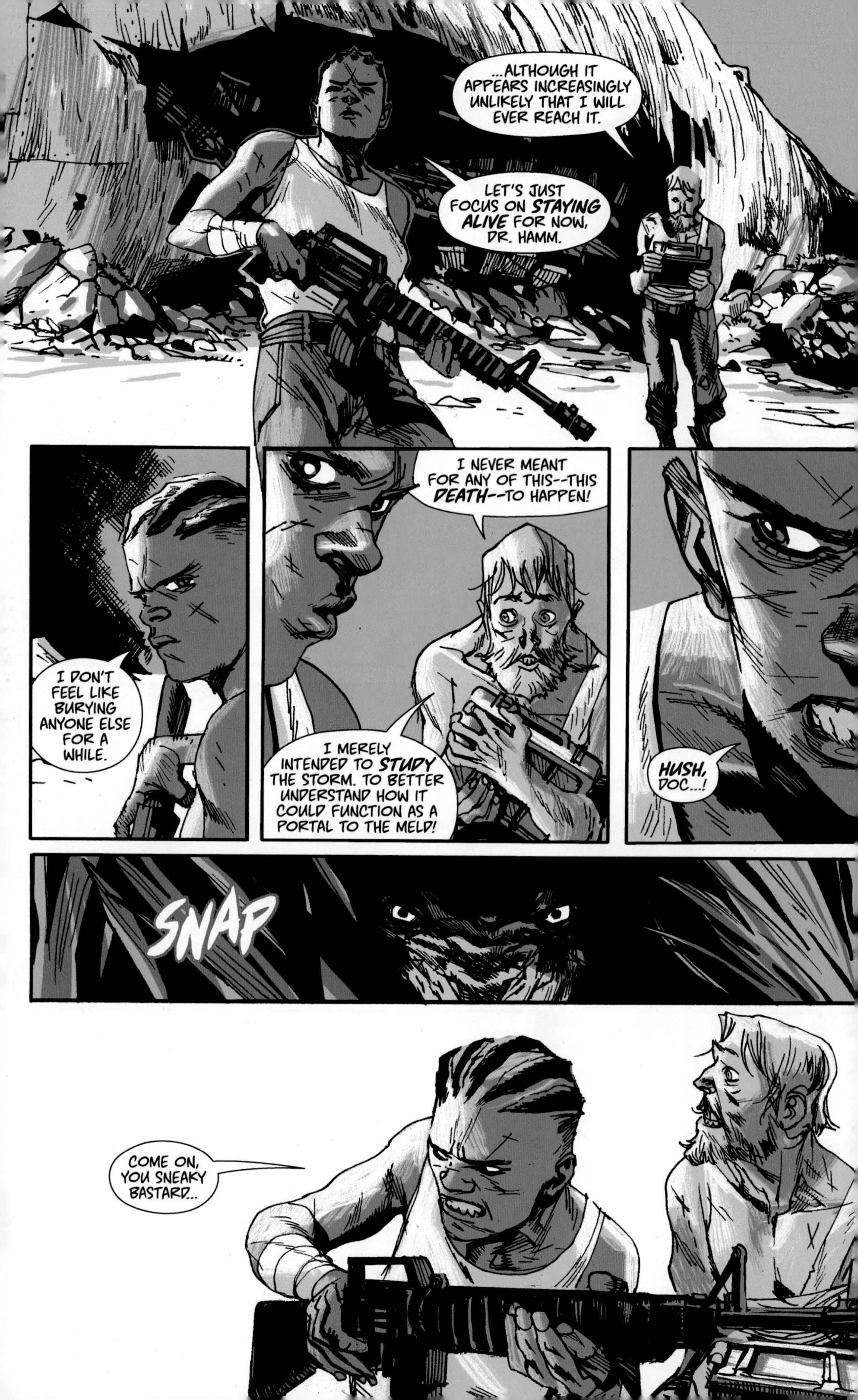
...ALTHOUGH IT APPEARS INCREASINGLY UNLIKELY THAT I WILL EVER REACH IT.
LET'S JUST FOCUS ON STAYING ALIVE FOR NOW, DR. HAMM.
I DON'T FEEL LIKE BURYING ANYONE ELSE FOR A WHILE.
I NEVER MEANT FOR ANY OF THIS--THIS DEATH--TO HAPPEN!
I MERELY INTENDED TO STUDY THE STORM. TO BETTER UNDERSTAND HOW IT COULD FUNCTION AS A PORTAL TO THE MELD!
HUSH, DOC...!
SNAP
COME ON, YOU SNEAKY BASTARD...

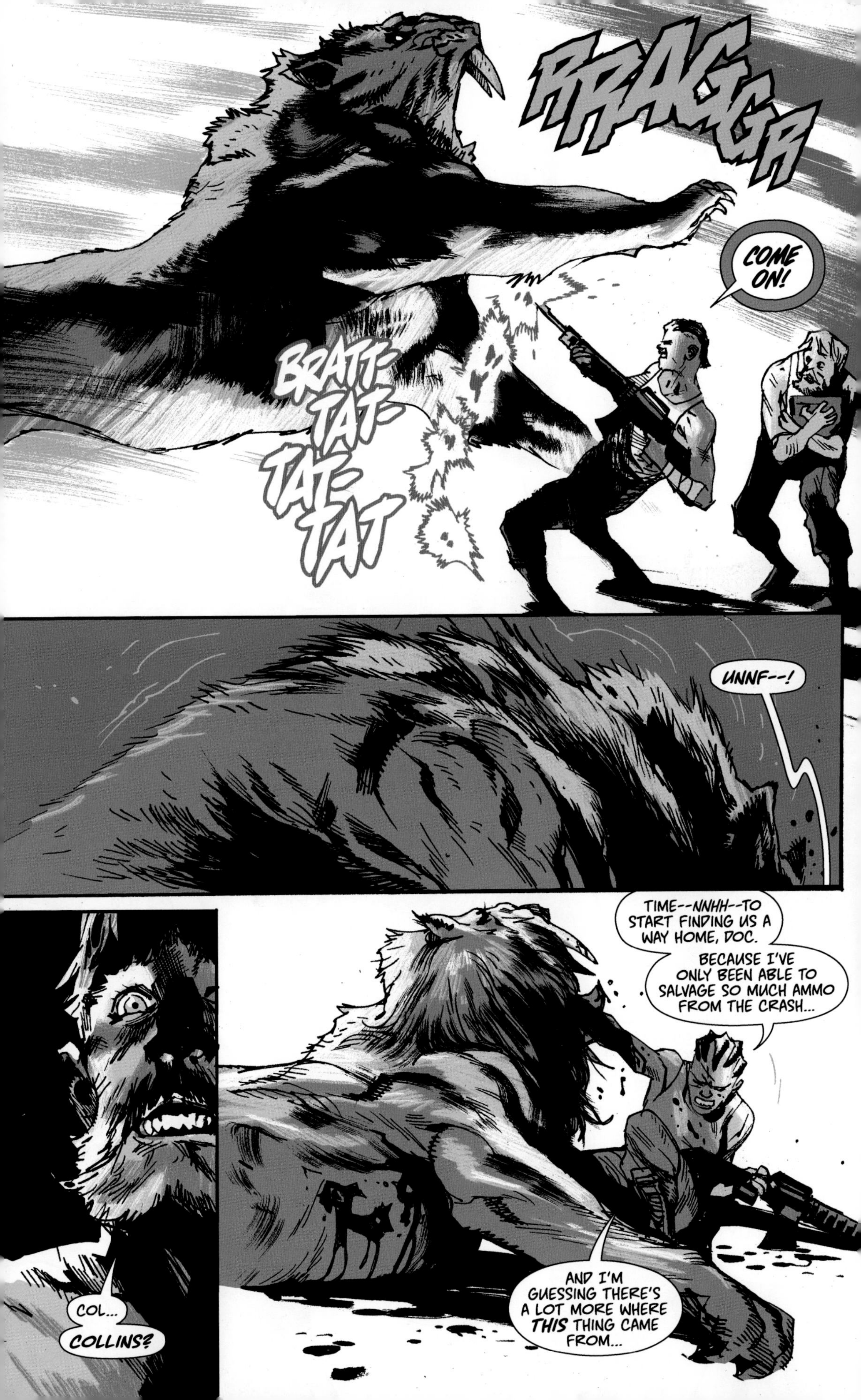
RRRAGGR
COME ON!
BRATT-TAT-TAT-TAT
UNNF--!
TIME--NNHH--TO START FINDING US A WAY HOME, DOC.
BECAUSE I'VE ONLY BEEN ABLE TO SALVAGE SO MUCH AMMO FROM THE CRASH...
AND I'M GUESSING THERE'S A LOT MORE WHERE THIS THING CAME FROM...
COL...
COLLINS?

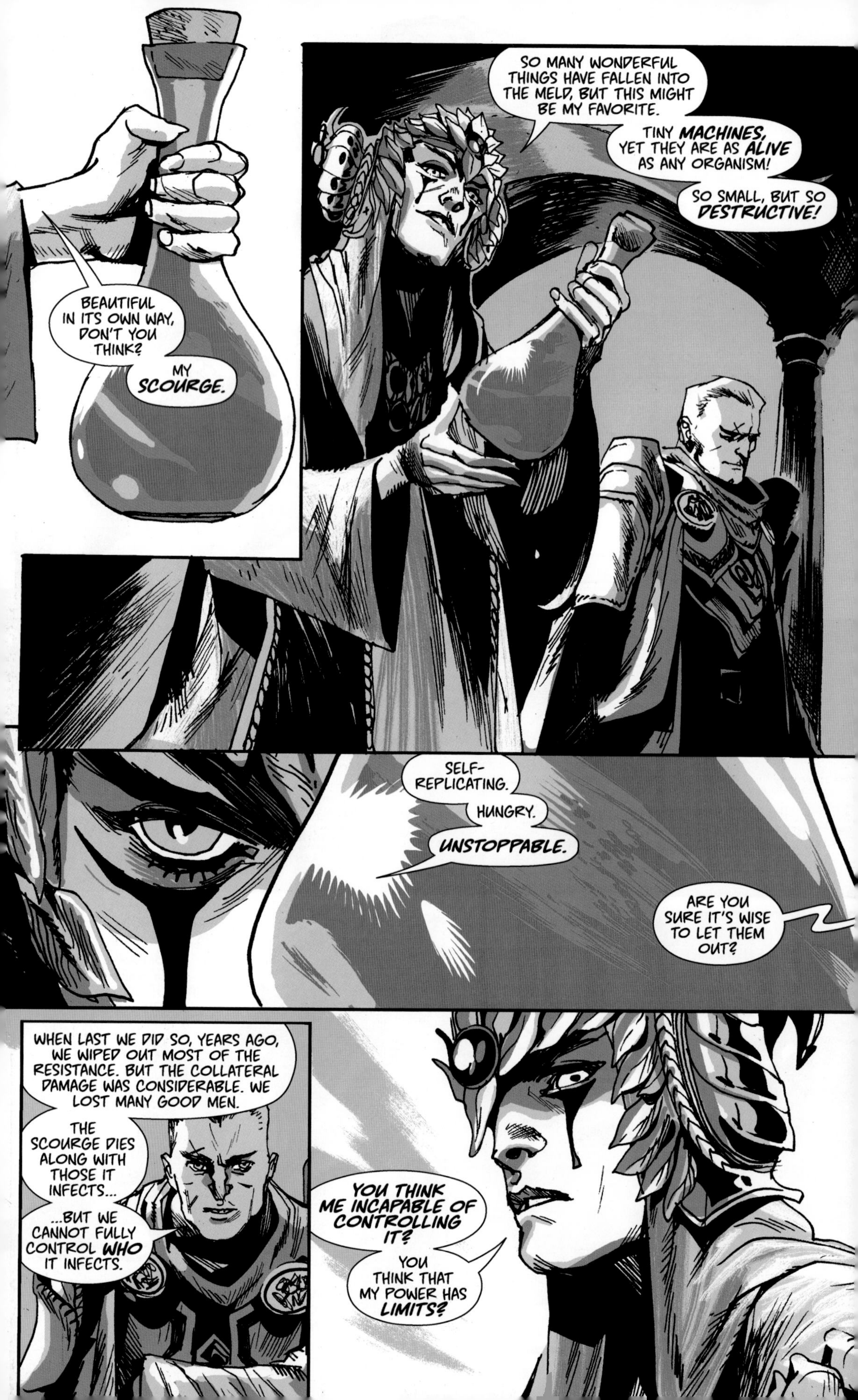
SO MANY WONDERFUL THINGS HAVE FALLEN INTO THE MELD, BUT THIS MIGHT BE MY FAVORITE.
TINY MACHINES, YET THEY ARE AS ALIVE AS ANY ORGANISM!
SO SMALL, BUT SO DESTRUCTIVE!
BEAUTIFUL IN ITS OWN WAY, DON'T YOU THINK?
MY SCOURGE.
SELF-REPLICATING.
HUNGRY.
UNSTOPPABLE.
ARE YOU SURE IT'S WISE TO LET THEM OUT?
WHEN LAST WE DID SO, YEARS AGO, WE WIPED OUT MOST OF THE RESISTANCE. BUT THE COLLATERAL DAMAGE WAS CONSIDERABLE. WE LOST MANY GOOD MEN.
THE SCOURGE DIES ALONG WITH THOSE IT INFECTS...
...BUT WE CANNOT FULLY CONTROL WHO IT INFECTS.
YOU THINK ME INCAPABLE OF CONTROLLING IT?
YOU THINK THAT MY POWER HAS LIMITS?

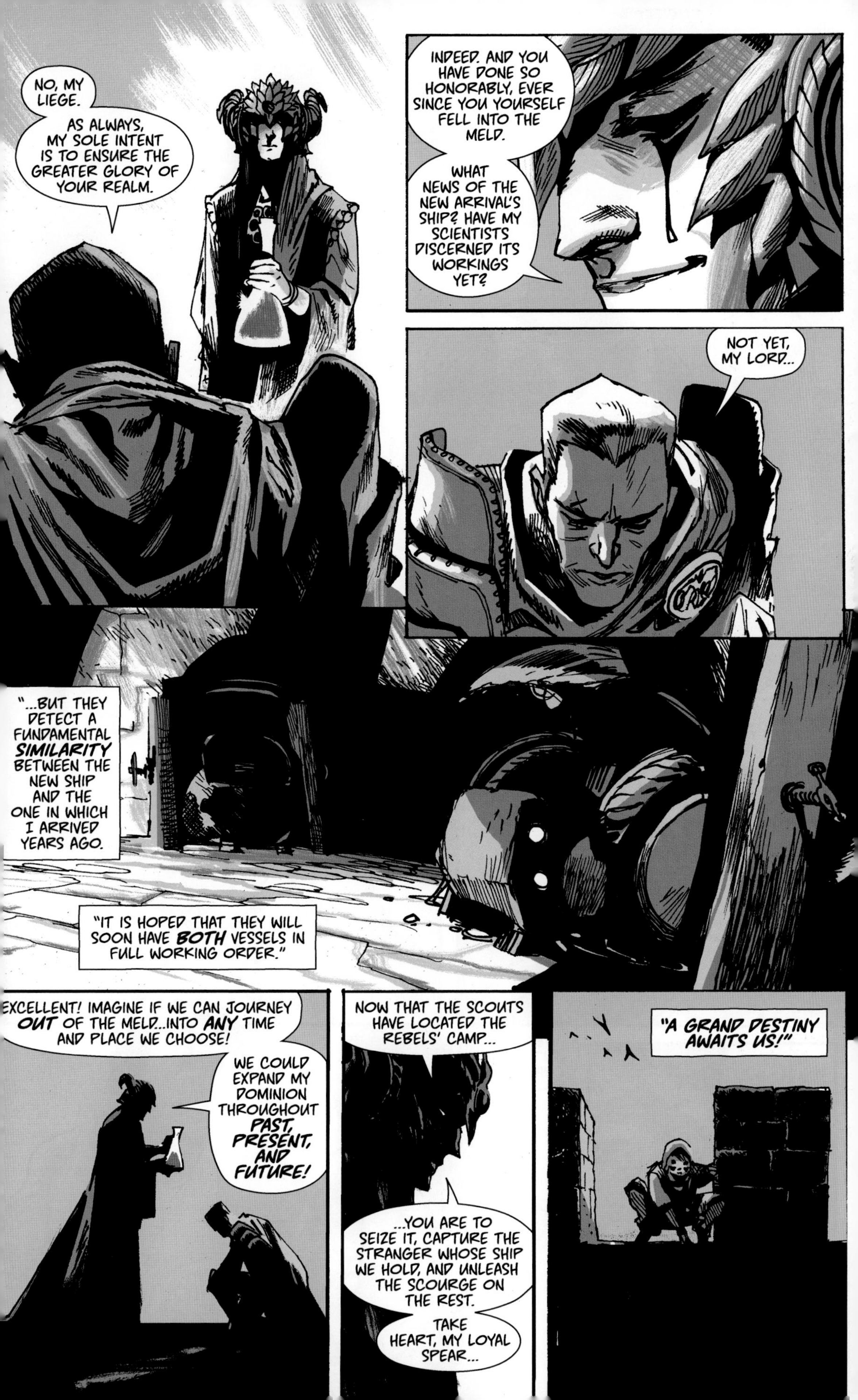
NO, MY LIEGE.
AS ALWAYS, MY SOLE INTENT IS TO ENSURE THE GREATER GLORY OF YOUR REALM.
INDEED. AND YOU HAVE DONE SO HONORABLY, EVER SINCE YOU YOURSELF FELL INTO THE MELD.
WHAT NEWS OF THE NEW ARRIVAL'S SHIP? HAVE MY SCIENTISTS DISCERNED ITS WORKINGS YET?
NOT YET, MY LORD...
"...BUT THEY DETECT A FUNDAMENTAL SIMILARITY BETWEEN THE NEW SHIP AND THE ONE IN WHICH I ARRIVED YEARS AGO.
"IT IS HOPED THAT THEY WILL SOON HAVE BOTH VESSELS IN FULL WORKING ORDER."
EXCELLENT! IMAGINE IF WE CAN JOURNEY OUT OF THE MELD...INTO ANY TIME AND PLACE WE CHOOSE!
WE COULD EXPAND MY DOMINION THROUGHOUT PAST, PRESENT, AND FUTURE!
NOW THAT THE SCOUTS HAVE LOCATED THE REBELS' CAMP...
...YOU ARE TO SEIZE IT, CAPTURE THE STRANGER WHOSE SHIP WE HOLD, AND UNLEASH THE SCOURGE ON THE REST.
TAKE HEART, MY LOYAL SPEAR...
"A GRAND DESTINY AWAITS US!"

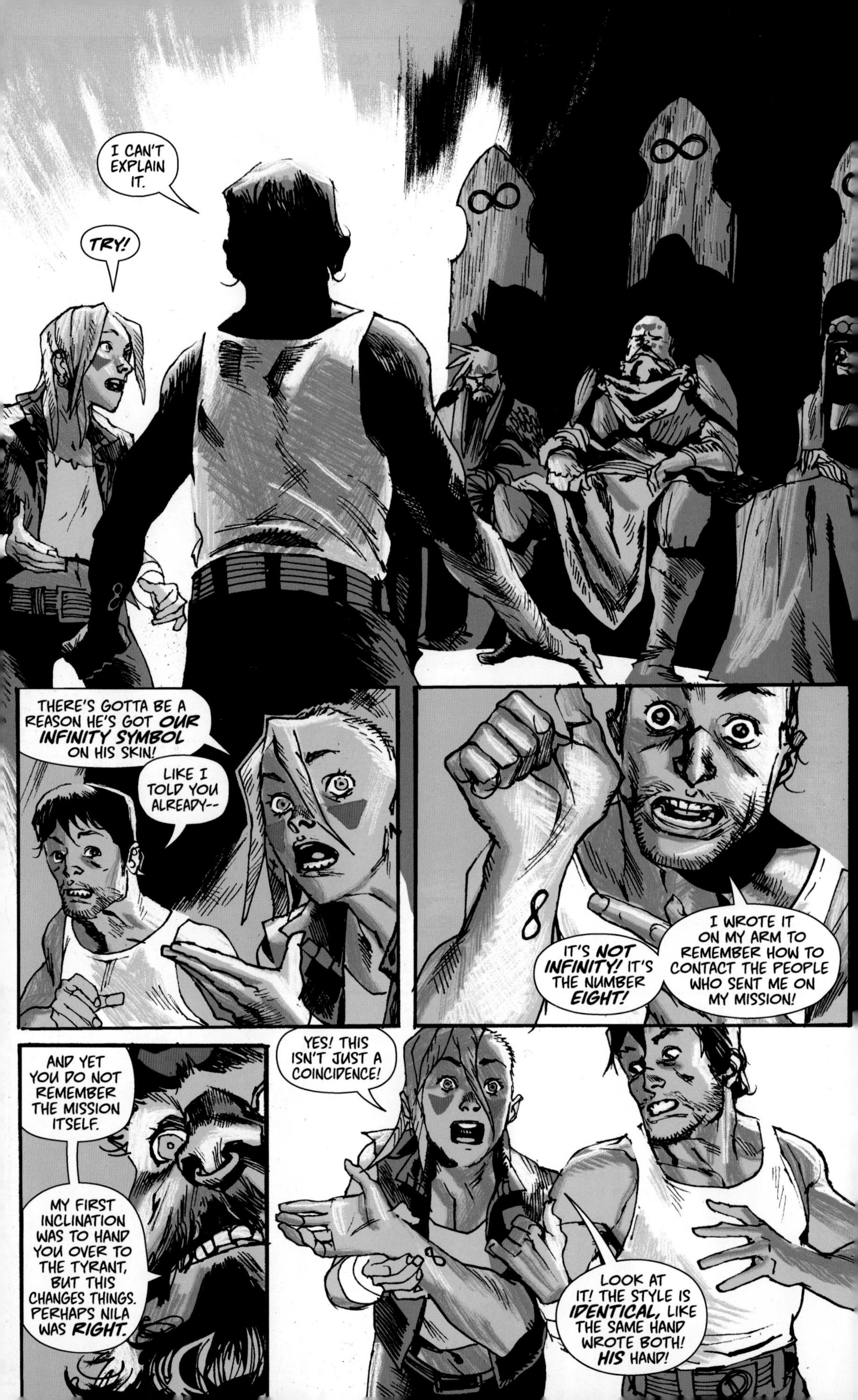
I CAN'T EXPLAIN IT.
TRY!
THERE'S GOTTA BE A REASON HE'S GOT OUR INFINITY SYMBOL ON HIS SKIN!
LIKE I TOLD YOU ALREADY--
IT'S NOT INFINITY! IT'S THE NUMBER EIGHT!
I WROTE IT ON MY ARM TO REMEMBER HOW TO CONTACT THE PEOPLE WHO SENT ME ON MY MISSION!
AND YET YOU DO NOT REMEMBER THE MISSION ITSELF.
MY FIRST INCLINATION WAS TO HAND YOU OVER TO THE TYRANT, BUT THIS CHANGES THINGS. PERHAPS NILA WAS RIGHT.
YES! THIS ISN'T JUST A COINCIDENCE!
LOOK AT IT! THE STYLE IS IDENTICAL, LIKE THE SAME HAND WROTE BOTH! HIS HAND!

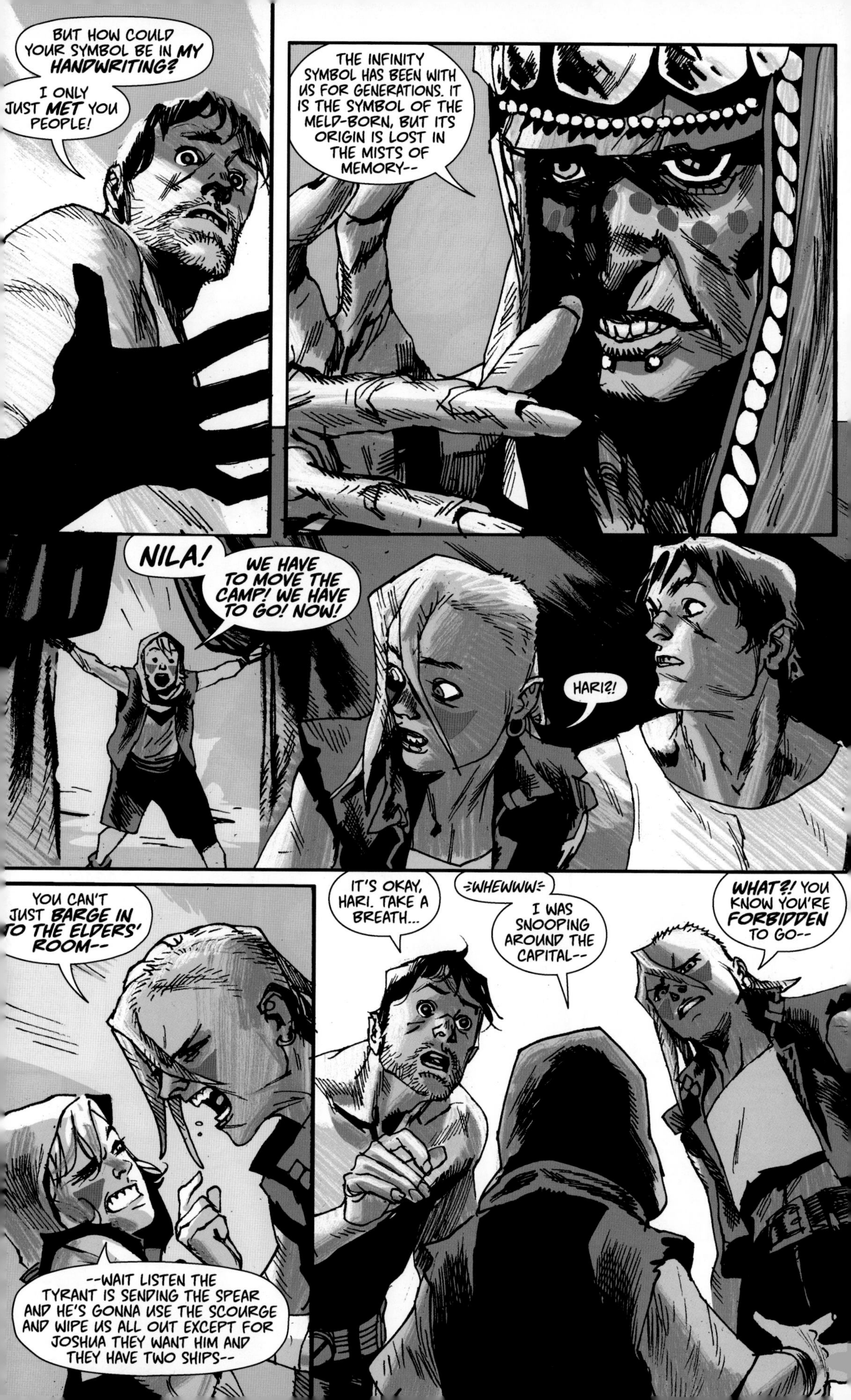

BUT HOW COULD YOUR SYMBOL BE IN **MY HANDWRITING?**
I ONLY JUST **MET** YOU PEOPLE!
THE INFINITY SYMBOL HAS BEEN WITH US FOR GENERATIONS. IT IS THE SYMBOL OF THE MELD-BORN, BUT ITS ORIGIN IS LOST IN THE MISTS OF MEMORY--
NILA!
WE HAVE TO MOVE THE CAMP! WE HAVE TO GO! NOW!
HARI?!
YOU CAN'T JUST **BARGE IN** TO THE ELDERS' ROOM--
--WAIT LISTEN THE TYRANT IS SENDING THE SPEAR AND HE'S GONNA USE THE SCOURGE AND WIPE US ALL OUT EXCEPT FOR JOSHUA THEY WANT HIM AND THEY HAVE TWO SHIPS--
IT'S OKAY, HARI. TAKE A BREATH...
=WHEWWW=
I WAS SNOOPING AROUND THE CAPITAL--
WHAT?! YOU KNOW YOU'RE **FORBIDDEN** TO GO--

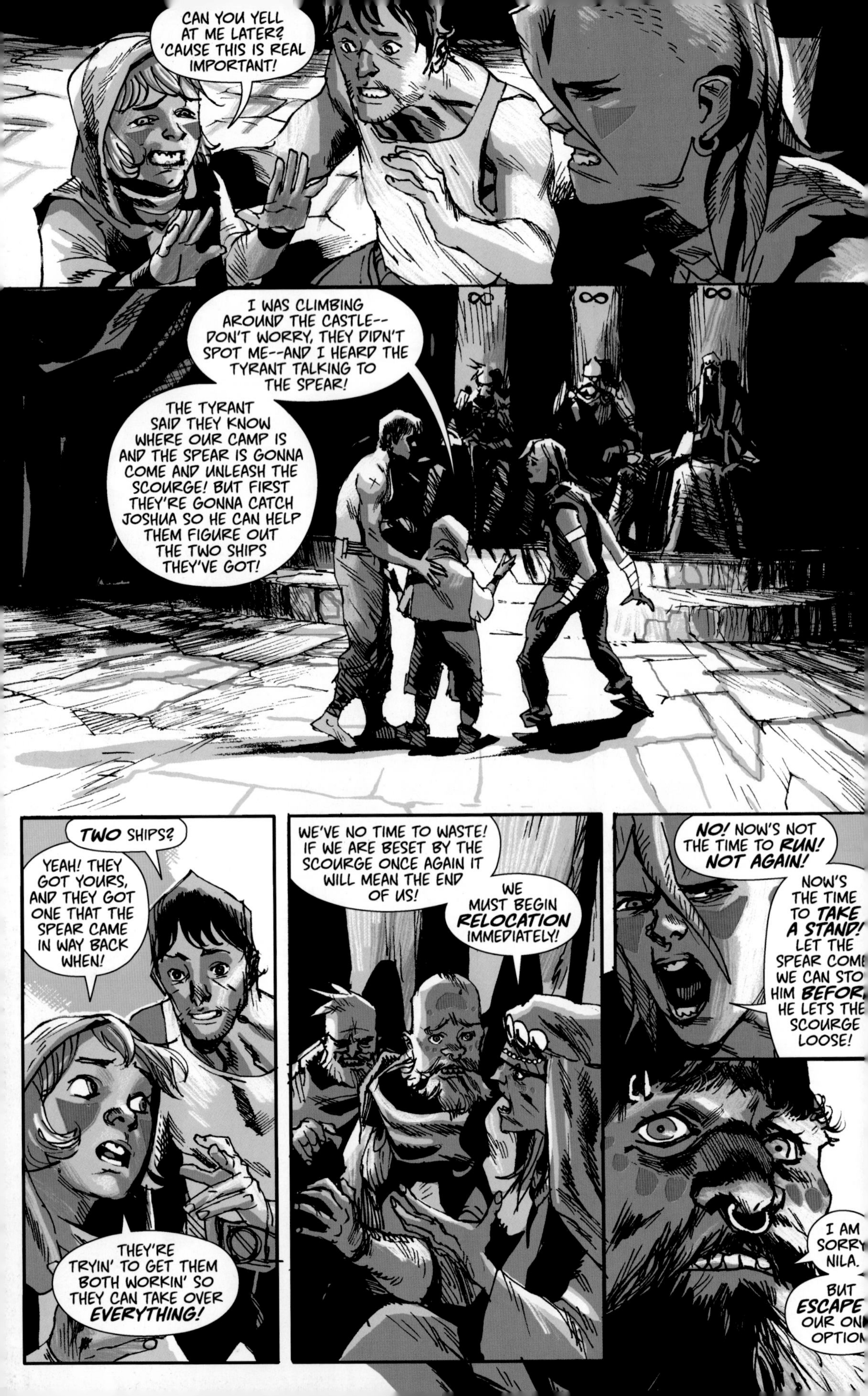
CAN YOU YELL AT ME LATER? 'CAUSE THIS IS REAL IMPORTANT!
I WAS CLIMBING AROUND THE CASTLE-- DON'T WORRY, THEY DIDN'T SPOT ME--AND I HEARD THE TYRANT TALKING TO THE SPEAR!
THE TYRANT SAID THEY KNOW WHERE OUR CAMP IS AND THE SPEAR IS GONNA COME AND UNLEASH THE SCOURGE! BUT FIRST THEY'RE GONNA CATCH JOSHUA SO HE CAN HELP THEM FIGURE OUT THE TWO SHIPS THEY'VE GOT!
TWO SHIPS?
YEAH! THEY GOT YOURS, AND THEY GOT ONE THAT THE SPEAR CAME IN WAY BACK WHEN!
THEY'RE TRYIN' TO GET THEM BOTH WORKIN' SO THEY CAN TAKE OVER EVERYTHING!
WE'VE NO TIME TO WASTE! IF WE ARE BESET BY THE SCOURGE ONCE AGAIN IT WILL MEAN THE END OF US!
WE MUST BEGIN RELOCATION IMMEDIATELY!
NO! NOW'S NOT THE TIME TO RUN! NOT AGAIN!
NOW'S THE TIME TO TAKE A STAND! LET THE SPEAR COM WE CAN STO HIM BEFOR HE LETS THE SCOURGE LOOSE!
I AM SORRY NILA.
BUT ESCAPE OUR ON OPTION

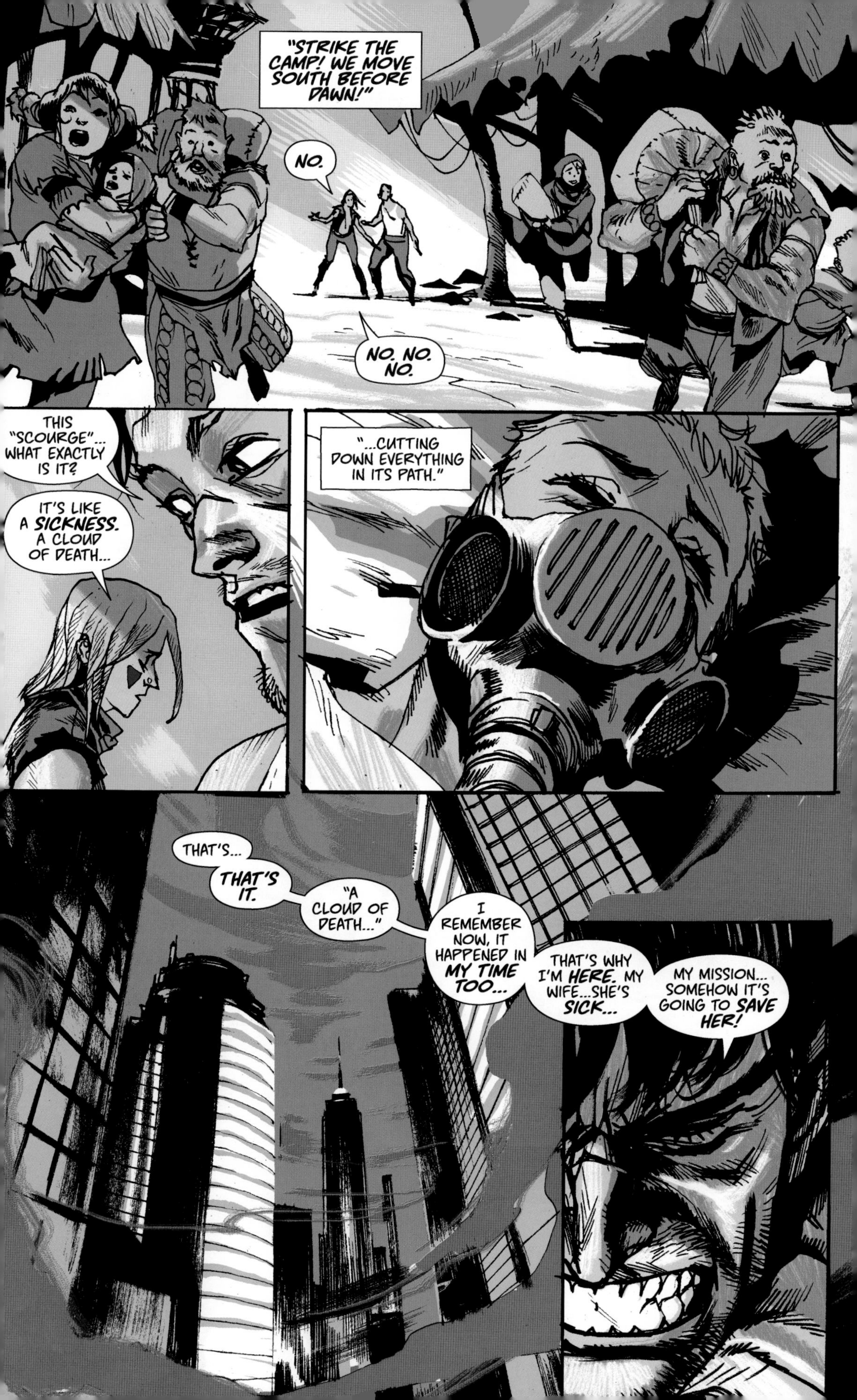
"STRIKE THE CAMP! WE MOVE SOUTH BEFORE DAWN!"
NO.
NO. NO. NO.
THIS "SCOURGE"... WHAT EXACTLY IS IT?
IT'S LIKE A SICKNESS. A CLOUD OF DEATH...
"...CUTTING DOWN EVERYTHING IN ITS PATH."
THAT'S... THAT'S IT.
"A CLOUD OF DEATH..."
I REMEMBER NOW, IT HAPPENED IN MY TIME TOO...
THAT'S WHY I'M HERE. MY WIFE...SHE'S SICK...
MY MISSION... SOMEHOW IT'S GOING TO SAVE HER!

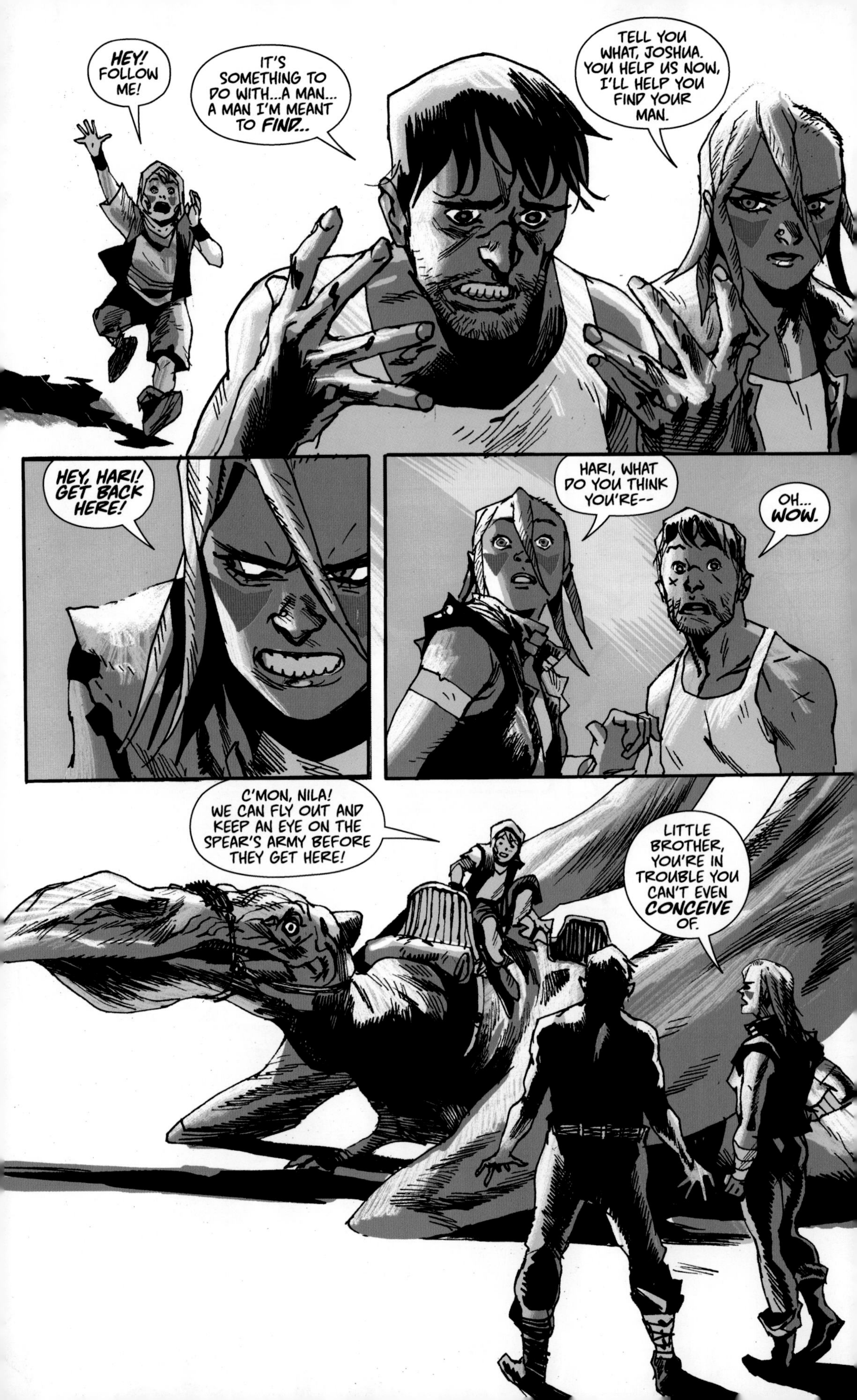
HEY! FOLLOW ME!
IT'S SOMETHING TO DO WITH...A MAN... A MAN I'M MEANT TO FIND...
TELL YOU WHAT, JOSHUA. YOU HELP US NOW, I'LL HELP YOU FIND YOUR MAN.
HEY, HARI! GET BACK HERE!
HARI, WHAT DO YOU THINK YOU'RE--
OH... WOW.
C'MON, NILA! WE CAN FLY OUT AND KEEP AN EYE ON THE SPEAR'S ARMY BEFORE THEY GET HERE!
LITTLE BROTHER, YOU'RE IN TROUBLE YOU CAN'T EVEN CONCEIVE OF.

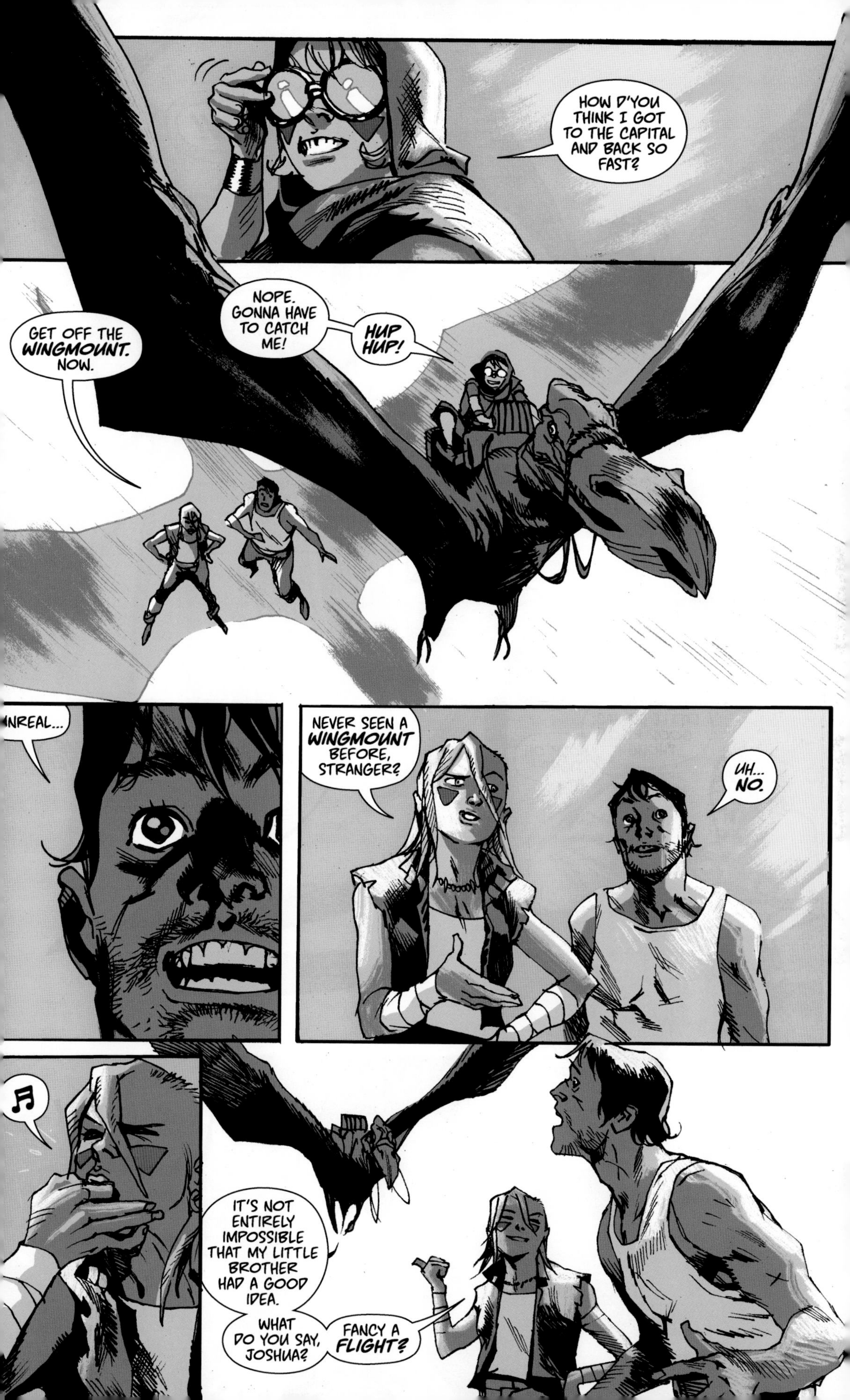
HOW D'YOU THINK I GOT TO THE CAPITAL AND BACK SO FAST?
GET OFF THE WINGMOUNT. NOW.
NOPE. GONNA HAVE TO CATCH ME!
HUP HUP!
NREAL...
NEVER SEEN A WINGMOUNT BEFORE, STRANGER?
UH... NO.
♫
IT'S NOT ENTIRELY IMPOSSIBLE THAT MY LITTLE BROTHER HAD A GOOD IDEA.
WHAT DO YOU SAY, JOSHUA?
FANCY A FLIGHT?

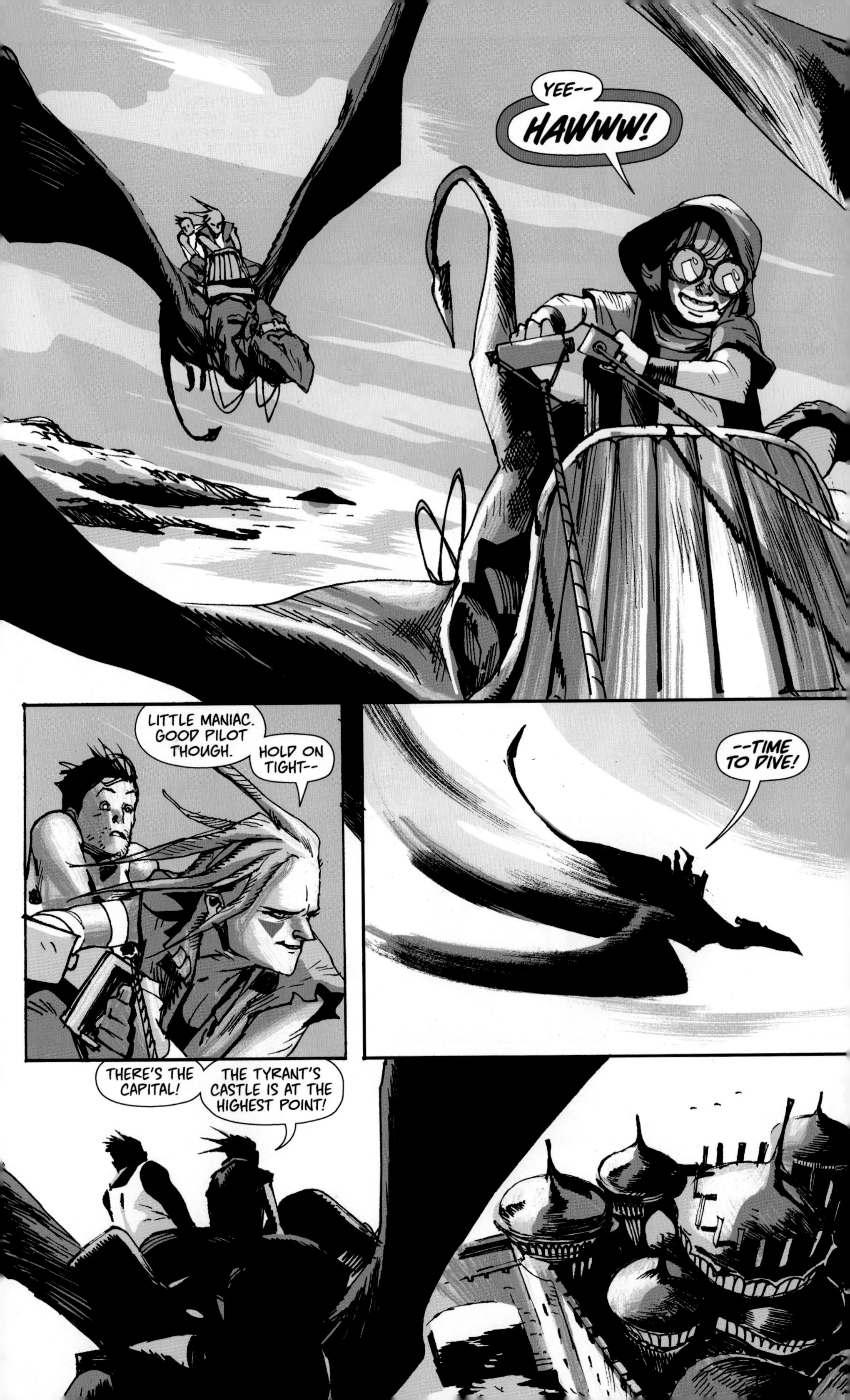
YEE--
HAWWW!
LITTLE MANIAC. GOOD PILOT THOUGH.
HOLD ON TIGHT--
--TIME TO DIVE!
THERE'S THE CAPITAL!
THE TYRANT'S CASTLE IS AT THE HIGHEST POINT!

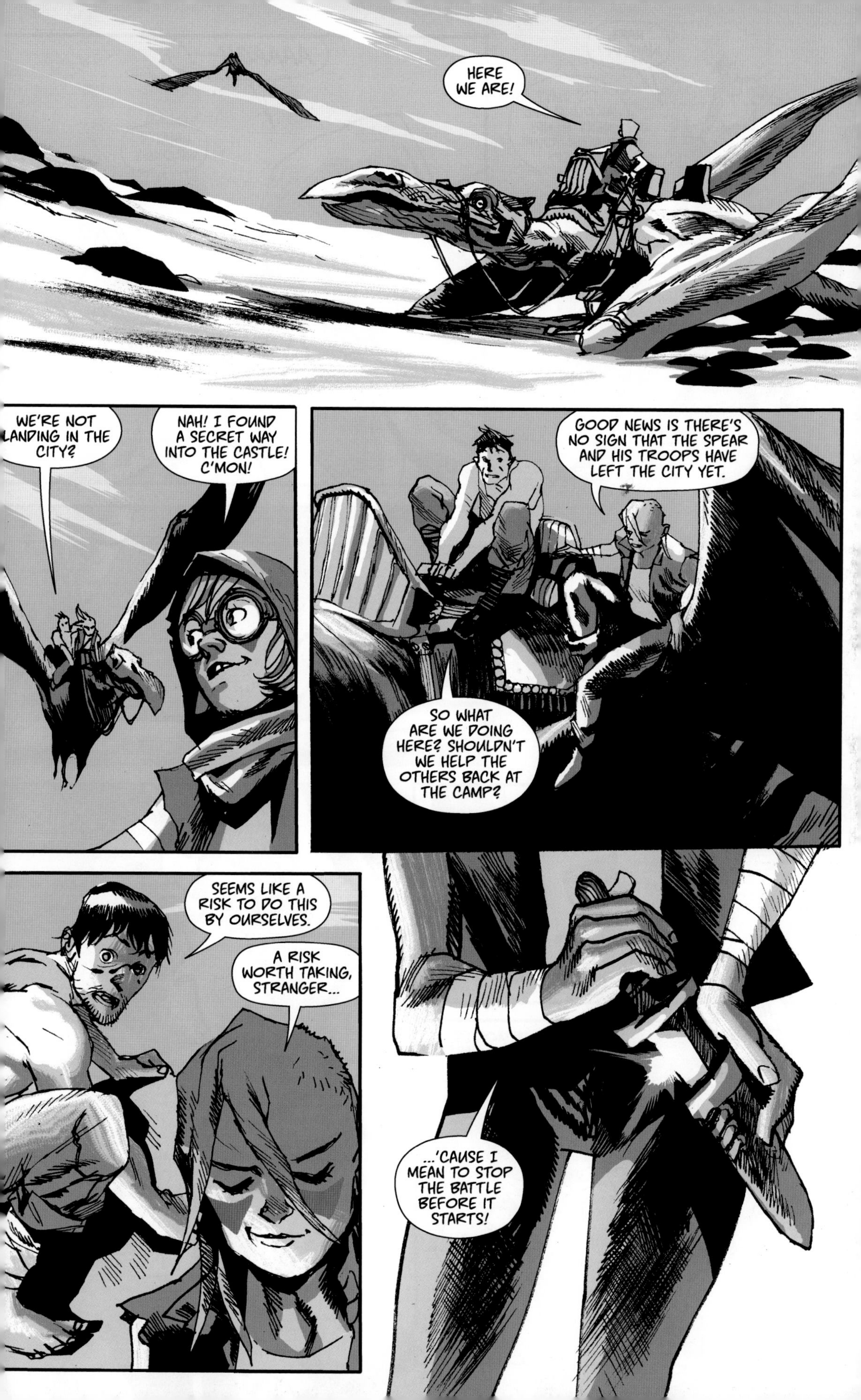
HERE WE ARE!
WE'RE NOT LANDING IN THE CITY?
NAH! I FOUND A SECRET WAY INTO THE CASTLE! C'MON!
GOOD NEWS IS THERE'S NO SIGN THAT THE SPEAR AND HIS TROOPS HAVE LEFT THE CITY YET.
SO WHAT ARE WE DOING HERE? SHOULDN'T WE HELP THE OTHERS BACK AT THE CAMP?
SEEMS LIKE A RISK TO DO THIS BY OURSELVES.
A RISK WORTH TAKING, STRANGER...
...'CAUSE I MEAN TO STOP THE BATTLE BEFORE IT STARTS!

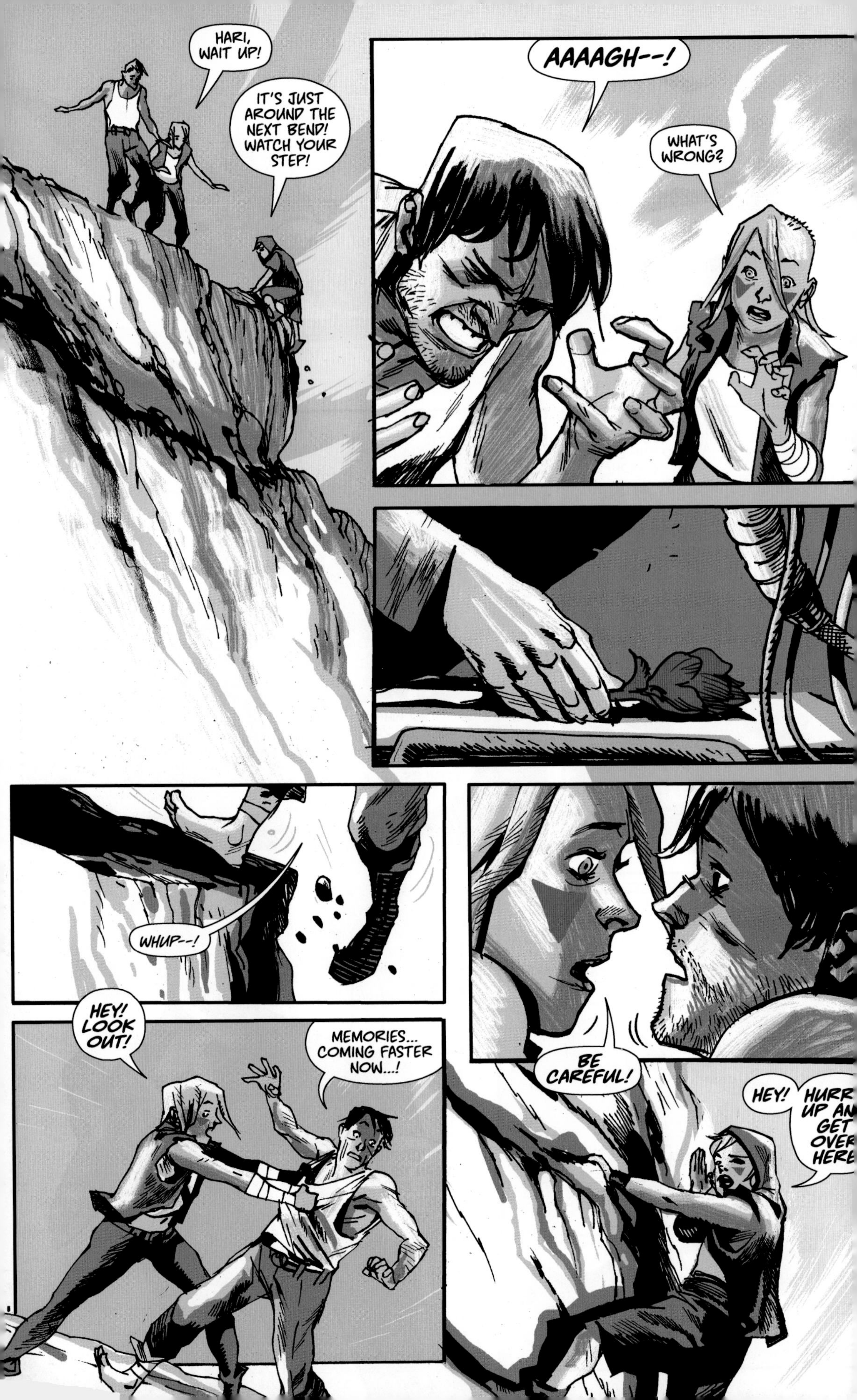
HARI, WAIT UP!
IT'S JUST AROUND THE NEXT BEND! WATCH YOUR STEP!
AAAAGH--!
WHAT'S WRONG?
WHUP--!
BE CAREFUL!
HEY! LOOK OUT!
MEMORIES... COMING FASTER NOW...!
HEY!

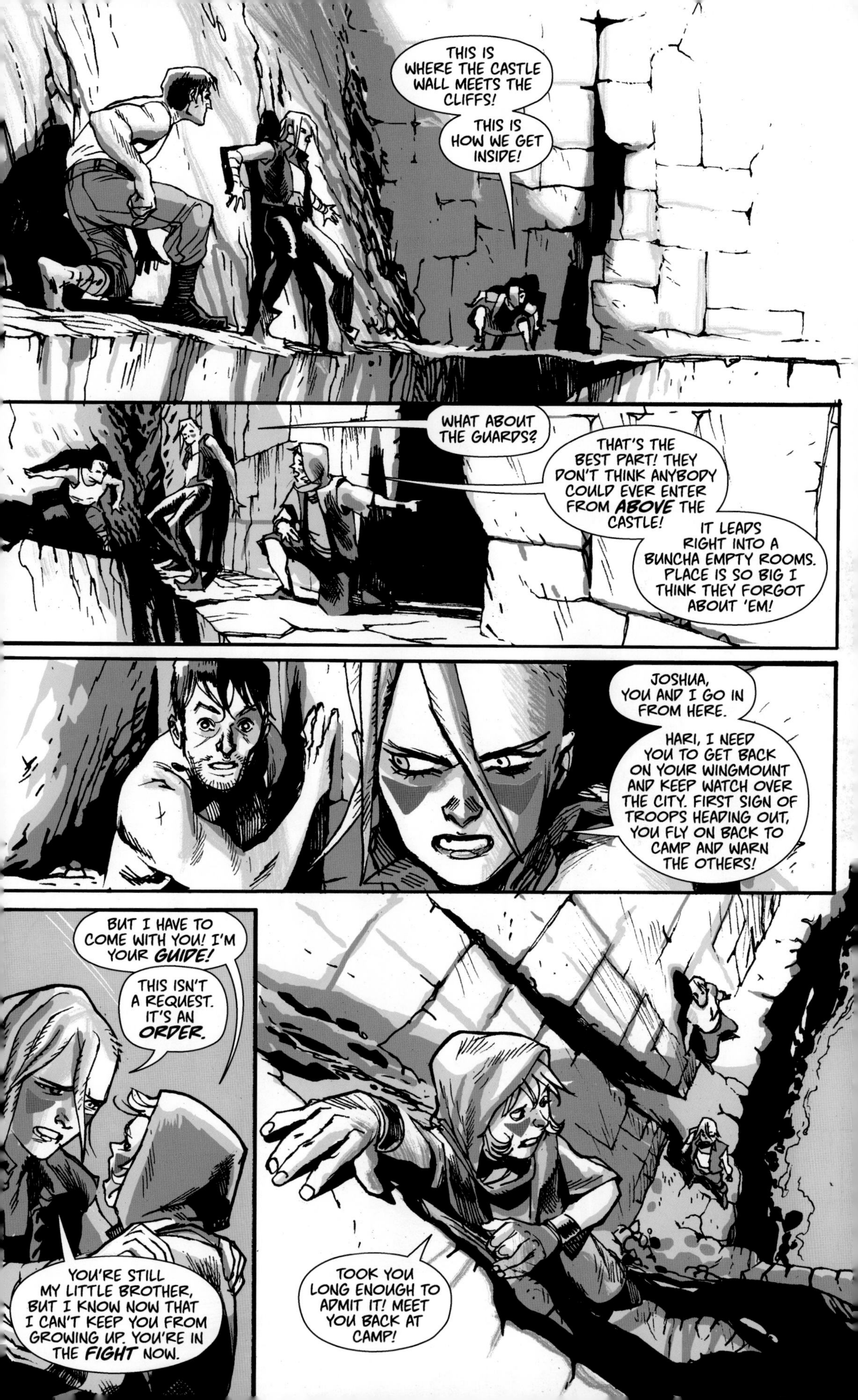
THIS IS WHERE THE CASTLE WALL MEETS THE CLIFFS!
THIS IS HOW WE GET INSIDE!
WHAT ABOUT THE GUARDS?
THAT'S THE BEST PART! THEY DON'T THINK ANYBODY COULD EVER ENTER FROM ABOVE THE CASTLE!
IT LEADS RIGHT INTO A BUNCHA EMPTY ROOMS. PLACE IS SO BIG I THINK THEY FORGOT ABOUT 'EM!
JOSHUA, YOU AND I GO IN FROM HERE.
HARI, I NEED YOU TO GET BACK ON YOUR WINGMOUNT AND KEEP WATCH OVER THE CITY. FIRST SIGN OF TROOPS HEADING OUT, YOU FLY ON BACK TO CAMP AND WARN THE OTHERS!
BUT I HAVE TO COME WITH YOU! I'M YOUR GUIDE!
THIS ISN'T A REQUEST. IT'S AN ORDER.
YOU'RE STILL MY LITTLE BROTHER, BUT I KNOW NOW THAT I CAN'T KEEP YOU FROM GROWING UP. YOU'RE IN THE FIGHT NOW.
TOOK YOU LONG ENOUGH TO ADMIT IT! MEET YOU BACK AT CAMP!

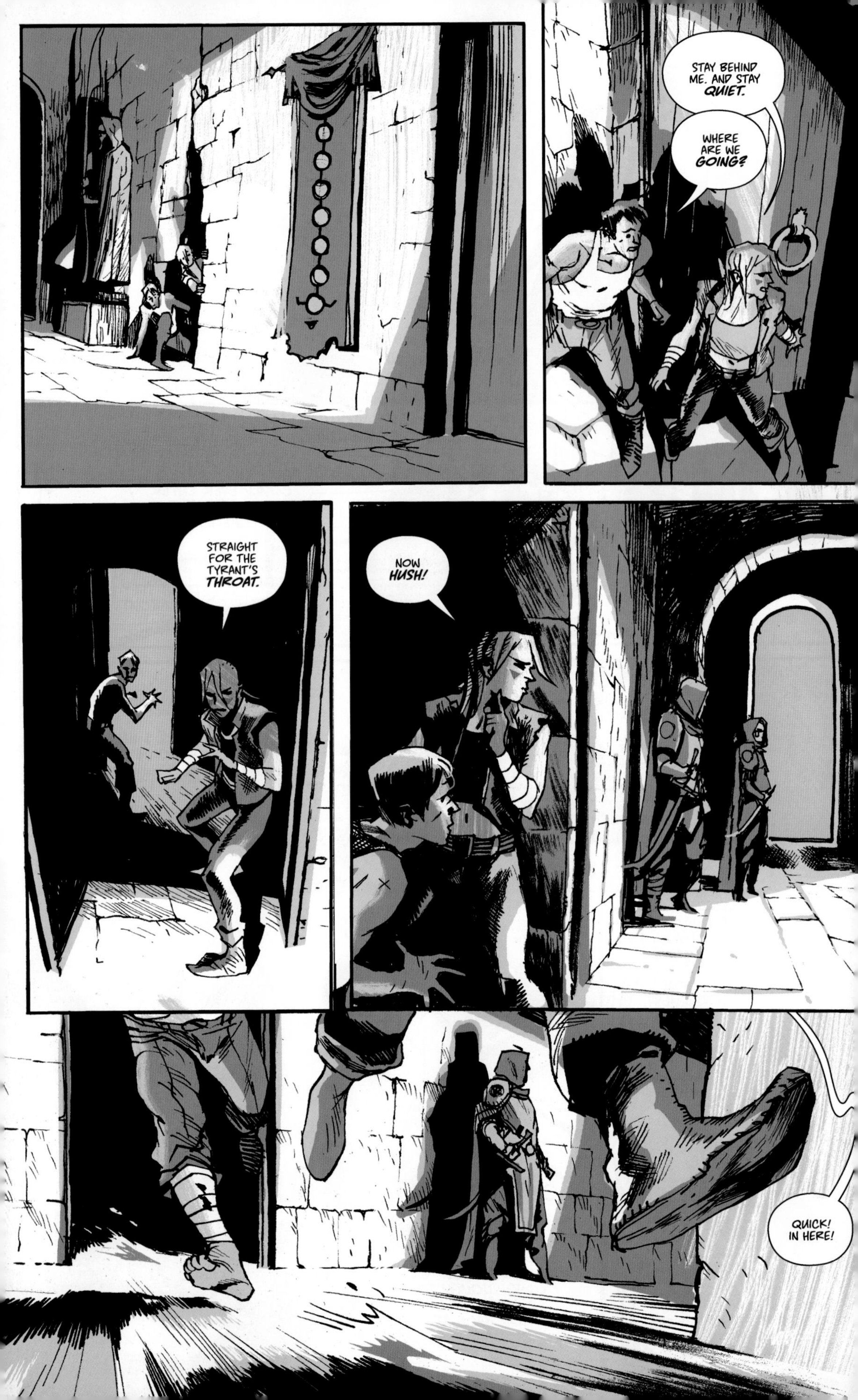
STAY BEHIND ME. AND STAY QUIET.
WHERE ARE WE GOING?
STRAIGHT FOR THE TYRANT'S THROAT.
NOW HUSH!
QUICK! IN HERE!

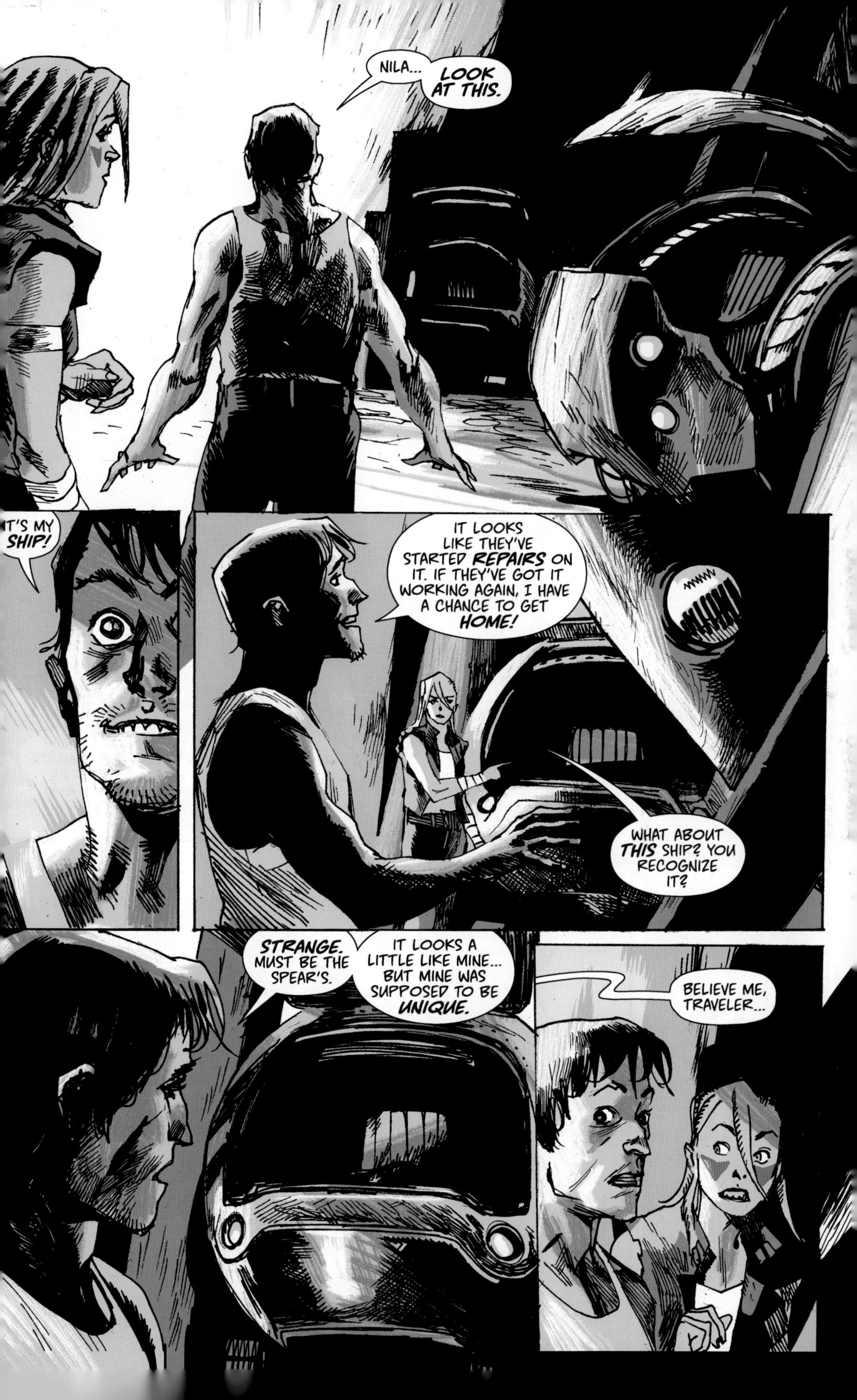
NILA... LOOK AT THIS.
IT'S MY SHIP!
IT LOOKS LIKE THEY'VE STARTED REPAIRS ON IT. IF THEY'VE GOT IT WORKING AGAIN, I HAVE A CHANCE TO GET HOME!
WHAT ABOUT THIS SHIP? YOU RECOGNIZE IT?
STRANGE. MUST BE THE SPEAR'S.
IT LOOKS A LITTLE LIKE MINE... BUT MINE WAS SUPPOSED TO BE UNIQUE.
BELIEVE ME, TRAVELER...

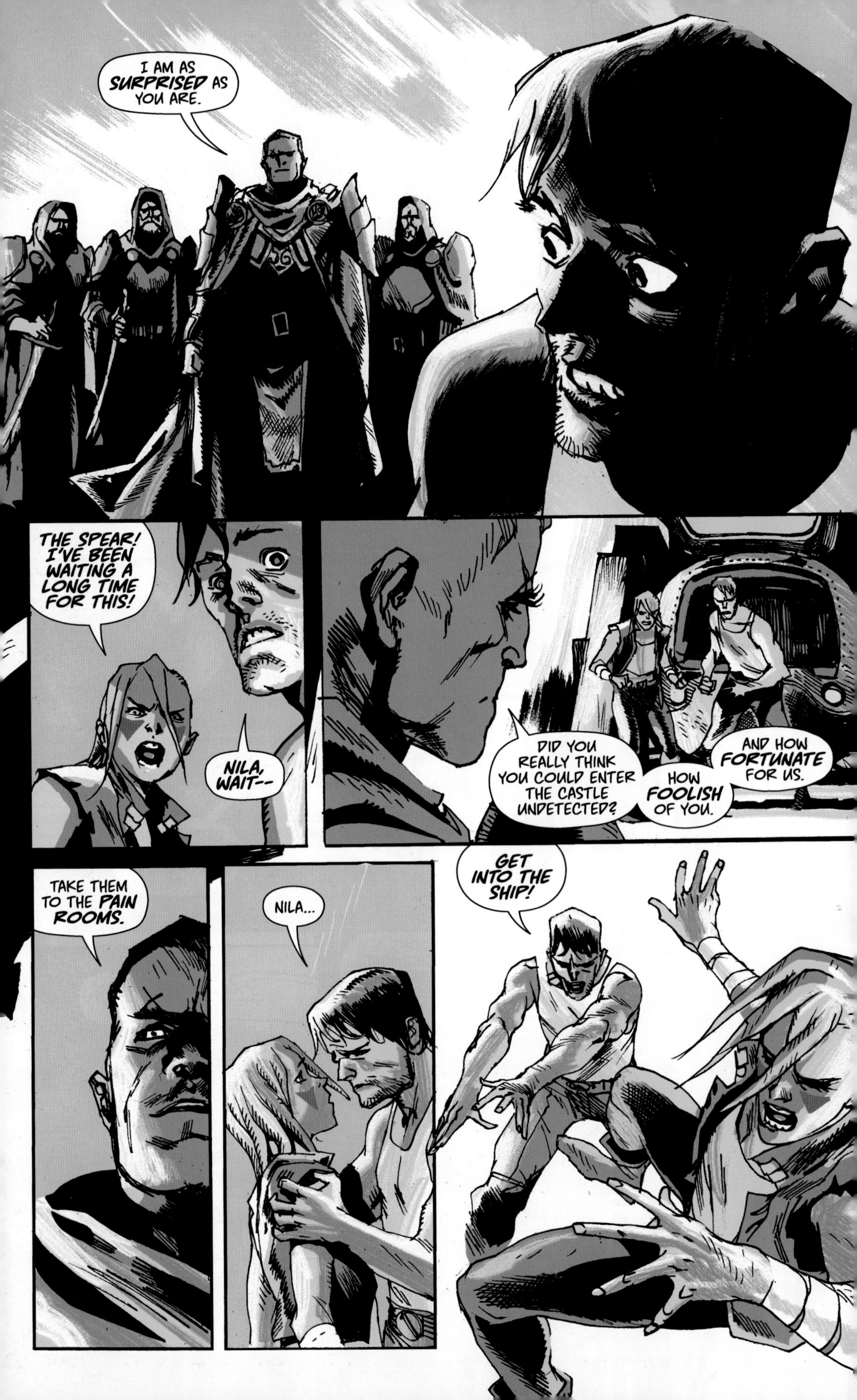
I AM AS SURPRISED AS YOU ARE.
THE SPEAR! I'VE BEEN WAITING A LONG TIME FOR THIS!
NILA, WAIT--
DID YOU REALLY THINK YOU COULD ENTER THE CASTLE UNDETECTED?
HOW FOOLISH OF YOU.
AND HOW FORTUNATE FOR US.
TAKE THEM TO THE PAIN ROOMS.
NILA...
GET INTO THE SHIP!

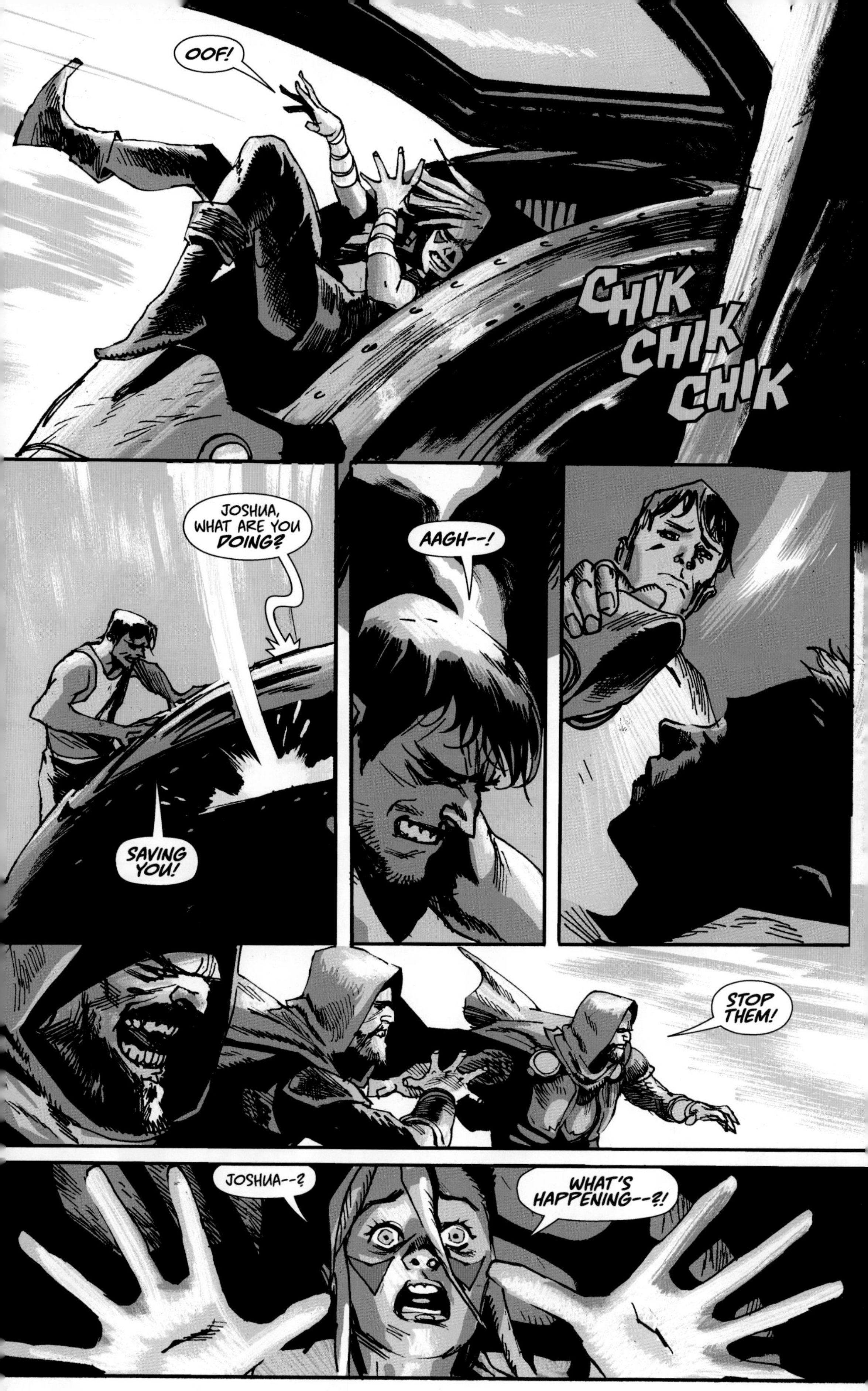
OOF!
CHIK CHIK CHIK
JOSHUA, WHAT ARE YOU DOING?
SAVING YOU!
AAGH--!
STOP THEM!
JOSHUA--?
WHAT'S HAPPENING--?!

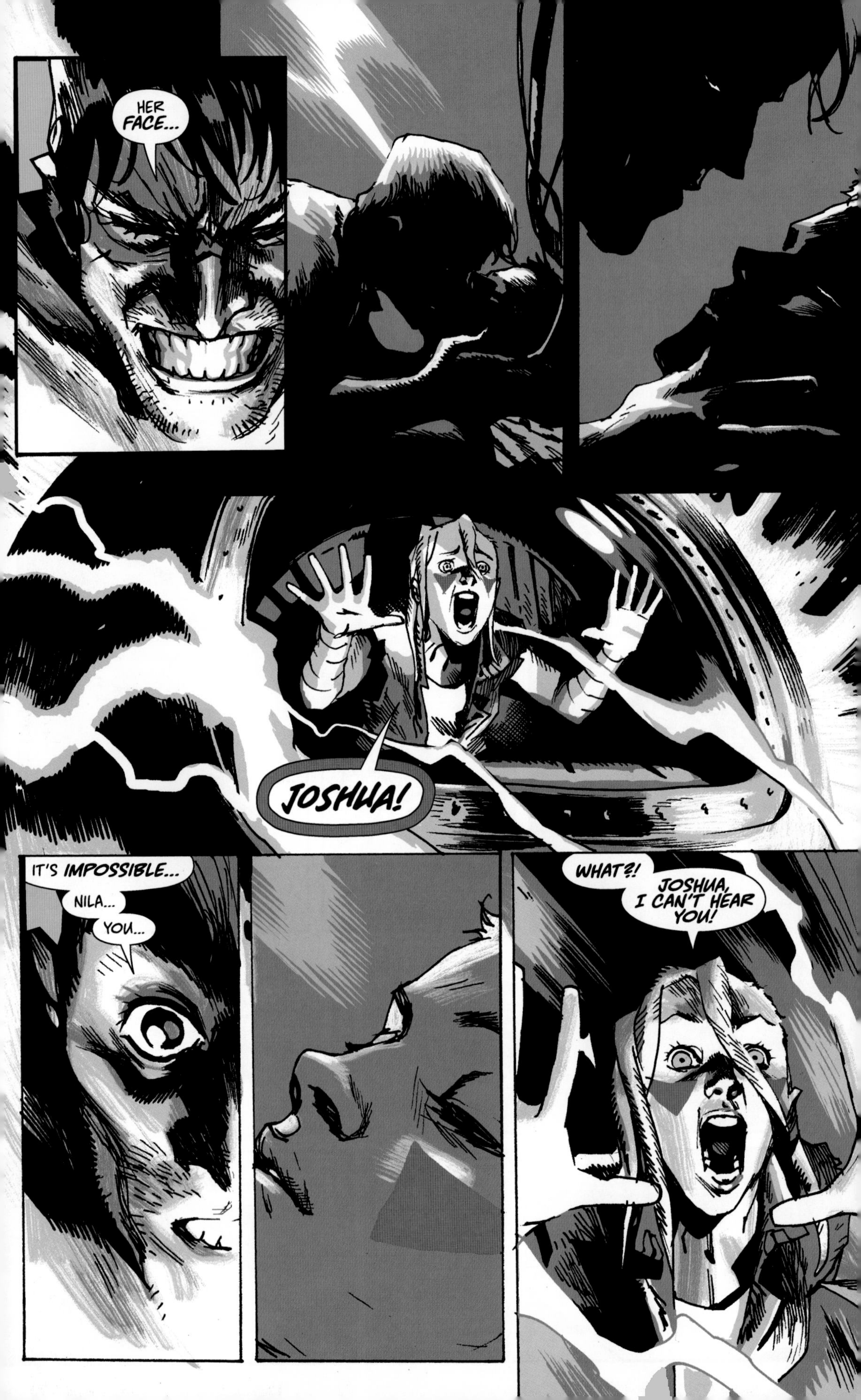
HER FACE...
JOSHUA!
IT'S IMPOSSIBLE...
NILA...
YOU...
WHAT?!
JOSHUA, I CAN'T HEAR YOU!

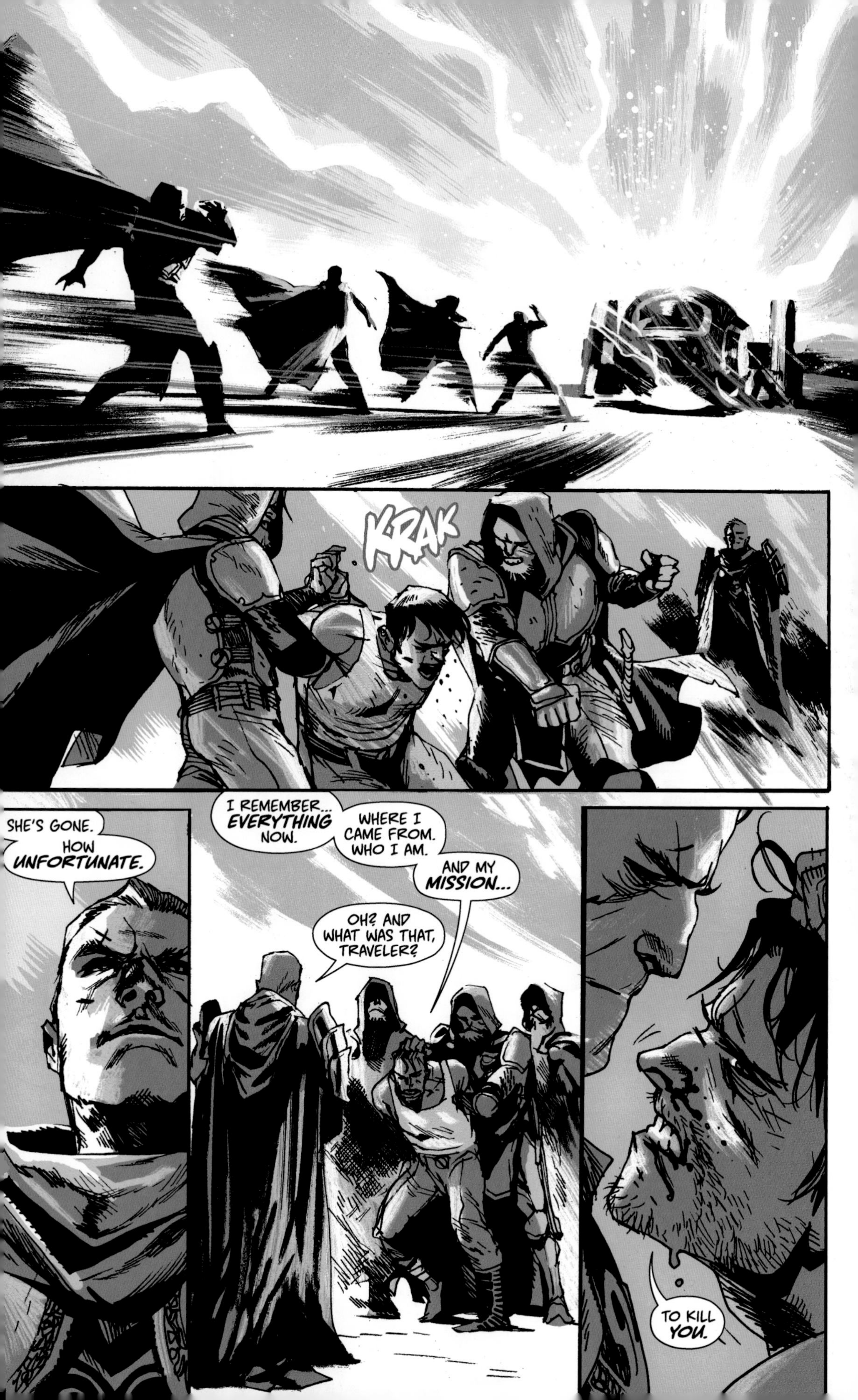
KRAK
SHE'S GONE.
HOW UNFORTUNATE.
I REMEMBER... EVERYTHING NOW.
WHERE I CAME FROM. WHO I AM.
AND MY MISSION...
OH? AND WHAT WAS THAT, TRAVELER?
TO KILL YOU.

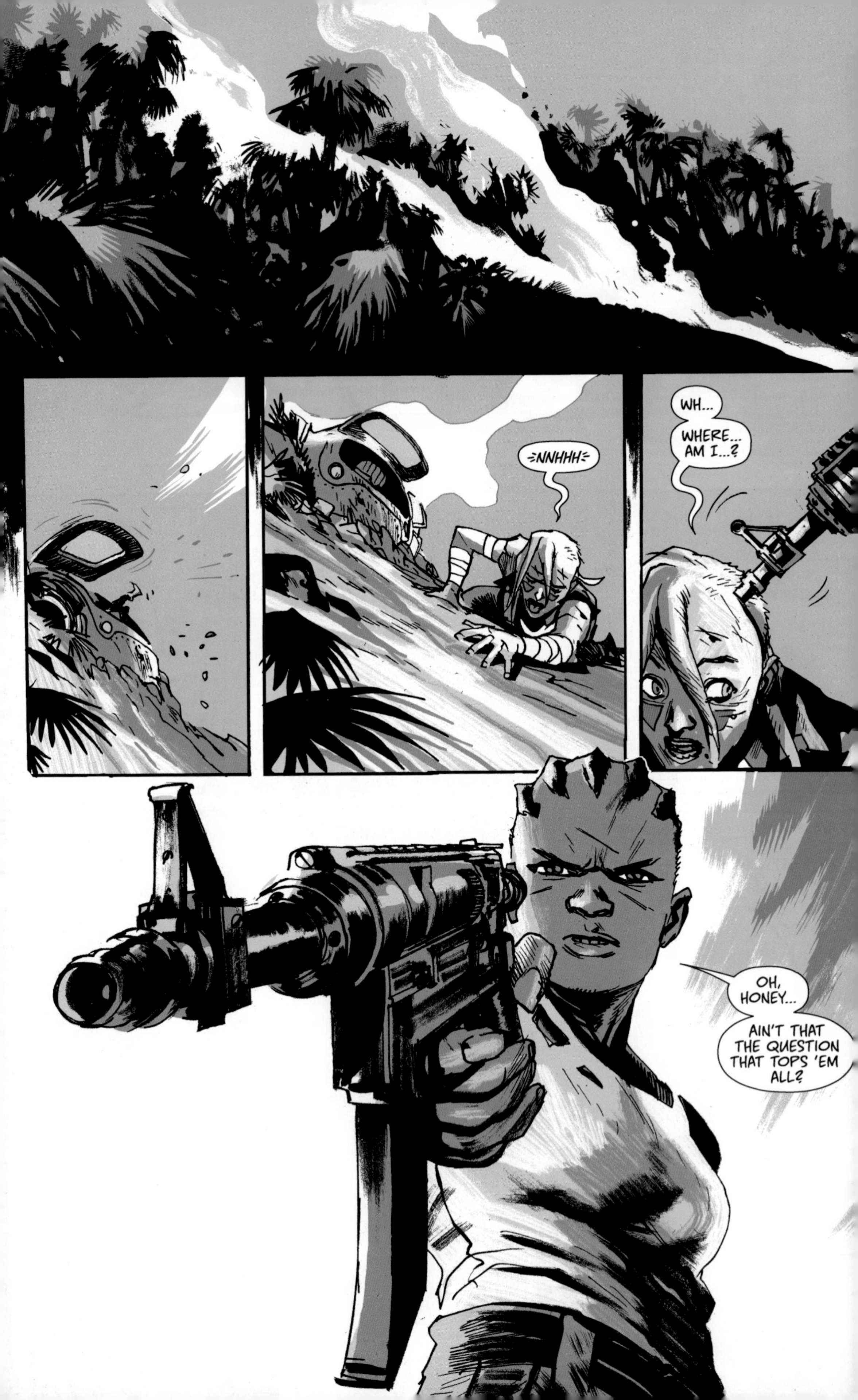
NNHHH
WH...
WHERE... AM I...?
OH, HONEY...
AIN'T THAT THE QUESTION THAT TOPS 'EM ALL?

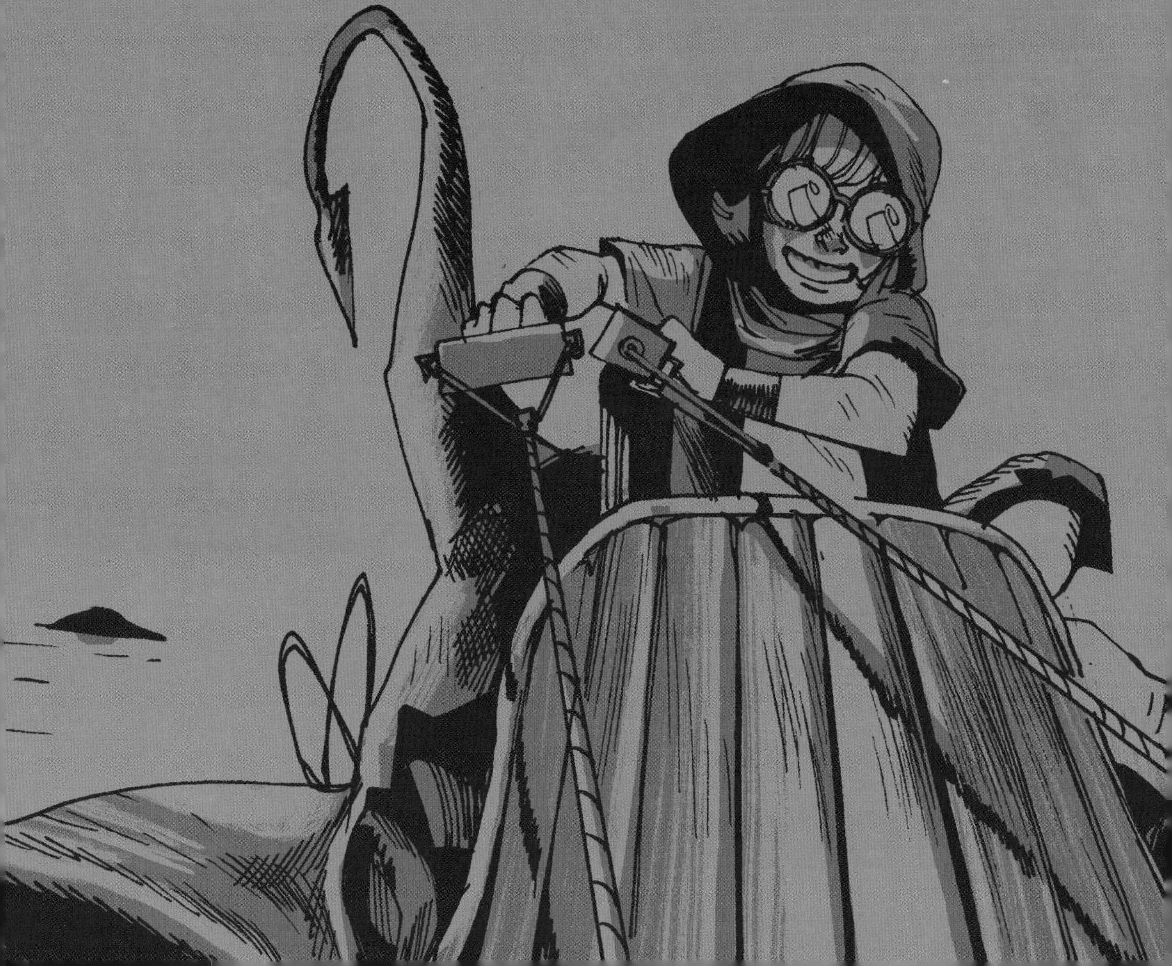

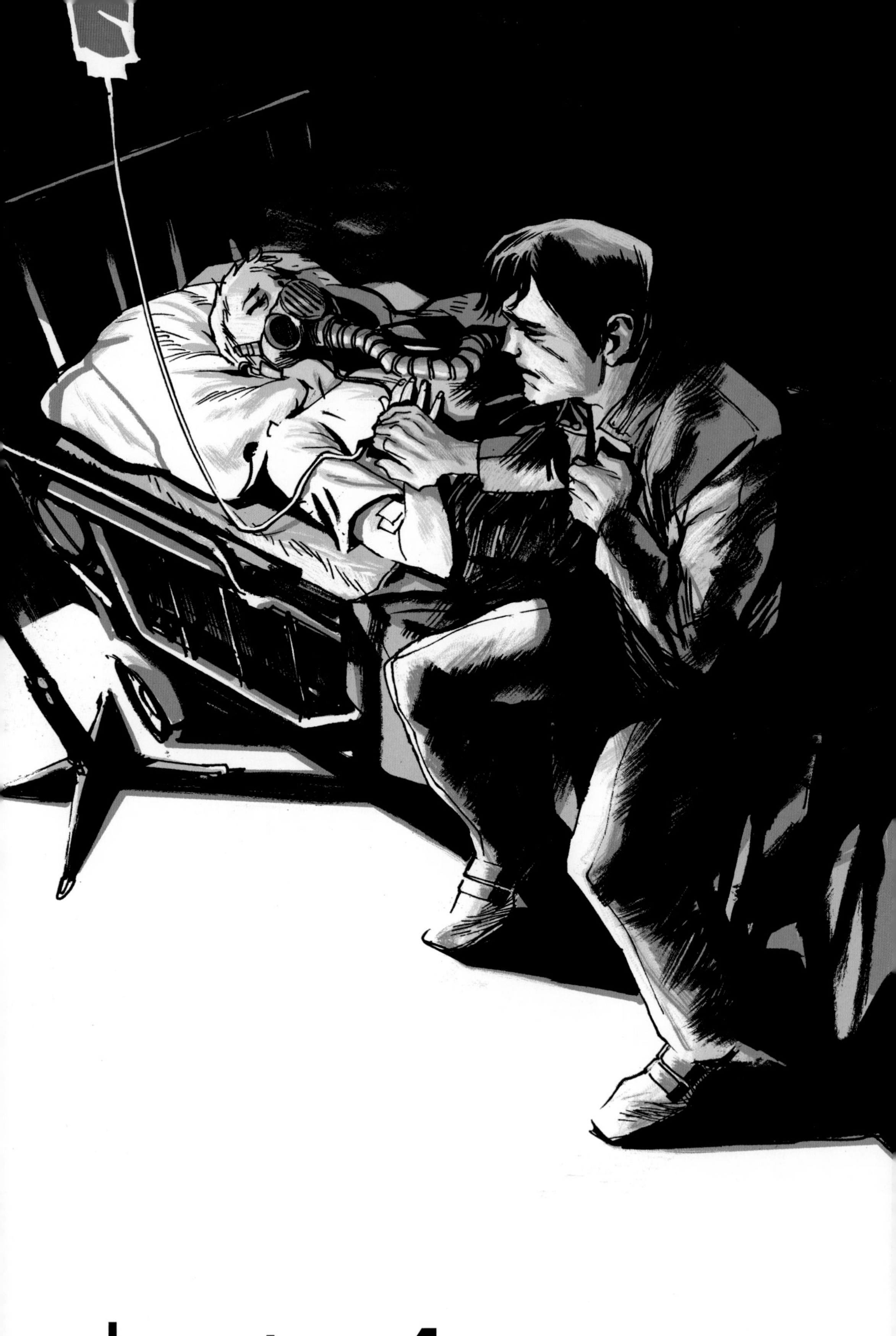

chapter 4

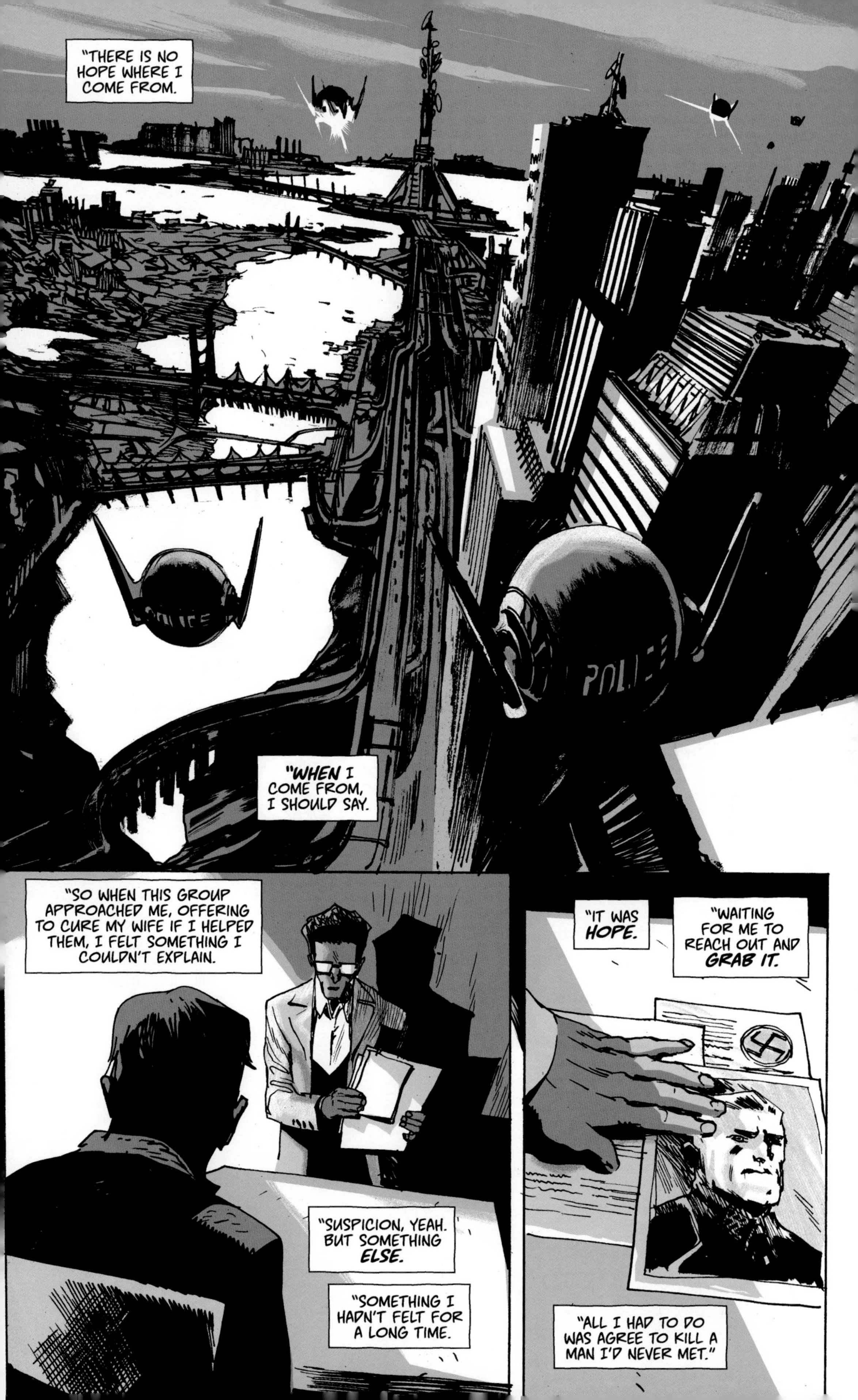
"THERE IS NO HOPE WHERE I COME FROM.
"WHEN I COME FROM, I SHOULD SAY.
"SO WHEN THIS GROUP APPROACHED ME, OFFERING TO CURE MY WIFE IF I HELPED THEM, I FELT SOMETHING I COULDN'T EXPLAIN.
"SUSPICION, YEAH. BUT SOMETHING ELSE.
"SOMETHING I HADN'T FELT FOR A LONG TIME.
"IT WAS HOPE.
"WAITING FOR ME TO REACH OUT AND GRAB IT.
"ALL I HAD TO DO WAS AGREE TO KILL A MAN I'D NEVER MET."

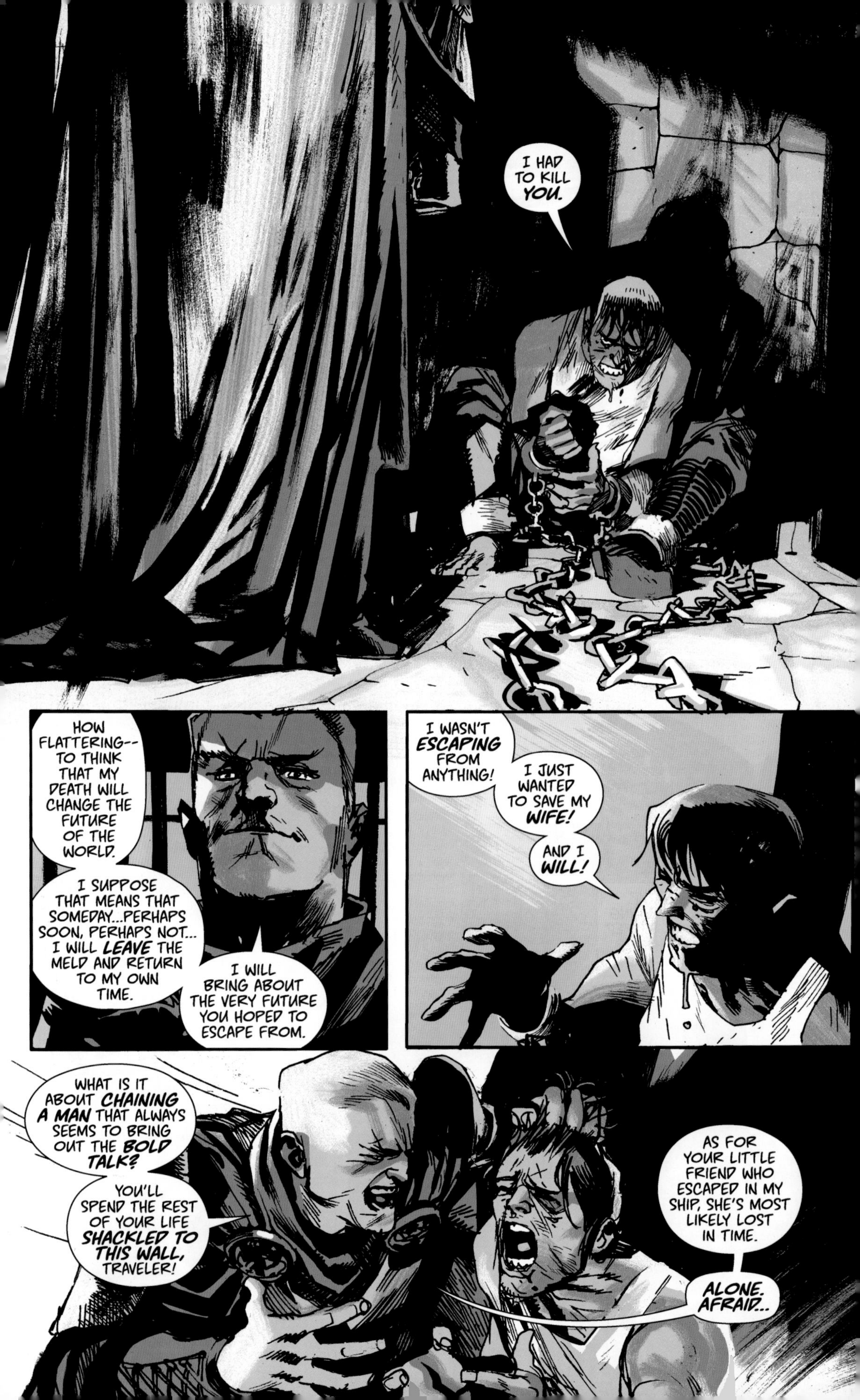
I HAD TO KILL YOU.
HOW FLATTERING--TO THINK THAT MY DEATH WILL CHANGE THE FUTURE OF THE WORLD.
I SUPPOSE THAT MEANS THAT SOMEDAY...PERHAPS SOON, PERHAPS NOT... I WILL LEAVE THE MELD AND RETURN TO MY OWN TIME.
I WILL BRING ABOUT THE VERY FUTURE YOU HOPED TO ESCAPE FROM.
I WASN'T ESCAPING FROM ANYTHING!
I JUST WANTED TO SAVE MY WIFE!
AND I WILL!
WHAT IS IT ABOUT CHAINING A MAN THAT ALWAYS SEEMS TO BRING OUT THE BOLD TALK?
YOU'LL SPEND THE REST OF YOUR LIFE SHACKLED TO THIS WALL, TRAVELER!
AS FOR YOUR LITTLE FRIEND WHO ESCAPED IN MY SHIP, SHE'S MOST LIKELY LOST IN TIME.
ALONE. AFRAID...

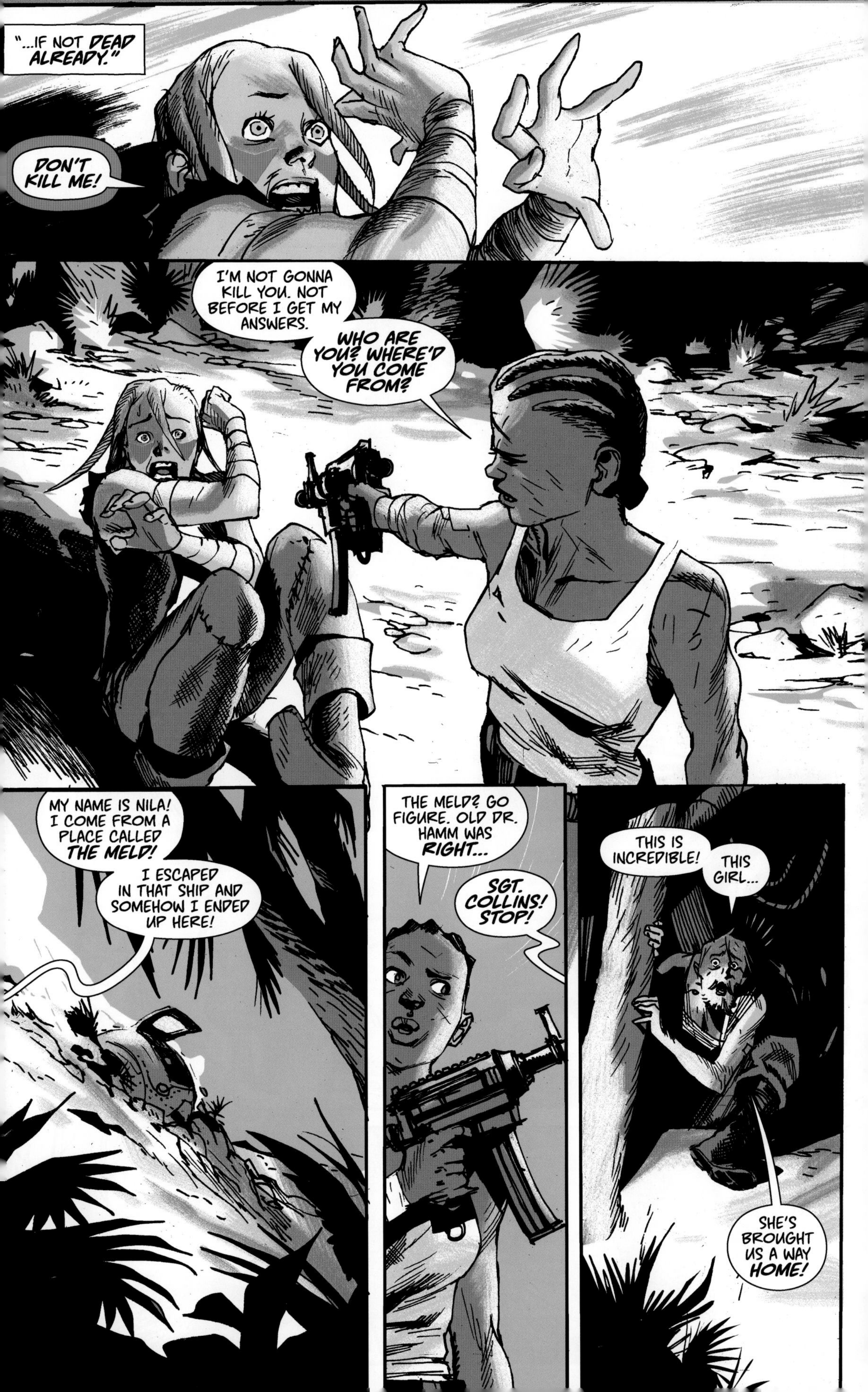
"...IF NOT DEAD ALREADY."
DON'T KILL ME!
I'M NOT GONNA KILL YOU. NOT BEFORE I GET MY ANSWERS.
WHO ARE YOU? WHERE'D YOU COME FROM?
MY NAME IS NILA! I COME FROM A PLACE CALLED THE MELD!
I ESCAPED IN THAT SHIP AND SOMEHOW I ENDED UP HERE!
THE MELD? GO FIGURE. OLD DR. HAMM WAS RIGHT...
SGT. COLLINS! STOP!
THIS IS INCREDIBLE!
THIS GIRL...
SHE'S BROUGHT US A WAY HOME!

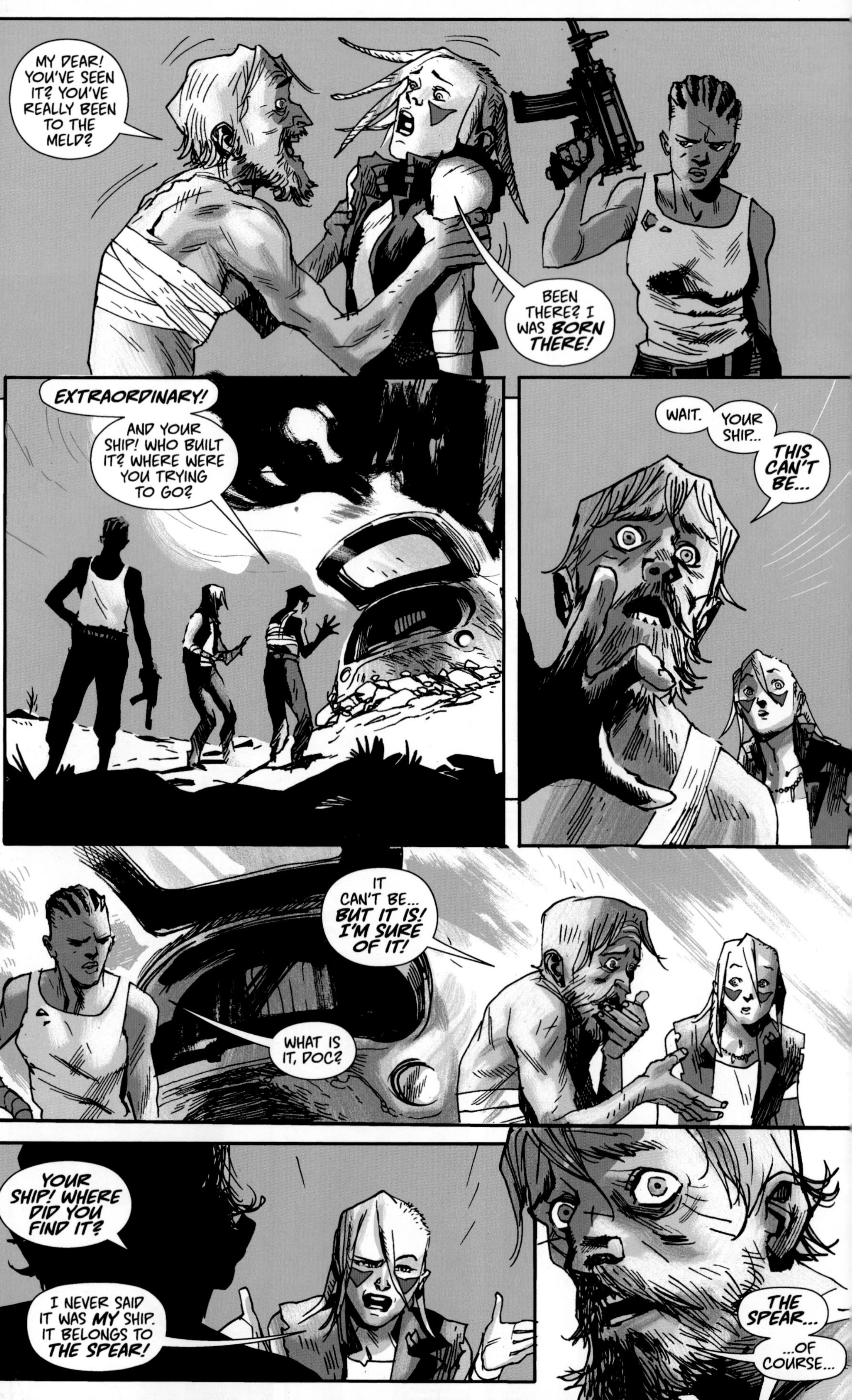
MY DEAR! YOU'VE SEEN IT? YOU'VE REALLY BEEN TO THE MELD?
BEEN THERE? I WAS BORN THERE!
EXTRAORDINARY!
AND YOUR SHIP! WHO BUILT IT? WHERE WERE YOU TRYING TO GO?
WAIT.
YOUR SHIP...
THIS CAN'T BE...
IT CAN'T BE... BUT IT IS! I'M SURE OF IT!
WHAT IS IT, DOC?
YOUR SHIP! WHERE DID YOU FIND IT?
I NEVER SAID IT WAS MY SHIP. IT BELONGS TO THE SPEAR!
THE SPEAR...
...OF COURSE...

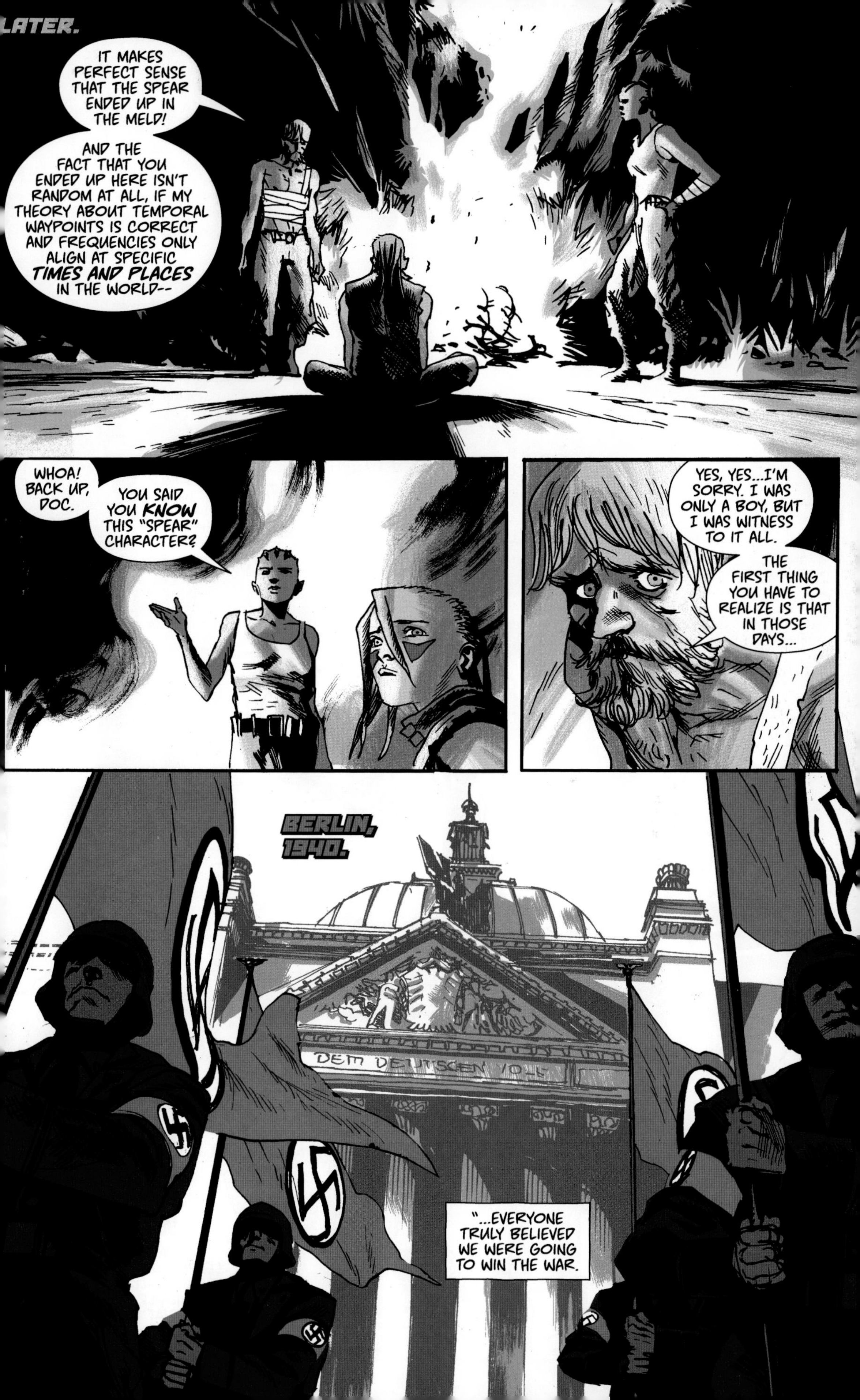
LATER.
IT MAKES PERFECT SENSE THAT THE SPEAR ENDED UP IN THE MELD!
AND THE FACT THAT YOU ENDED UP HERE ISN'T RANDOM AT ALL, IF MY THEORY ABOUT TEMPORAL WAYPOINTS IS CORRECT AND FREQUENCIES ONLY ALIGN AT SPECIFIC TIMES AND PLACES IN THE WORLD--
WHOA! BACK UP, DOC.
YOU SAID YOU KNOW THIS "SPEAR" CHARACTER?
YES, YES...I'M SORRY. I WAS ONLY A BOY, BUT I WAS WITNESS TO IT ALL.
THE FIRST THING YOU HAVE TO REALIZE IS THAT IN THOSE DAYS...
BERLIN, 1940.
"...EVERYONE TRULY BELIEVED WE WERE GOING TO WIN THE WAR.

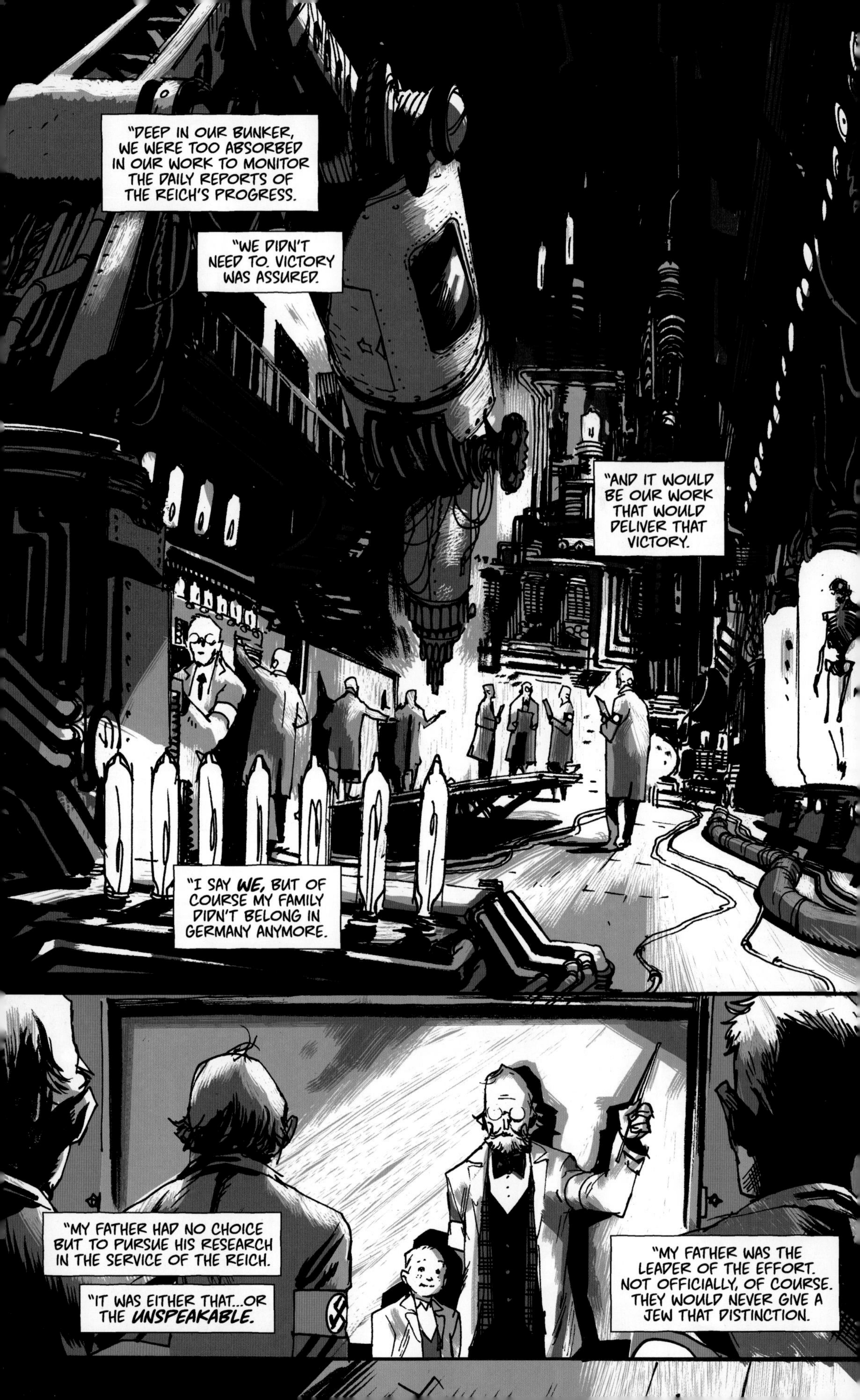
"DEEP IN OUR BUNKER, WE WERE TOO ABSORBED IN OUR WORK TO MONITOR THE DAILY REPORTS OF THE REICH'S PROGRESS.
"WE DIDN'T NEED TO. VICTORY WAS ASSURED.
"AND IT WOULD BE OUR WORK THAT WOULD DELIVER THAT VICTORY.
"I SAY *WE*, BUT OF COURSE MY FAMILY DIDN'T BELONG IN GERMANY ANYMORE.
"MY FATHER HAD NO CHOICE BUT TO PURSUE HIS RESEARCH IN THE SERVICE OF THE REICH.
"IT WAS EITHER THAT...OR THE *UNSPEAKABLE*.
"MY FATHER WAS THE LEADER OF THE EFFORT. NOT OFFICIALLY, OF COURSE. THEY WOULD NEVER GIVE A JEW THAT DISTINCTION.

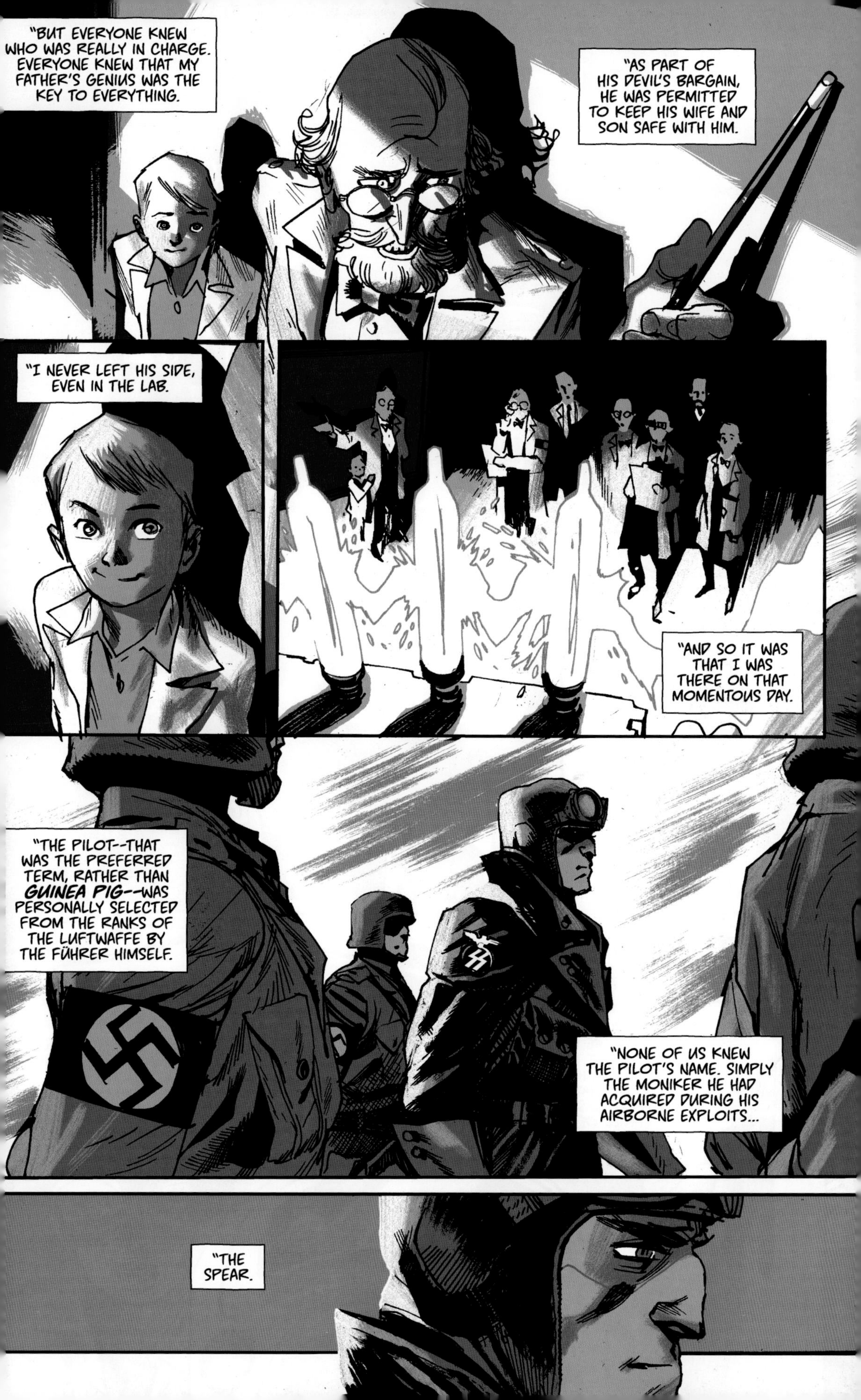

"BUT EVERYONE KNEW WHO WAS REALLY IN CHARGE. EVERYONE KNEW THAT MY FATHER'S GENIUS WAS THE KEY TO EVERYTHING.
"AS PART OF HIS DEVIL'S BARGAIN, HE WAS PERMITTED TO KEEP HIS WIFE AND SON SAFE WITH HIM.
"I NEVER LEFT HIS SIDE, EVEN IN THE LAB.
"AND SO IT WAS THAT I WAS THERE ON THAT MOMENTOUS DAY.
"THE PILOT--THAT WAS THE PREFERRED TERM, RATHER THAN *GUINEA PIG*--WAS PERSONALLY SELECTED FROM THE RANKS OF THE LUFTWAFFE BY THE FÜHRER HIMSELF.
"NONE OF US KNEW THE PILOT'S NAME. SIMPLY THE MONIKER HE HAD ACQUIRED DURING HIS AIRBORNE EXPLOITS...
"THE SPEAR.

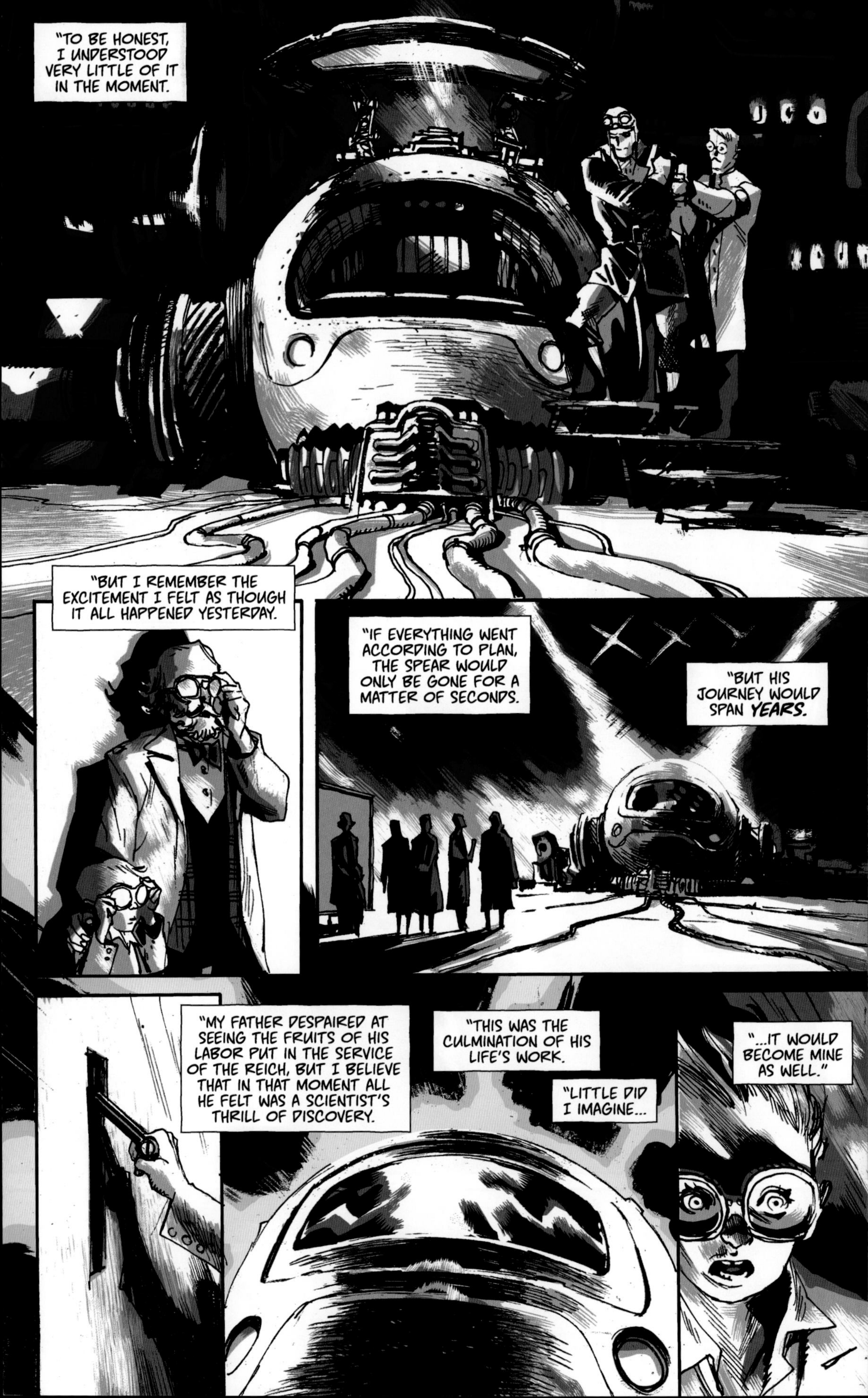
"TO BE HONEST, I UNDERSTOOD VERY LITTLE OF IT IN THE MOMENT.
"BUT I REMEMBER THE EXCITEMENT I FELT AS THOUGH IT ALL HAPPENED YESTERDAY.
"IF EVERYTHING WENT ACCORDING TO PLAN, THE SPEAR WOULD ONLY BE GONE FOR A MATTER OF SECONDS.
"BUT HIS JOURNEY WOULD SPAN ***YEARS.***
"MY FATHER DESPAIRED AT SEEING THE FRUITS OF HIS LABOR PUT IN THE SERVICE OF THE REICH, BUT I BELIEVE THAT IN THAT MOMENT ALL HE FELT WAS A SCIENTIST'S THRILL OF DISCOVERY.
"THIS WAS THE CULMINATION OF HIS LIFE'S WORK.
"LITTLE DID I IMAGINE...
"...IT WOULD BECOME MINE AS WELL."

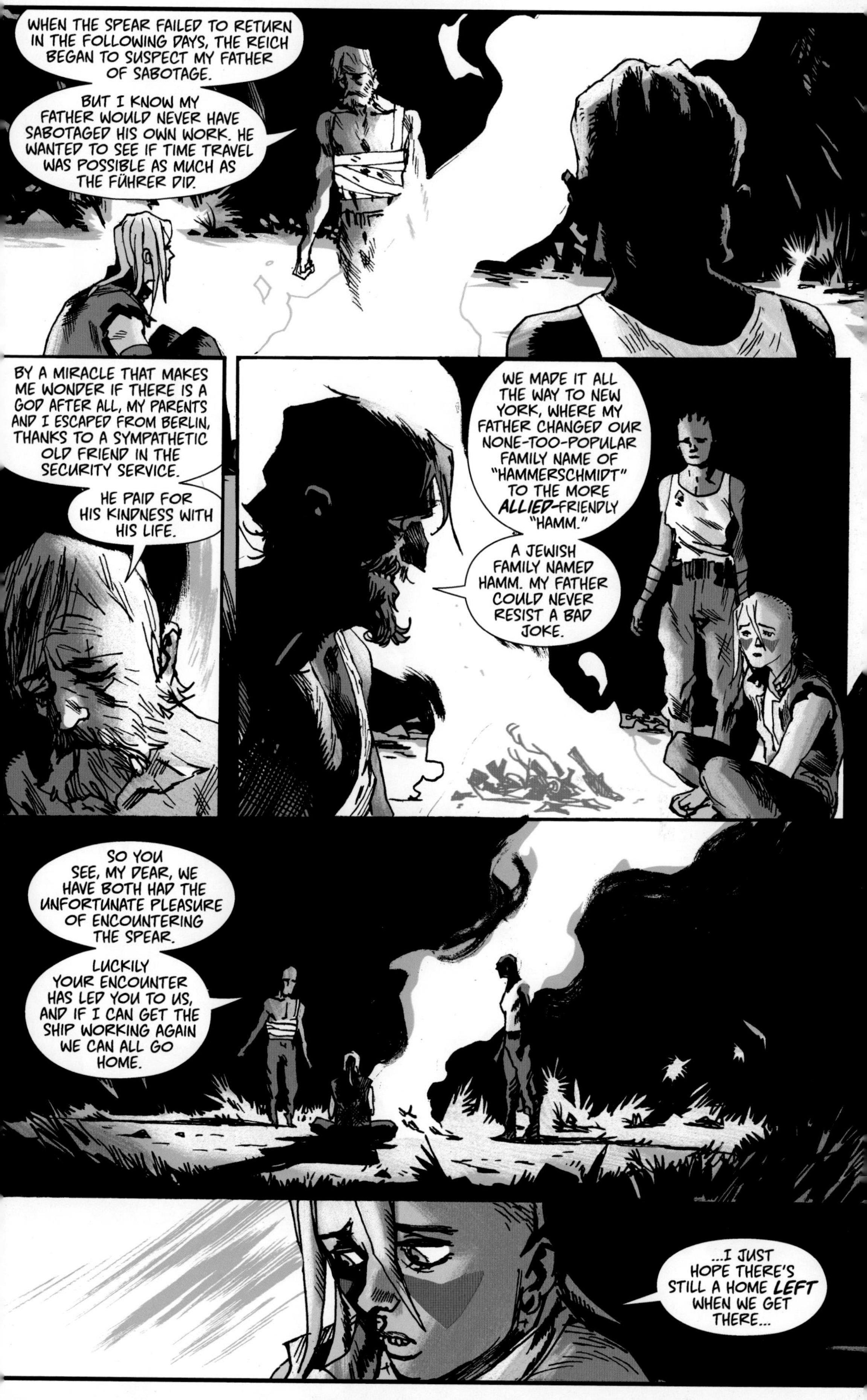
WHEN THE SPEAR FAILED TO RETURN IN THE FOLLOWING DAYS, THE REICH BEGAN TO SUSPECT MY FATHER OF SABOTAGE.
BUT I KNOW MY FATHER WOULD NEVER HAVE SABOTAGED HIS OWN WORK. HE WANTED TO SEE IF TIME TRAVEL WAS POSSIBLE AS MUCH AS THE FÜHRER DID.
BY A MIRACLE THAT MAKES ME WONDER IF THERE IS A GOD AFTER ALL, MY PARENTS AND I ESCAPED FROM BERLIN, THANKS TO A SYMPATHETIC OLD FRIEND IN THE SECURITY SERVICE.
HE PAID FOR HIS KINDNESS WITH HIS LIFE.
WE MADE IT ALL THE WAY TO NEW YORK, WHERE MY FATHER CHANGED OUR NONE-TOO-POPULAR FAMILY NAME OF "HAMMERSCHMIDT" TO THE MORE ***ALLIED***-FRIENDLY "HAMM."
A JEWISH FAMILY NAMED HAMM. MY FATHER COULD NEVER RESIST A BAD JOKE.
SO YOU SEE, MY DEAR, WE HAVE BOTH HAD THE UNFORTUNATE PLEASURE OF ENCOUNTERING THE SPEAR.
LUCKILY YOUR ENCOUNTER HAS LED YOU TO US, AND IF I CAN GET THE SHIP WORKING AGAIN WE CAN ALL GO HOME.
...I JUST HOPE THERE'S STILL A HOME ***LEFT*** WHEN WE GET THERE...

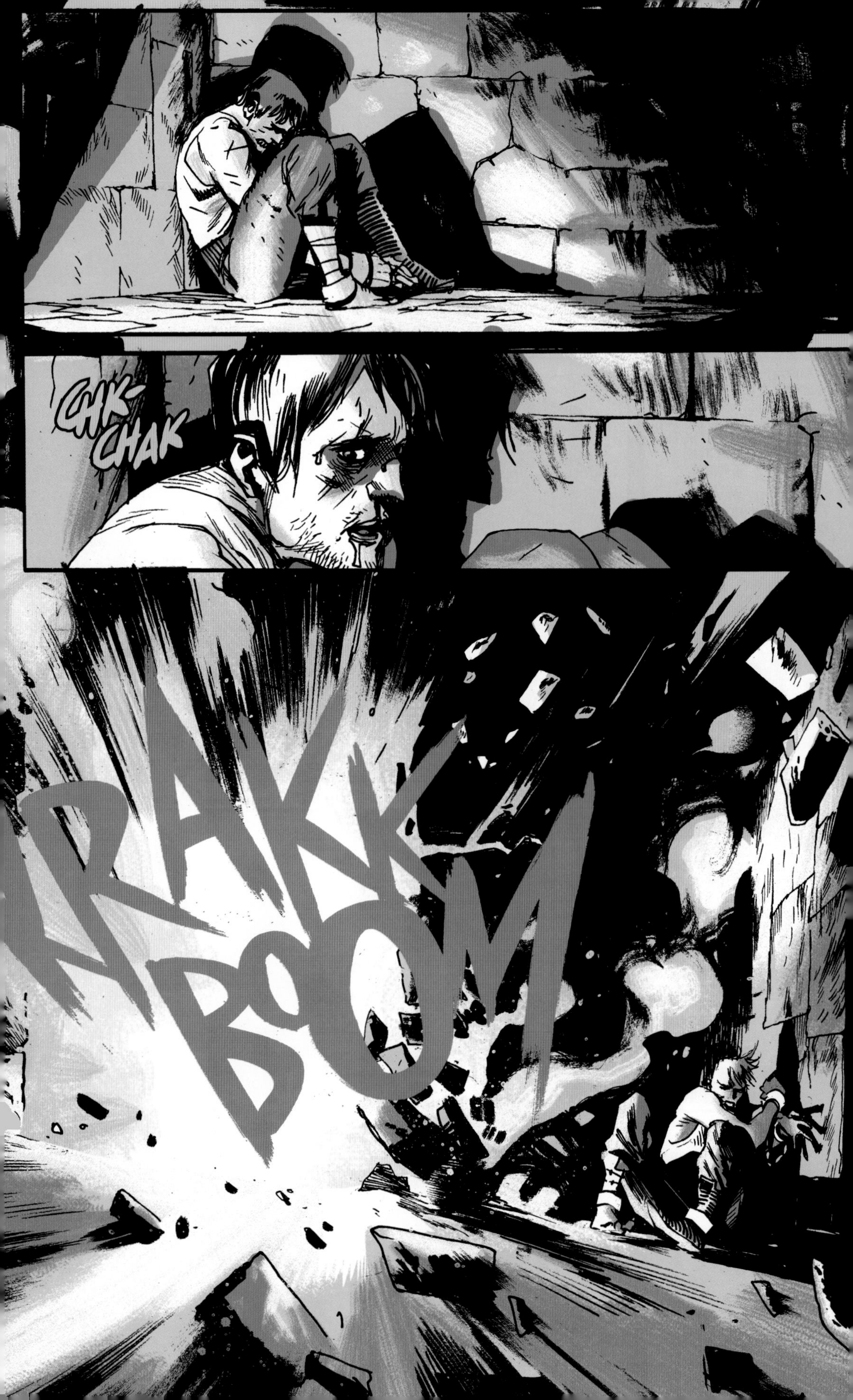
CHK-
CHAK
KRAK
BOOM

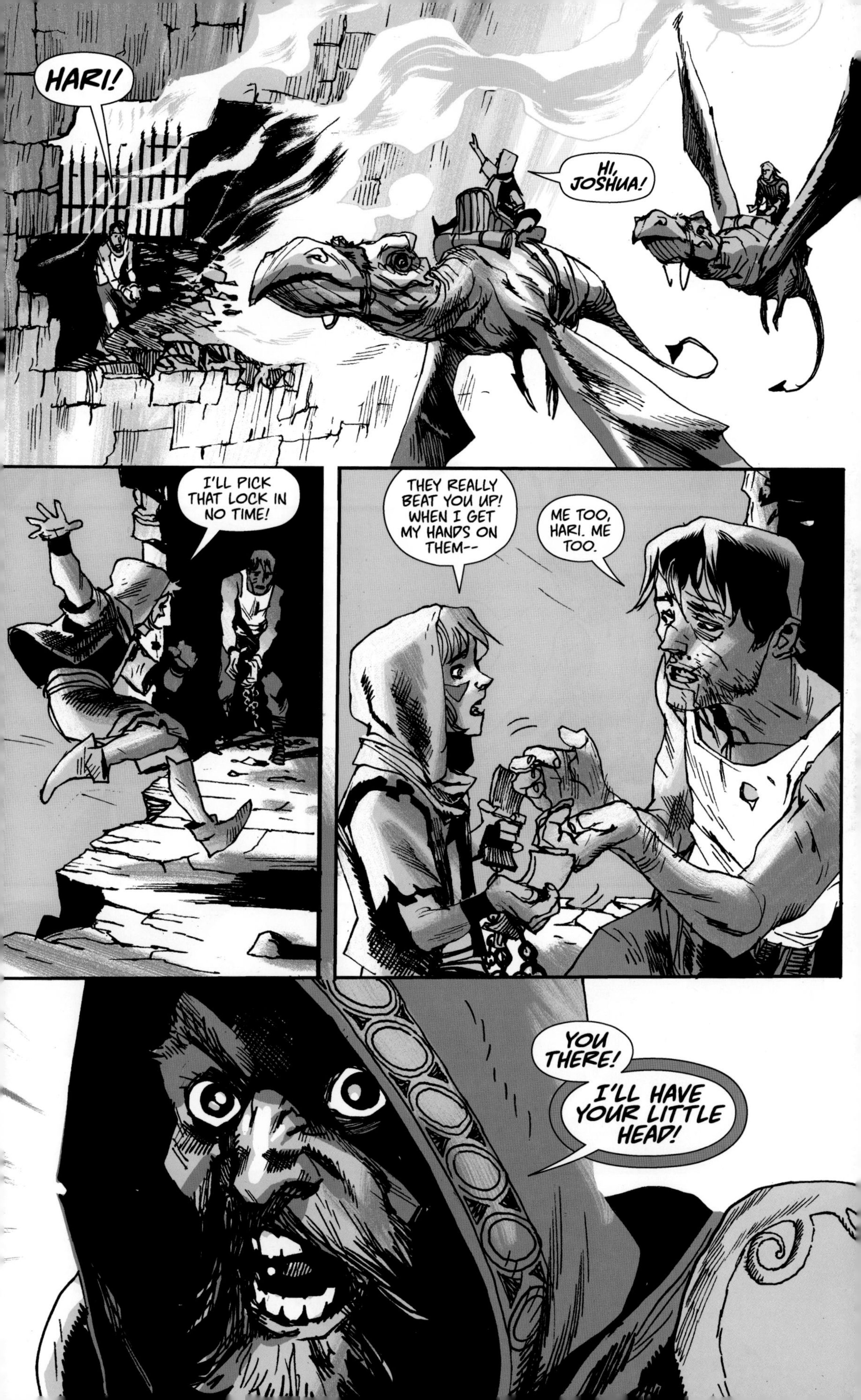
HARI!
HI, JOSHUA!
I'LL PICK THAT LOCK IN NO TIME!
THEY REALLY BEAT YOU UP! WHEN I GET MY HANDS ON THEM--
ME TOO, HARI. ME TOO.
YOU THERE!
I'LL HAVE YOUR LITTLE HEAD!

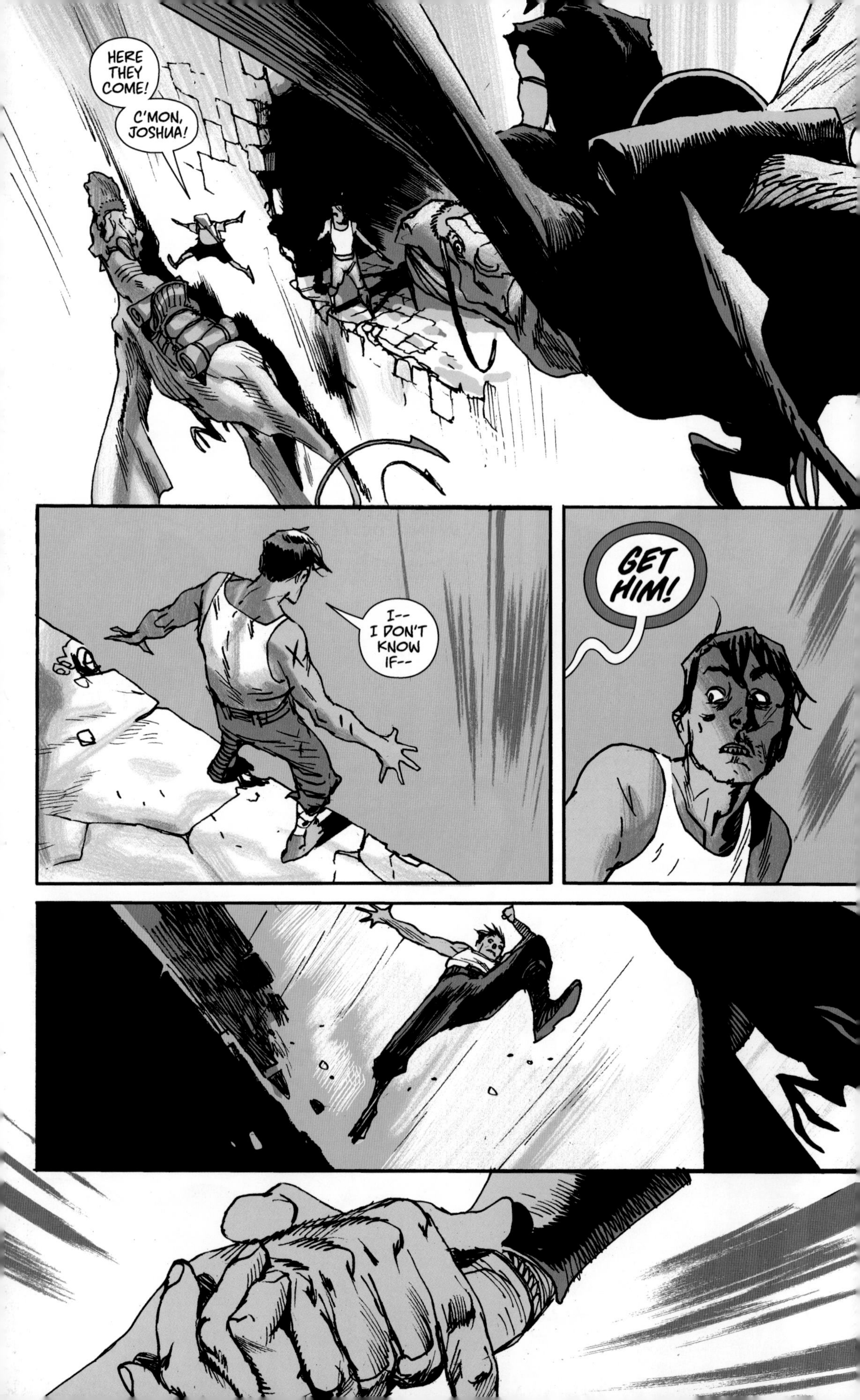
HERE THEY COME!
C'MON, JOSHUA!
I-- I DON'T KNOW IF--
GET HIM!

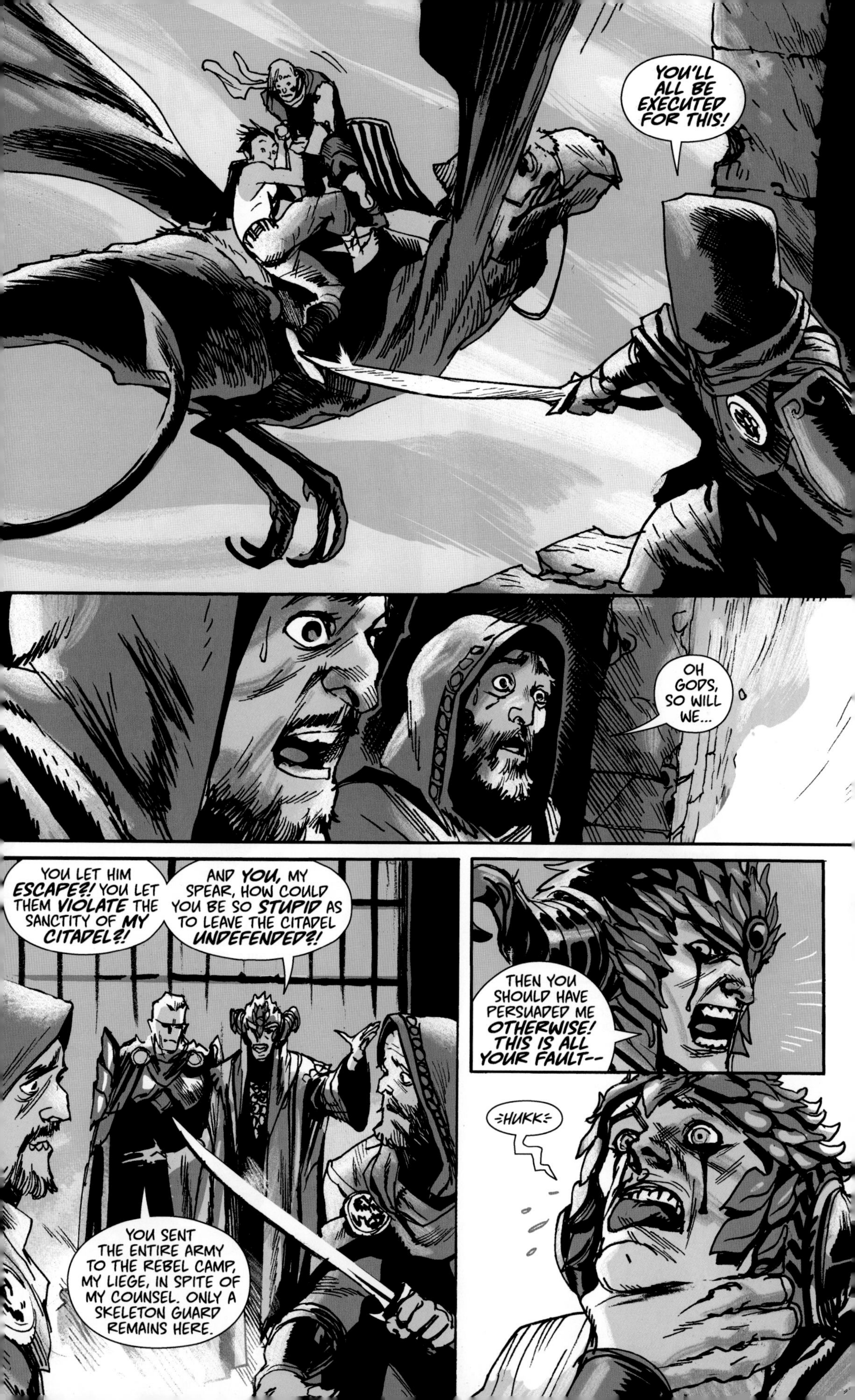
YOU'LL ALL BE EXECUTED FOR THIS!
OH GODS, SO WILL WE...
YOU LET HIM ESCAPE?! YOU LET THEM VIOLATE THE SANCTITY OF MY CITADEL?!
AND YOU, MY SPEAR, HOW COULD YOU BE SO STUPID AS TO LEAVE THE CITADEL UNDEFENDED?!
YOU SENT THE ENTIRE ARMY TO THE REBEL CAMP, MY LIEGE, IN SPITE OF MY COUNSEL. ONLY A SKELETON GUARD REMAINS HERE.
THEN YOU SHOULD HAVE PERSUADED ME OTHERWISE! THIS IS ALL YOUR FAULT--
HUKK

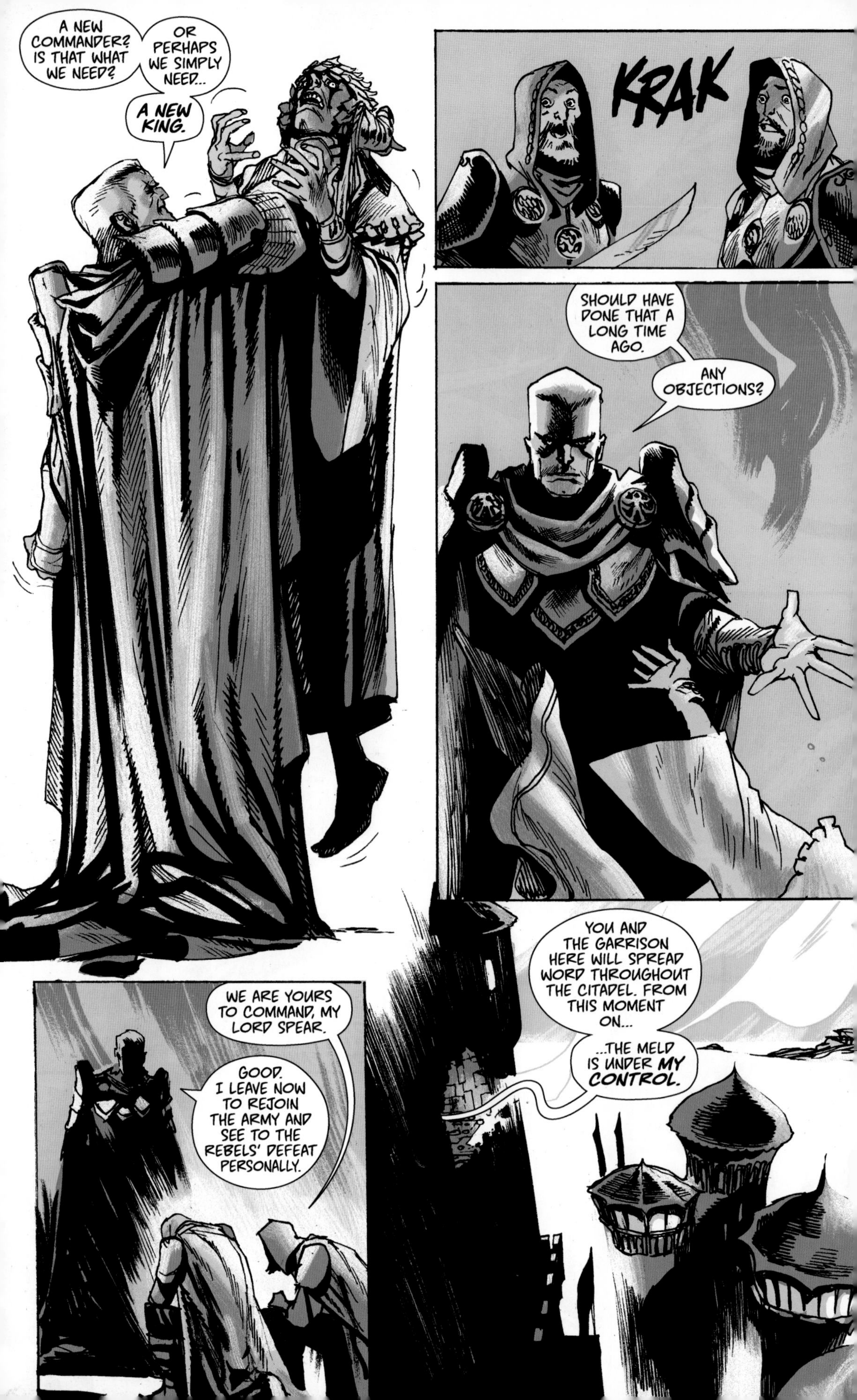
A NEW COMMANDER? IS THAT WHAT WE NEED?
OR PERHAPS WE SIMPLY NEED...
A NEW KING.
KRAK
SHOULD HAVE DONE THAT A LONG TIME AGO.
ANY OBJECTIONS?
WE ARE YOURS TO COMMAND, MY LORD SPEAR.
GOOD. I LEAVE NOW TO REJOIN THE ARMY AND SEE TO THE REBELS' DEFEAT PERSONALLY.
YOU AND THE GARRISON HERE WILL SPREAD WORD THROUGHOUT THE CITADEL. FROM THIS MOMENT ON...
...THE MELD IS UNDER MY CONTROL.

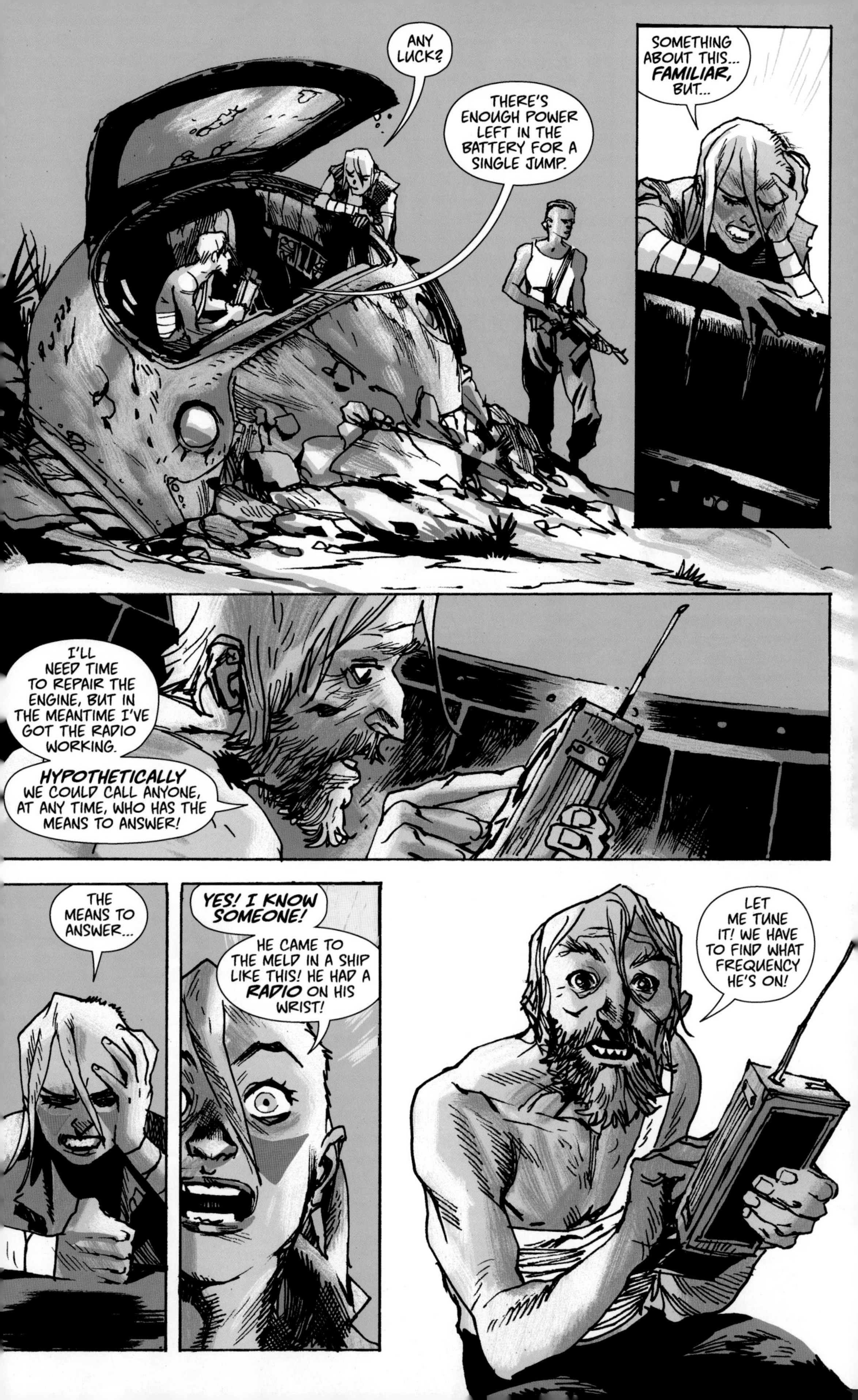
ANY LUCK?
THERE'S ENOUGH POWER LEFT IN THE BATTERY FOR A SINGLE JUMP.
SOMETHING ABOUT THIS... **FAMILIAR,** BUT...
I'LL NEED TIME TO REPAIR THE ENGINE, BUT IN THE MEANTIME I'VE GOT THE RADIO WORKING.
HYPOTHETICALLY WE COULD CALL ANYONE, AT ANY TIME, WHO HAS THE MEANS TO ANSWER!
THE MEANS TO ANSWER...
YES! I KNOW SOMEONE!
HE CAME TO THE MELD IN A SHIP LIKE THIS! HE HAD A **RADIO** ON HIS WRIST!
LET ME TUNE IT! WE HAVE TO FIND WHAT FREQUENCY HE'S ON!

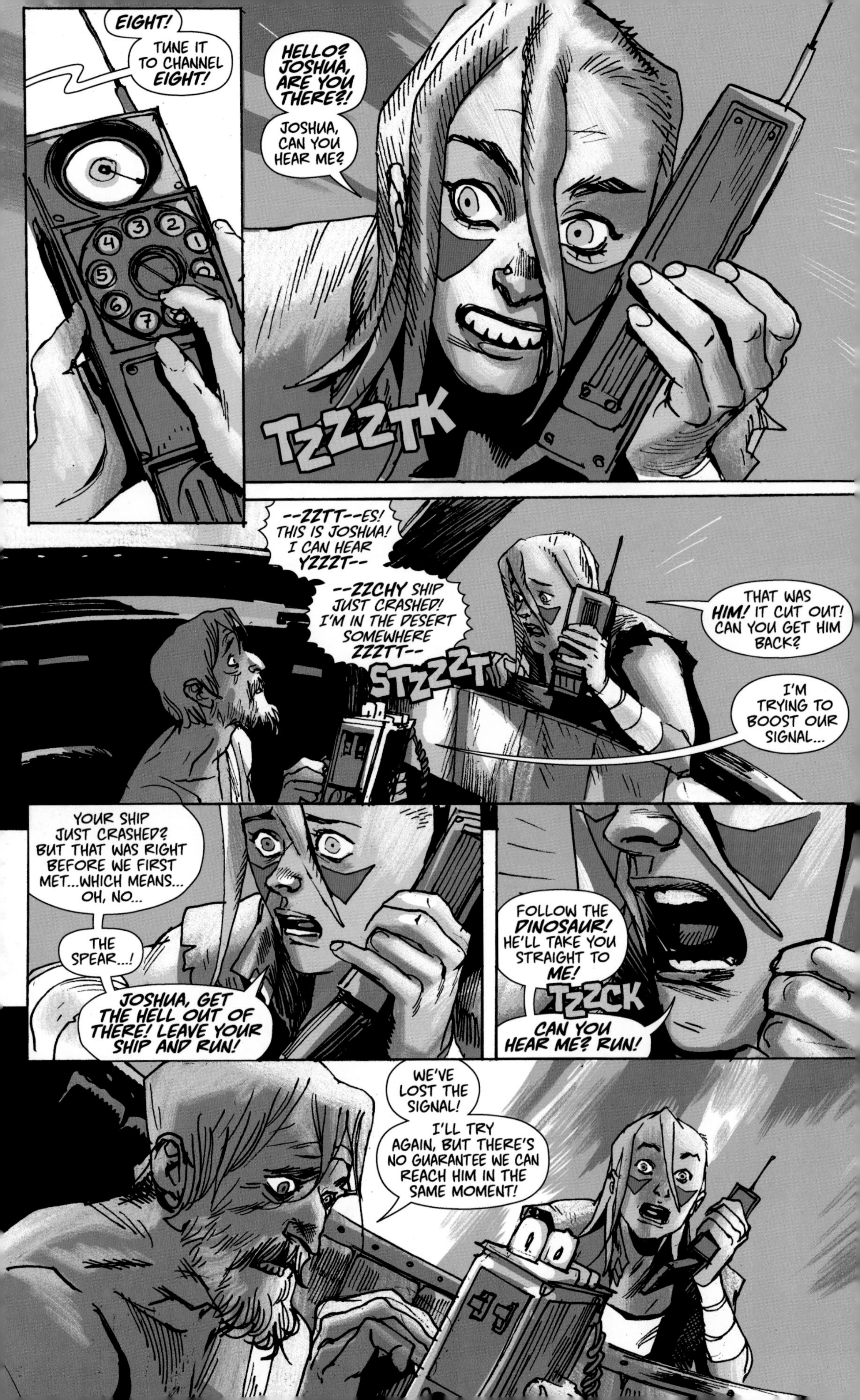
EIGHT!
TUNE IT TO CHANNEL EIGHT!
HELLO? JOSHUA, ARE YOU THERE?!
JOSHUA, CAN YOU HEAR ME?
TZZZTK
--ZZTT--ES! THIS IS JOSHUA! I CAN HEAR YZZZT--
--ZZCHY SHIP JUST CRASHED! I'M IN THE DESERT SOMEWHERE ZZZTT--
STZZZT
THAT WAS HIM! IT CUT OUT! CAN YOU GET HIM BACK?
I'M TRYING TO BOOST OUR SIGNAL...
YOUR SHIP JUST CRASHED? BUT THAT WAS RIGHT BEFORE WE FIRST MET...WHICH MEANS... OH, NO...
THE SPEAR...!
JOSHUA, GET THE HELL OUT OF THERE! LEAVE YOUR SHIP AND RUN!
FOLLOW THE DINOSAUR! HE'LL TAKE YOU STRAIGHT TO ME!
TZZCK
CAN YOU HEAR ME? RUN!
WE'VE LOST THE SIGNAL!
I'LL TRY AGAIN, BUT THERE'S NO GUARANTEE WE CAN REACH HIM IN THE SAME MOMENT!

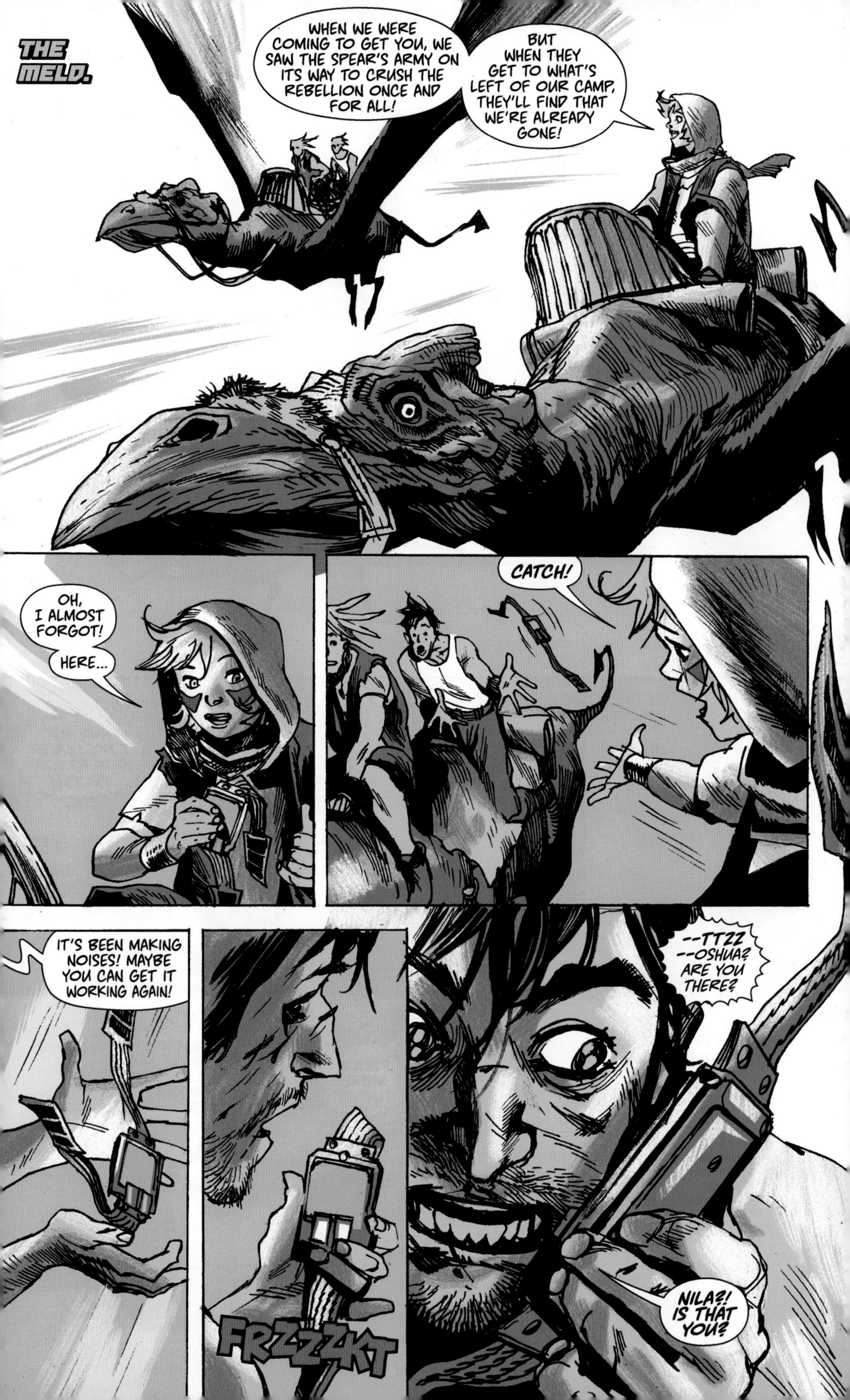
THE MELD.
WHEN WE WERE COMING TO GET YOU, WE SAW THE SPEAR'S ARMY ON ITS WAY TO CRUSH THE REBELLION ONCE AND FOR ALL!
BUT WHEN THEY GET TO WHAT'S LEFT OF OUR CAMP, THEY'LL FIND THAT WE'RE ALREADY GONE!
OH, I ALMOST FORGOT!
HERE...
CATCH!
IT'S BEEN MAKING NOISES! MAYBE YOU CAN GET IT WORKING AGAIN!
FRZZZKT
--TTZZ --OSHUA? ARE YOU THERE?
NILA?! IS THAT YOU?

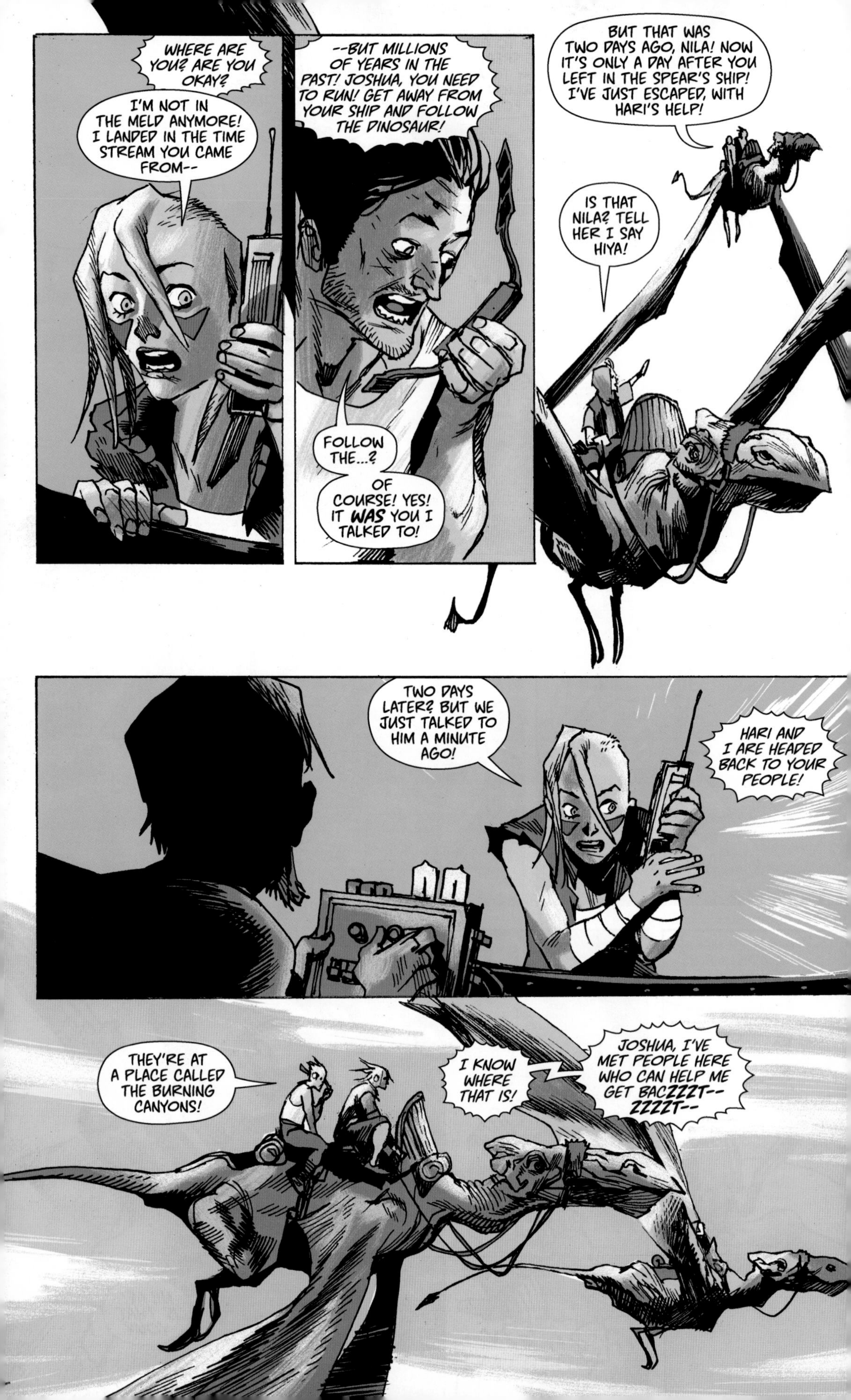
WHERE ARE YOU? ARE YOU OKAY?
I'M NOT IN THE MELD ANYMORE! I LANDED IN THE TIME STREAM YOU CAME FROM--
--BUT MILLIONS OF YEARS IN THE PAST! JOSHUA, YOU NEED TO RUN! GET AWAY FROM YOUR SHIP AND FOLLOW THE DINOSAUR!
FOLLOW THE...?
OF COURSE! YES! IT **WAS** YOU I TALKED TO!
BUT THAT WAS TWO DAYS AGO, NILA! NOW IT'S ONLY A DAY AFTER YOU LEFT IN THE SPEAR'S SHIP! I'VE JUST ESCAPED, WITH HARI'S HELP!
IS THAT NILA? TELL HER I SAY HIYA!
TWO DAYS LATER? BUT WE JUST TALKED TO HIM A MINUTE AGO!
HARI AND I ARE HEADED BACK TO YOUR PEOPLE!
THEY'RE AT A PLACE CALLED THE BURNING CANYONS!
I KNOW WHERE THAT IS!
JOSHUA, I'VE MET PEOPLE HERE WHO CAN HELP ME GET BACZZZT-- ZZZZT--

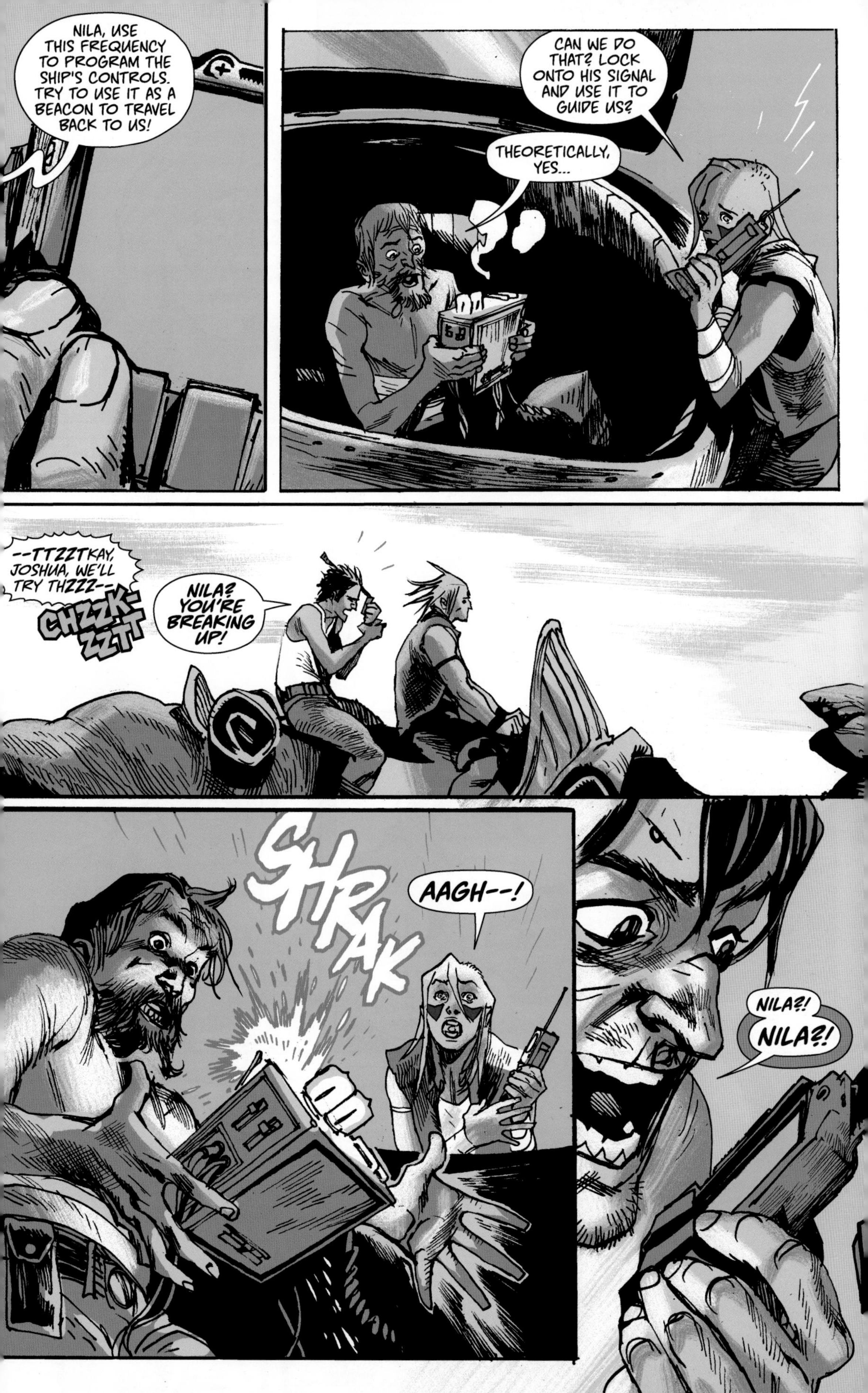
NILA, USE THIS FREQUENCY TO PROGRAM THE SHIP'S CONTROLS. TRY TO USE IT AS A BEACON TO TRAVEL BACK TO US!
CAN WE DO THAT? LOCK ONTO HIS SIGNAL AND USE IT TO GUIDE US?
THEORETICALLY, YES...
--TTZZTKAY, JOSHUA, WE'LL TRY THZZZ--
CHZZK-ZZTT
NILA? YOU'RE BREAKING UP!
SHRAK
AAGH--!
NILA?!
NILA?!

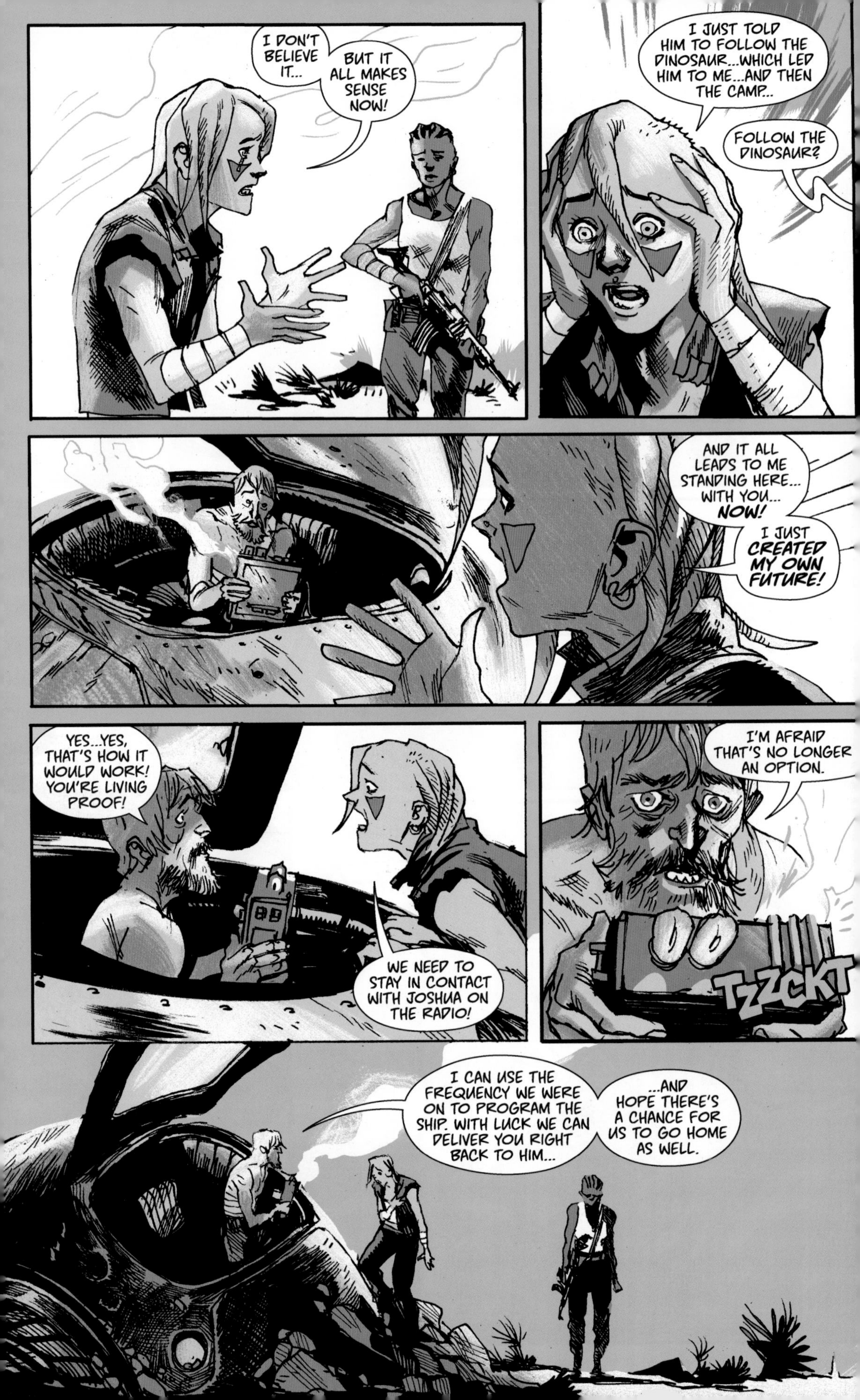
I DON'T BELIEVE IT...
BUT IT ALL MAKES SENSE NOW!
I JUST TOLD HIM TO FOLLOW THE DINOSAUR...WHICH LED HIM TO ME...AND THEN THE CAMP...
FOLLOW THE DINOSAUR?
AND IT ALL LEADS TO ME STANDING HERE... WITH YOU... NOW!
I JUST CREATED MY OWN FUTURE!
YES...YES, THAT'S HOW IT WOULD WORK! YOU'RE LIVING PROOF!
WE NEED TO STAY IN CONTACT WITH JOSHUA ON THE RADIO!
I'M AFRAID THAT'S NO LONGER AN OPTION.
TZZCKT
I CAN USE THE FREQUENCY WE WERE ON TO PROGRAM THE SHIP. WITH LUCK WE CAN DELIVER YOU RIGHT BACK TO HIM...
...AND HOPE THERE'S A CHANCE FOR US TO GO HOME AS WELL.

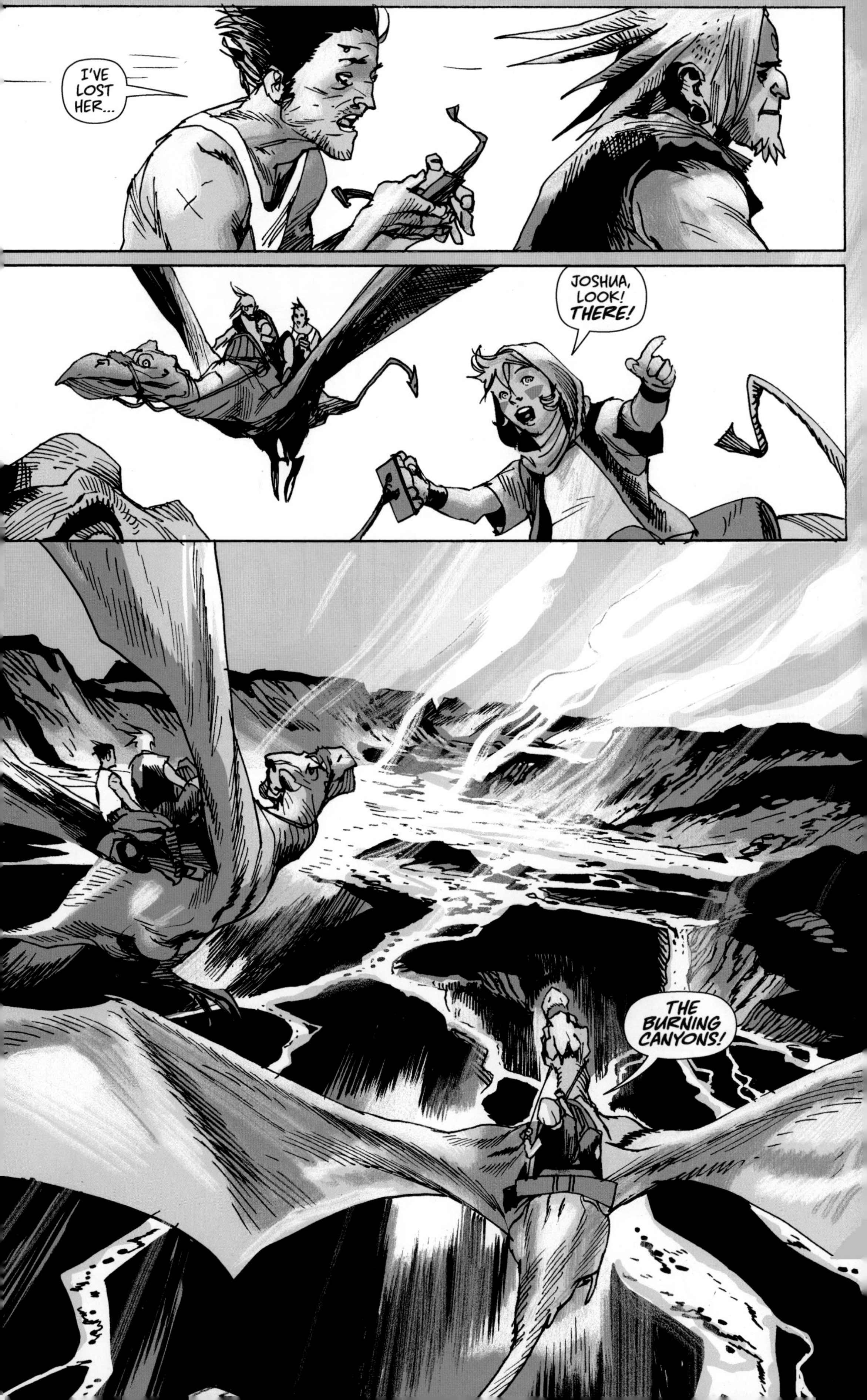
I'VE LOST HER...
JOSHUA, LOOK! THERE!
THE BURNING CANYONS!

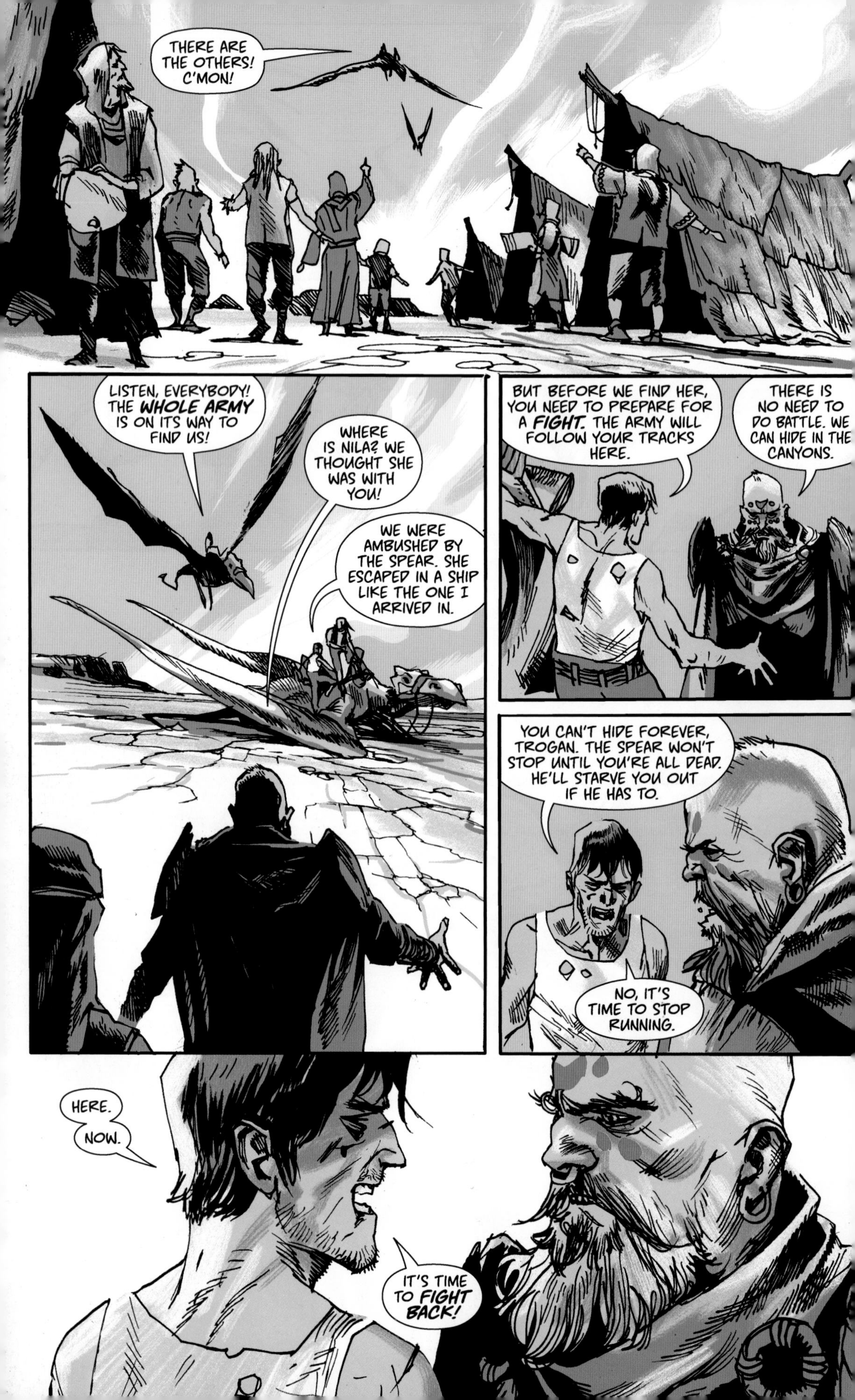
THERE ARE THE OTHERS! C'MON!
LISTEN, EVERYBODY! THE WHOLE ARMY IS ON ITS WAY TO FIND US!
WHERE IS NILA? WE THOUGHT SHE WAS WITH YOU!
WE WERE AMBUSHED BY THE SPEAR. SHE ESCAPED IN A SHIP LIKE THE ONE I ARRIVED IN.
BUT BEFORE WE FIND HER, YOU NEED TO PREPARE FOR A FIGHT. THE ARMY WILL FOLLOW YOUR TRACKS HERE.
THERE IS NO NEED TO DO BATTLE. WE CAN HIDE IN THE CANYONS.
YOU CAN'T HIDE FOREVER, TROGAN. THE SPEAR WON'T STOP UNTIL YOU'RE ALL DEAD. HE'LL STARVE YOU OUT IF HE HAS TO.
NO, IT'S TIME TO STOP RUNNING.
HERE.
NOW.
IT'S TIME TO FIGHT BACK!

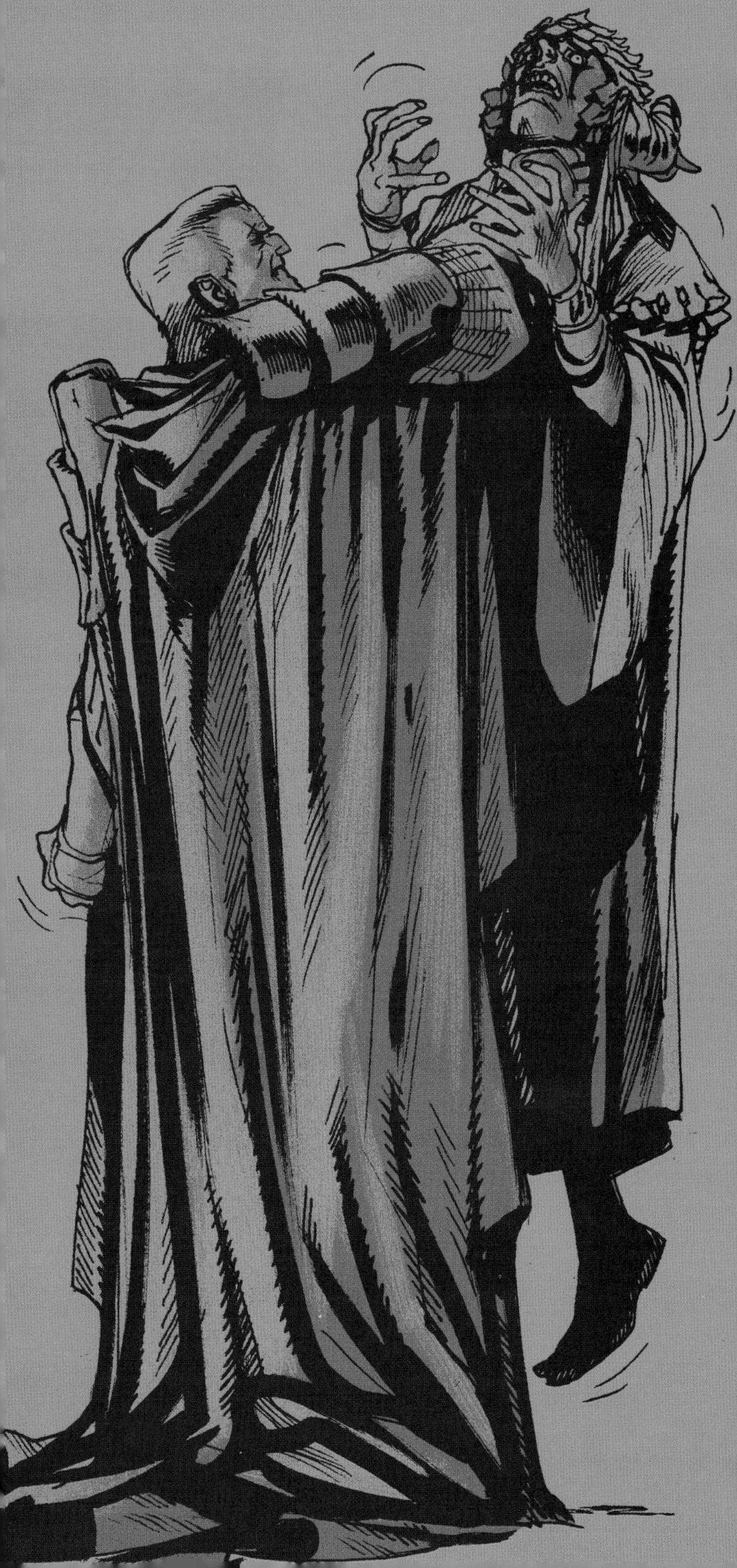

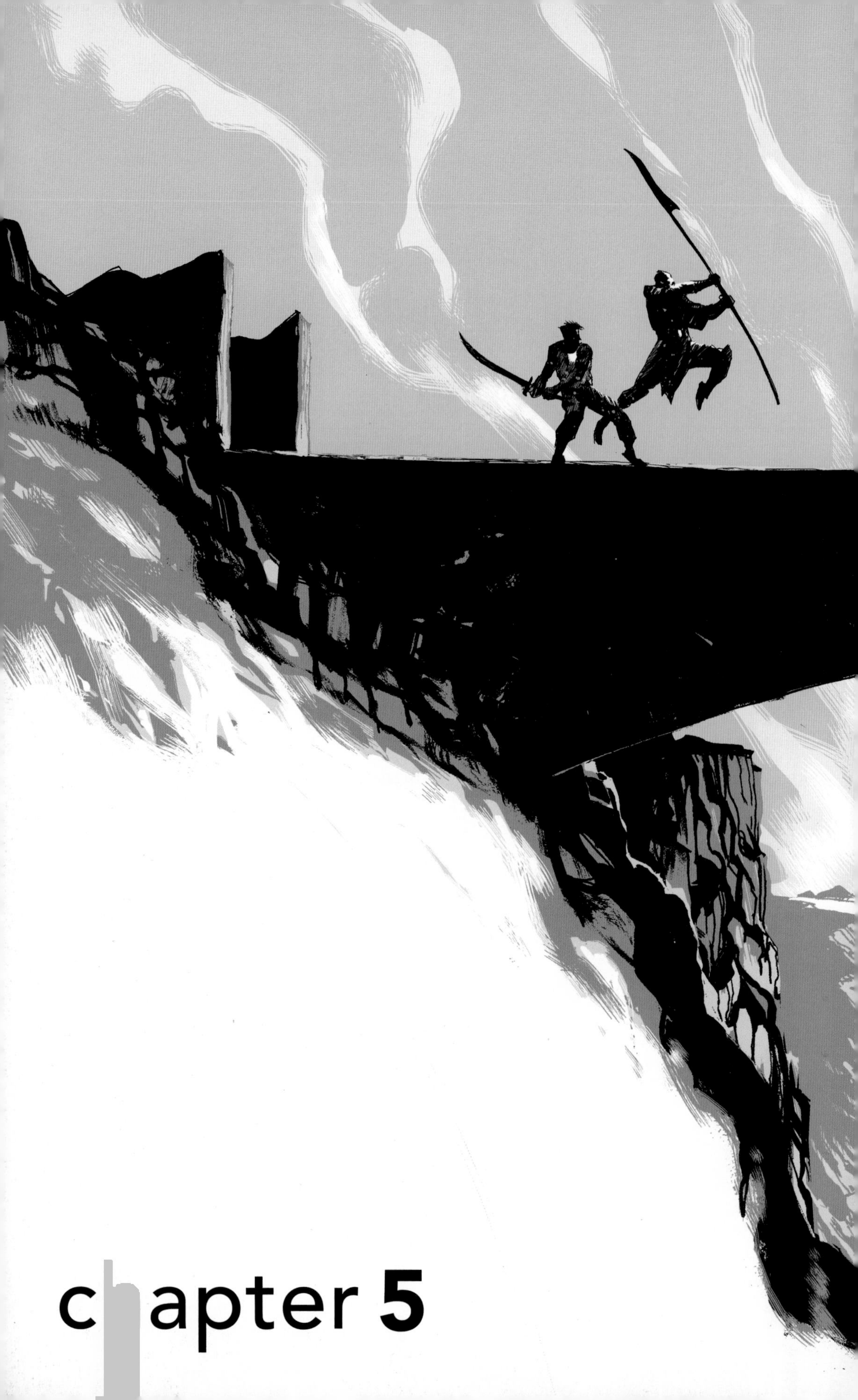

chapter 5

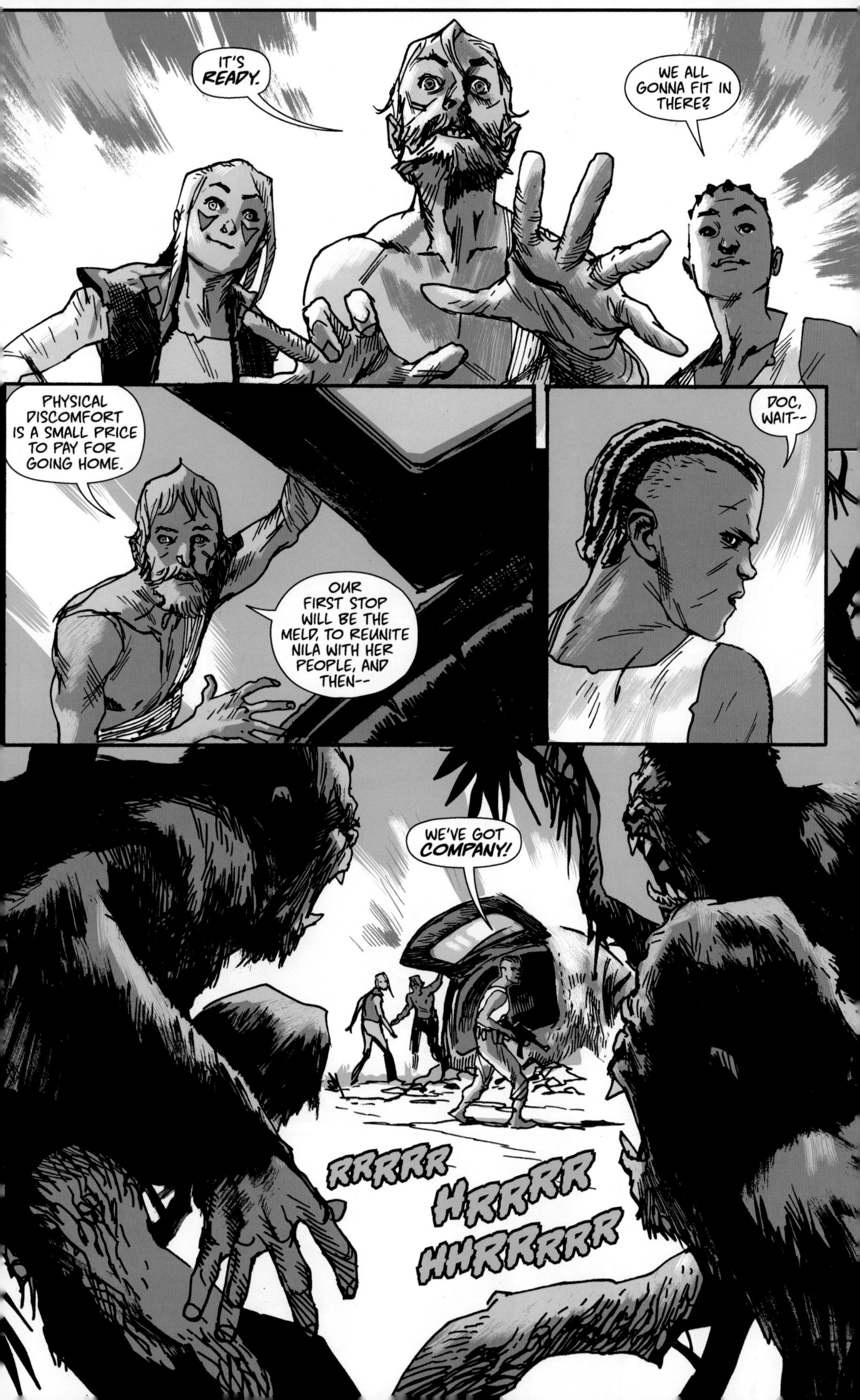
IT'S READY.
WE ALL GONNA FIT IN THERE?
PHYSICAL DISCOMFORT IS A SMALL PRICE TO PAY FOR GOING HOME.
OUR FIRST STOP WILL BE THE MELD, TO REUNITE NILA WITH HER PEOPLE, AND THEN--
DOC, WAIT--
WE'VE GOT COMPANY!
RRRRR
HRRRR
HHRRRRR

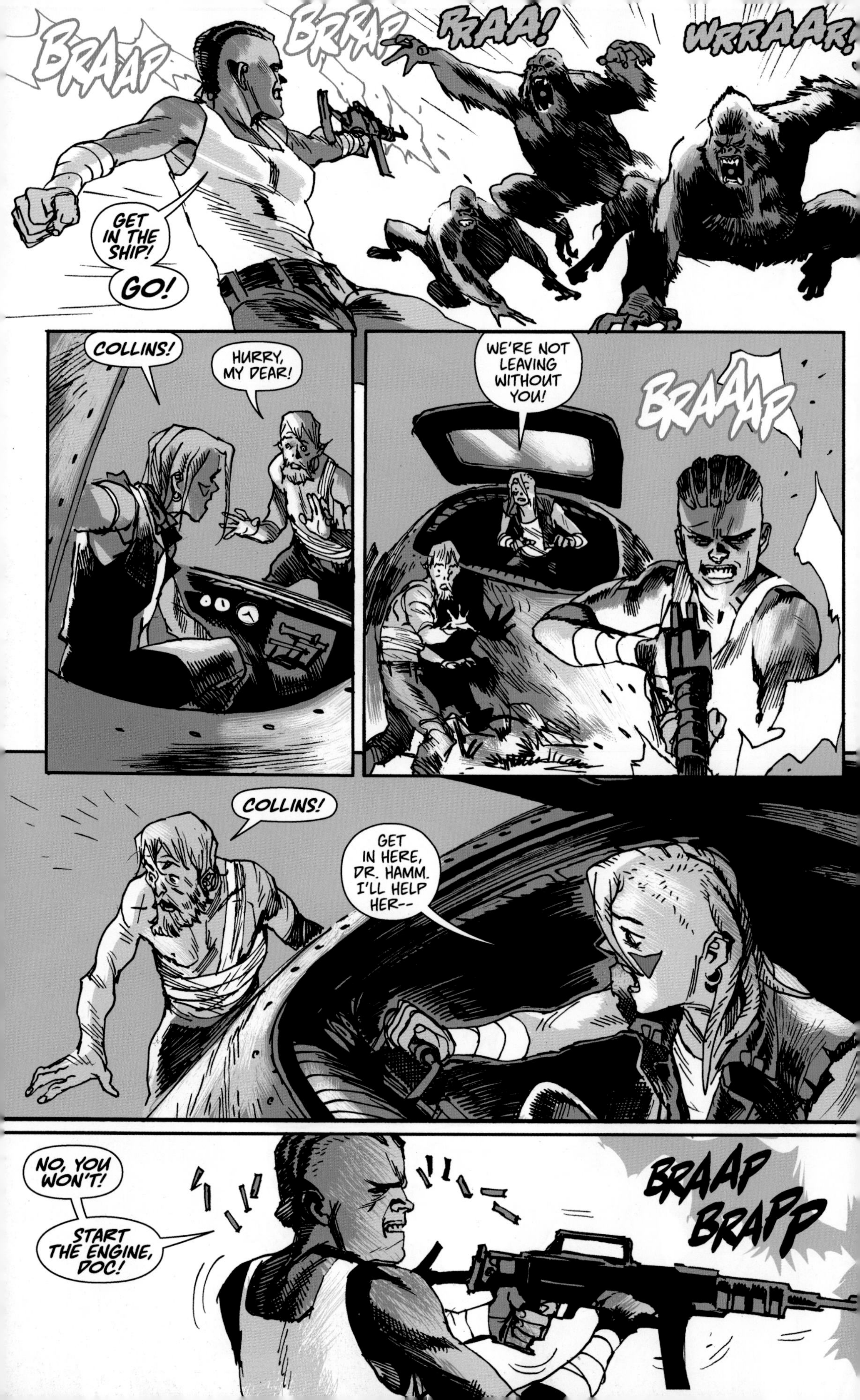
BRAAP
BRRAP
RAA!
WRRAAR!
GET IN THE SHIP!
GO!
COLLINS!
HURRY, MY DEAR!
WE'RE NOT LEAVING WITHOUT YOU!
BRAAAP
COLLINS!
GET IN HERE, DR. HAMM. I'LL HELP HER--
NO, YOU WON'T!
START THE ENGINE, DOC!
BRAAP
BRAPP

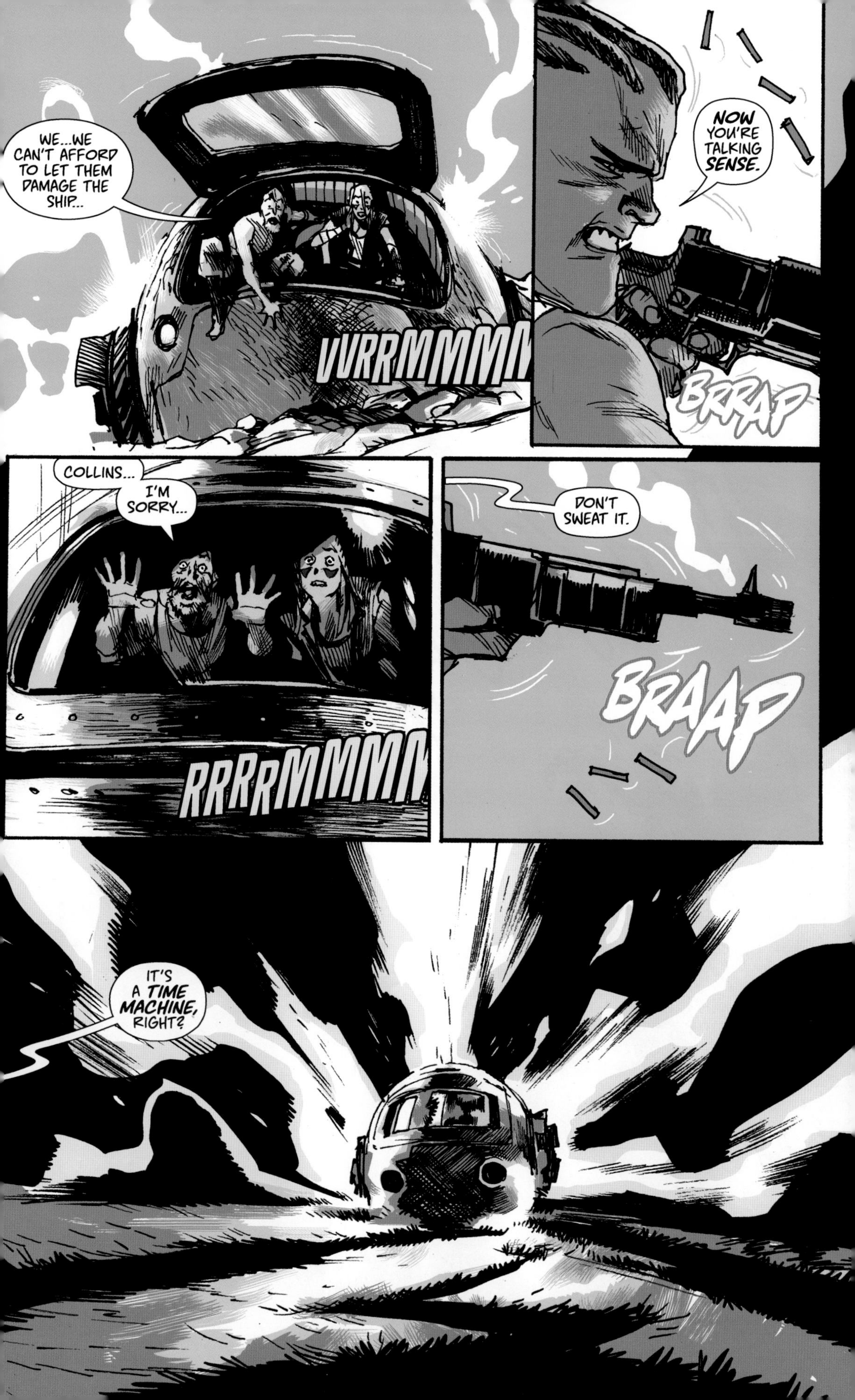
WE...WE CAN'T AFFORD TO LET THEM DAMAGE THE SHIP...
VVRRMMMMM
NOW YOU'RE TALKING SENSE.
BRRAP
COLLINS...
I'M SORRY...
RRRRMMMMM
DON'T SWEAT IT.
BRAAP
IT'S A TIME MACHINE, RIGHT?

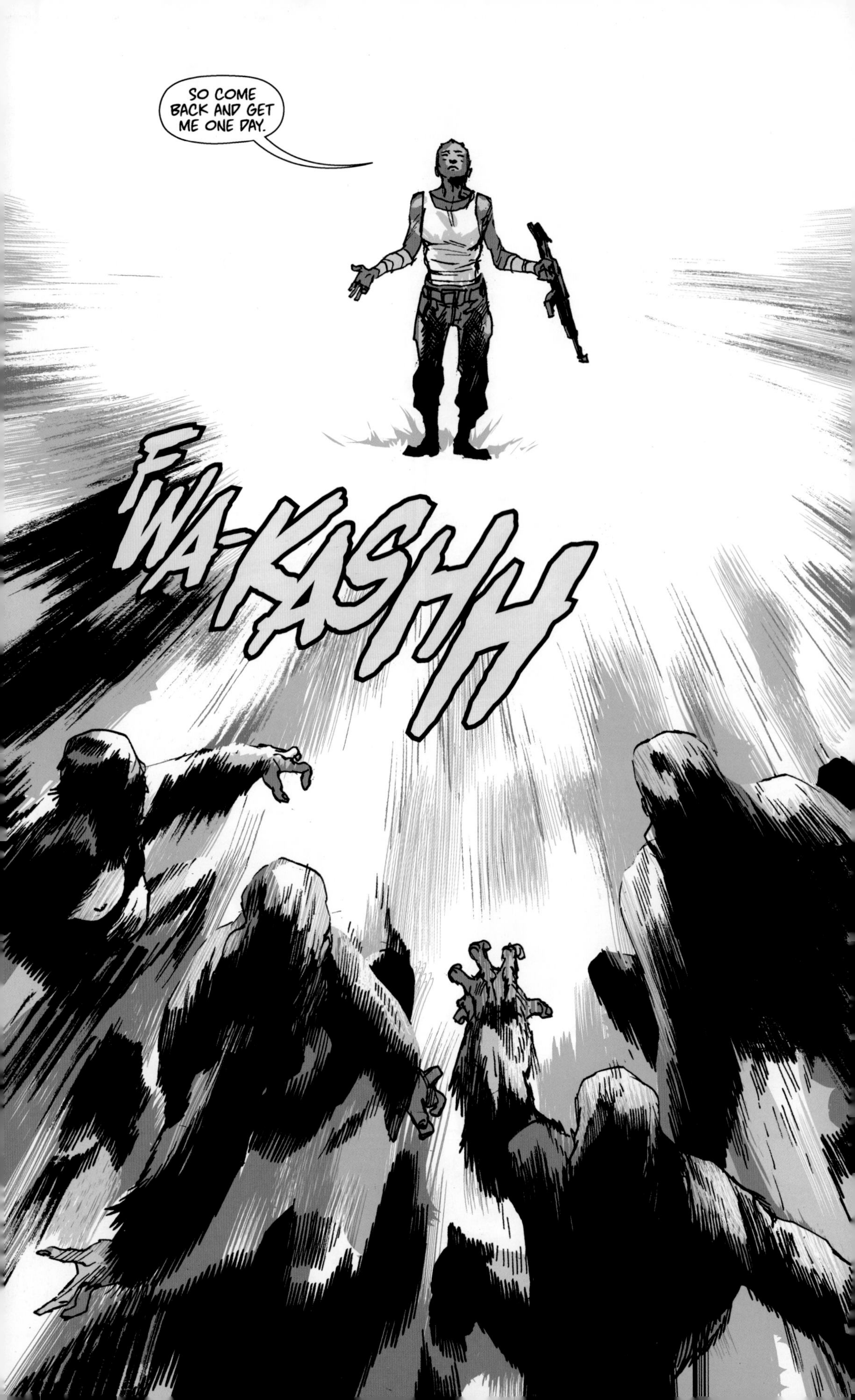
SO COME BACK AND GET ME ONE DAY.
FWA-KASHH

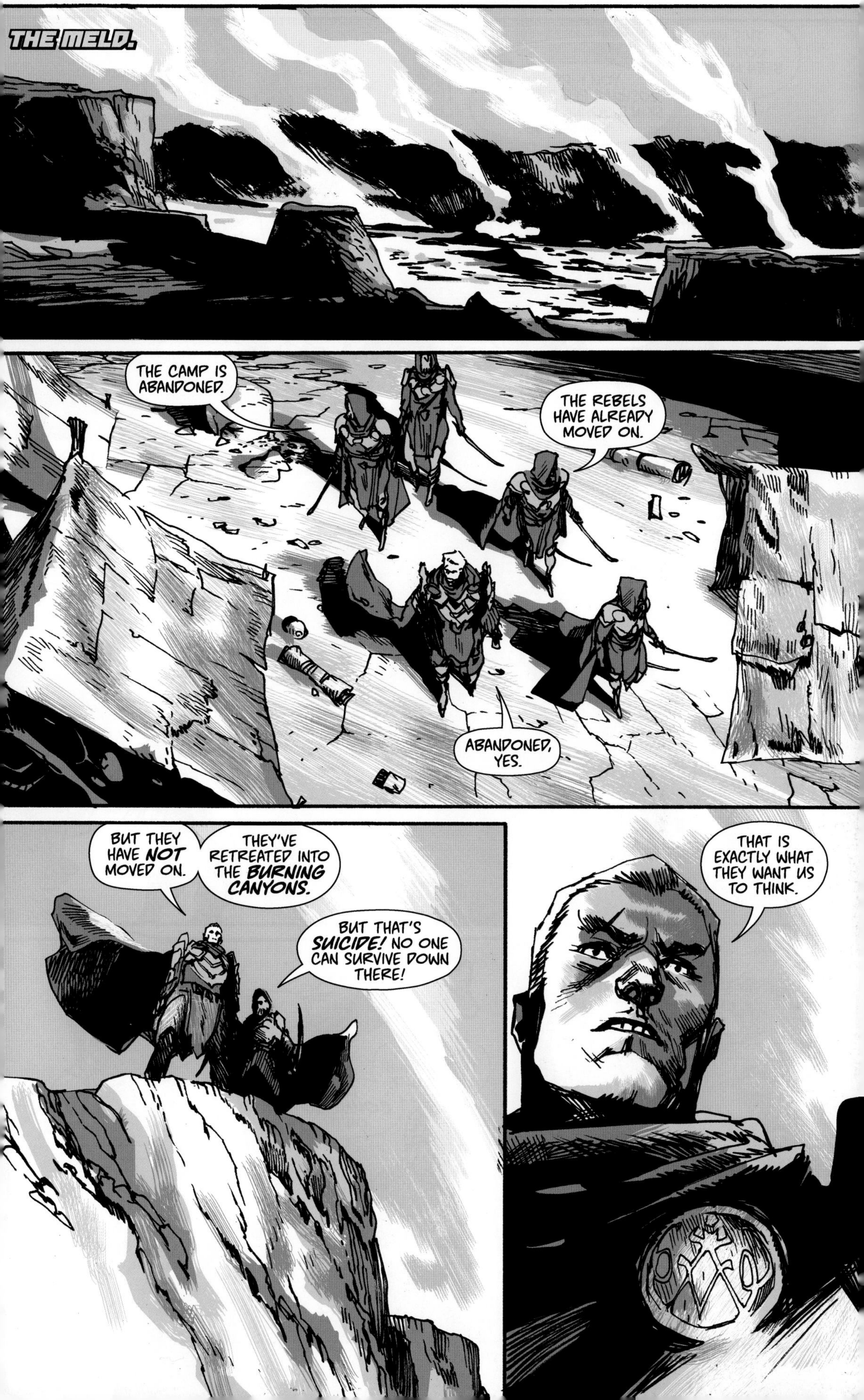
THE MELD.
THE CAMP IS ABANDONED.
THE REBELS HAVE ALREADY MOVED ON.
ABANDONED, YES.
BUT THEY HAVE NOT MOVED ON.
THEY'VE RETREATED INTO THE BURNING CANYONS.
BUT THAT'S SUICIDE! NO ONE CAN SURVIVE DOWN THERE!
THAT IS EXACTLY WHAT THEY WANT US TO THINK.

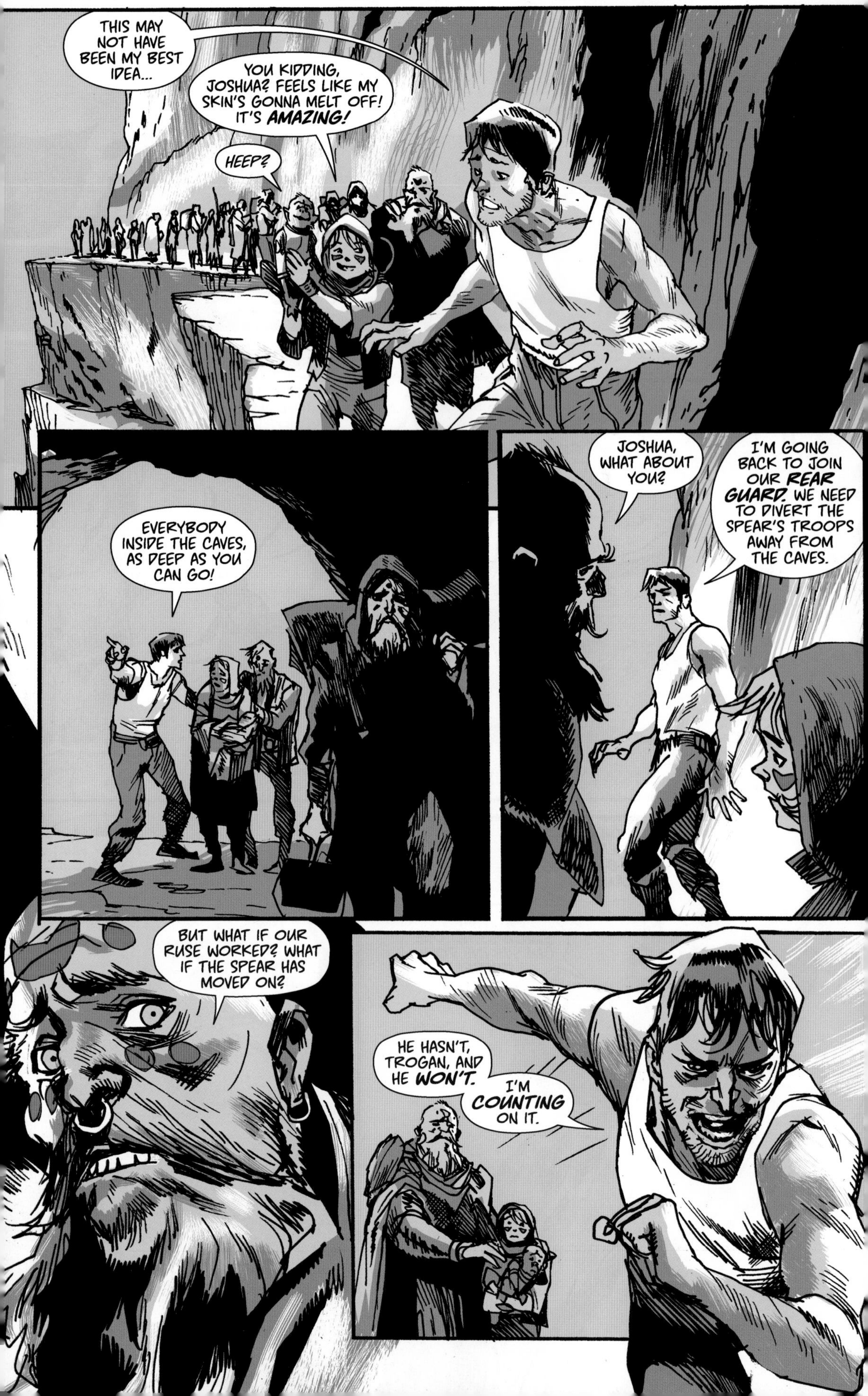
THIS MAY NOT HAVE BEEN MY BEST IDEA...
YOU KIDDING, JOSHUA? FEELS LIKE MY SKIN'S GONNA MELT OFF! IT'S AMAZING!
HEEP?
EVERYBODY INSIDE THE CAVES, AS DEEP AS YOU CAN GO!
JOSHUA, WHAT ABOUT YOU?
I'M GOING BACK TO JOIN OUR REAR GUARD. WE NEED TO DIVERT THE SPEAR'S TROOPS AWAY FROM THE CAVES.
BUT WHAT IF OUR RUSE WORKED? WHAT IF THE SPEAR HAS MOVED ON?
HE HASN'T, TROGAN, AND HE WON'T.
I'M COUNTING ON IT.

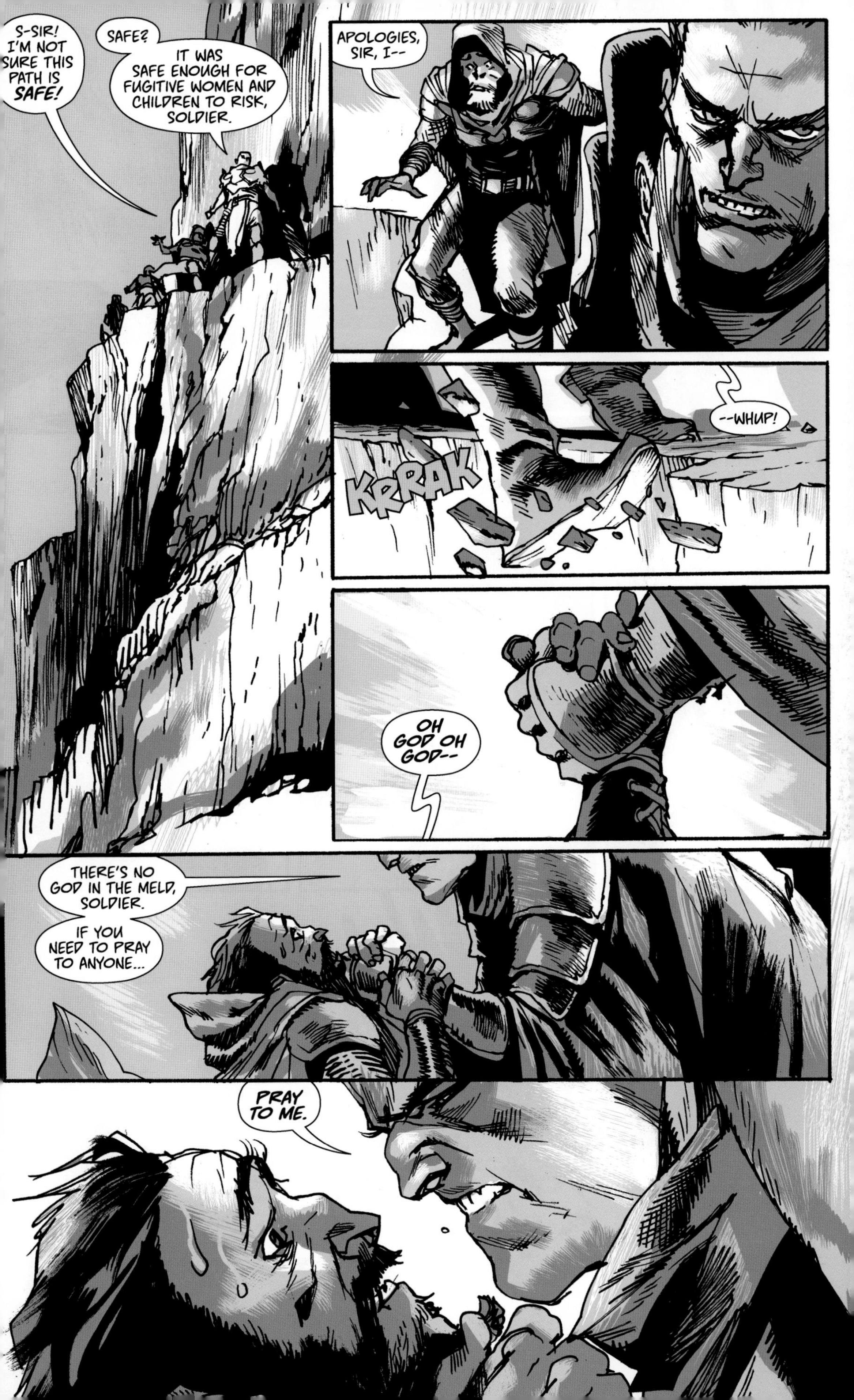
S-SIR! I'M NOT SURE THIS PATH IS SAFE!
SAFE?
IT WAS SAFE ENOUGH FOR FUGITIVE WOMEN AND CHILDREN TO RISK, SOLDIER.
APOLOGIES, SIR, I--
KRRAK
--WHUP!
OH GOD OH GOD--
THERE'S NO GOD IN THE MELD, SOLDIER.
IF YOU NEED TO PRAY TO ANYONE...
PRAY TO ME.

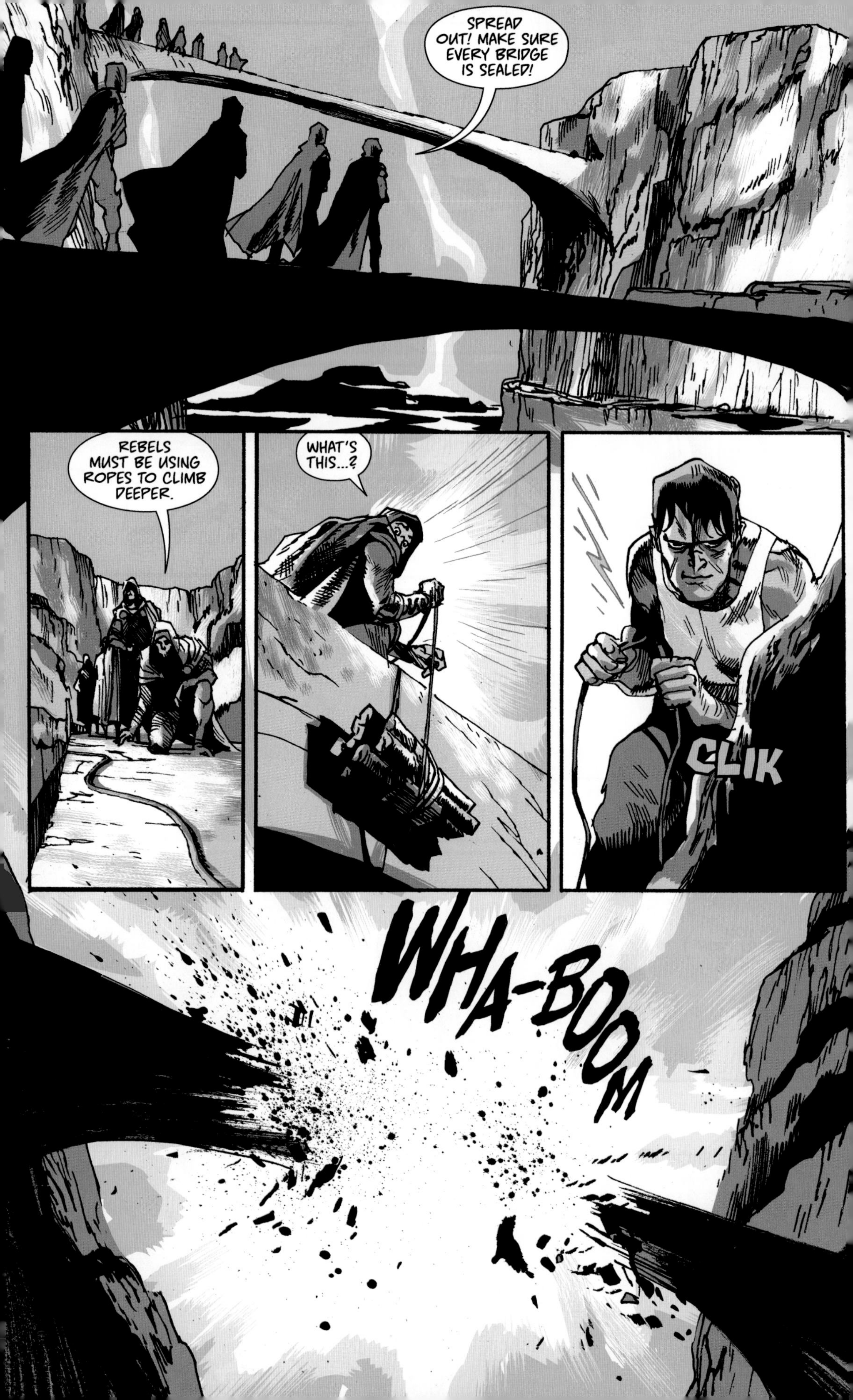
SPREAD OUT! MAKE SURE EVERY BRIDGE IS SEALED!
REBELS MUST BE USING ROPES TO CLIMB DEEPER.
WHAT'S THIS...?
CLIK
WHA-BOOM

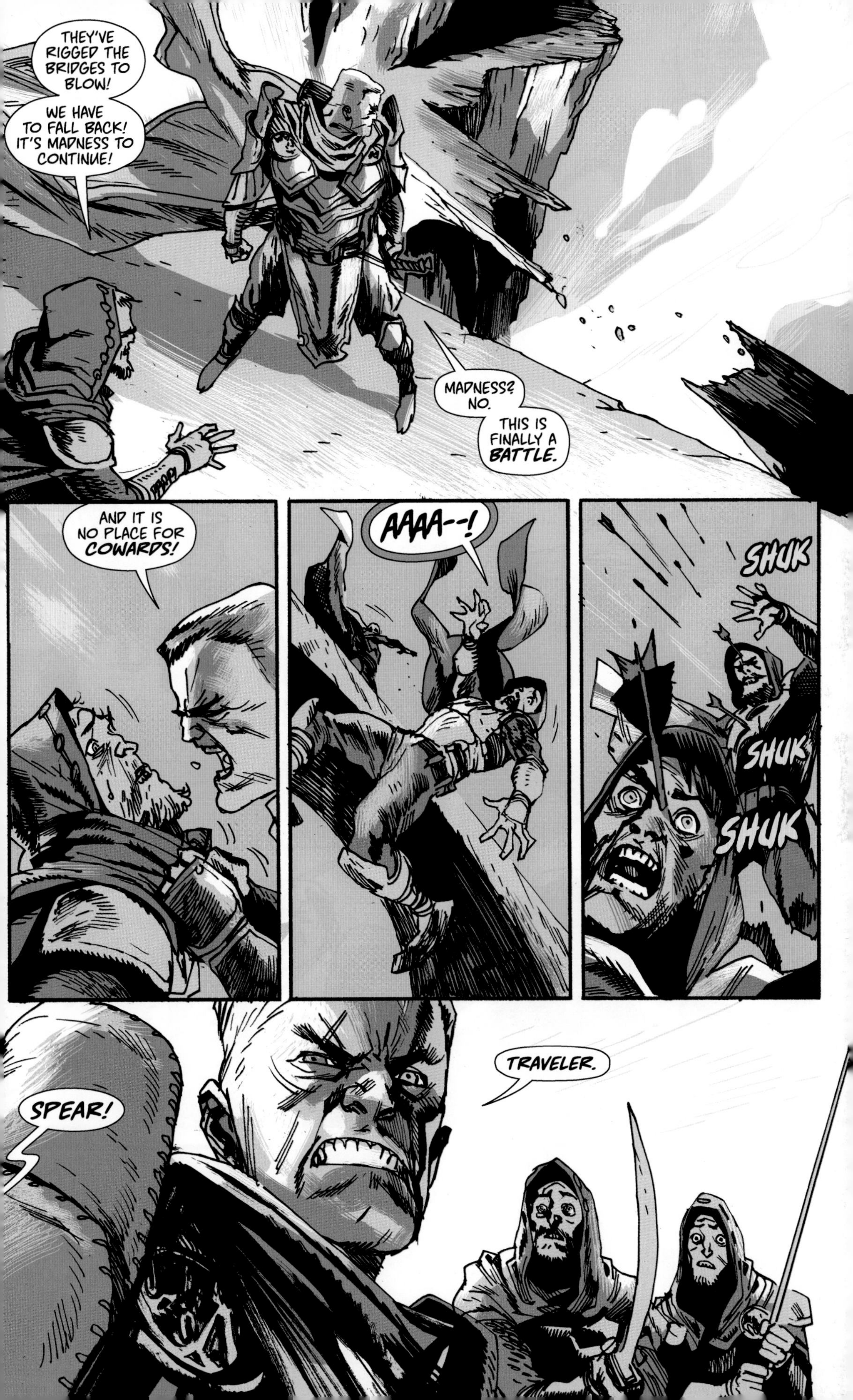
THEY'VE RIGGED THE BRIDGES TO BLOW!
WE HAVE TO FALL BACK! IT'S MADNESS TO CONTINUE!
MADNESS? NO.
THIS IS FINALLY A BATTLE.
AND IT IS NO PLACE FOR COWARDS!
AAAA--!
SHUK
SHUK
SHUK
TRAVELER.
SPEAR!

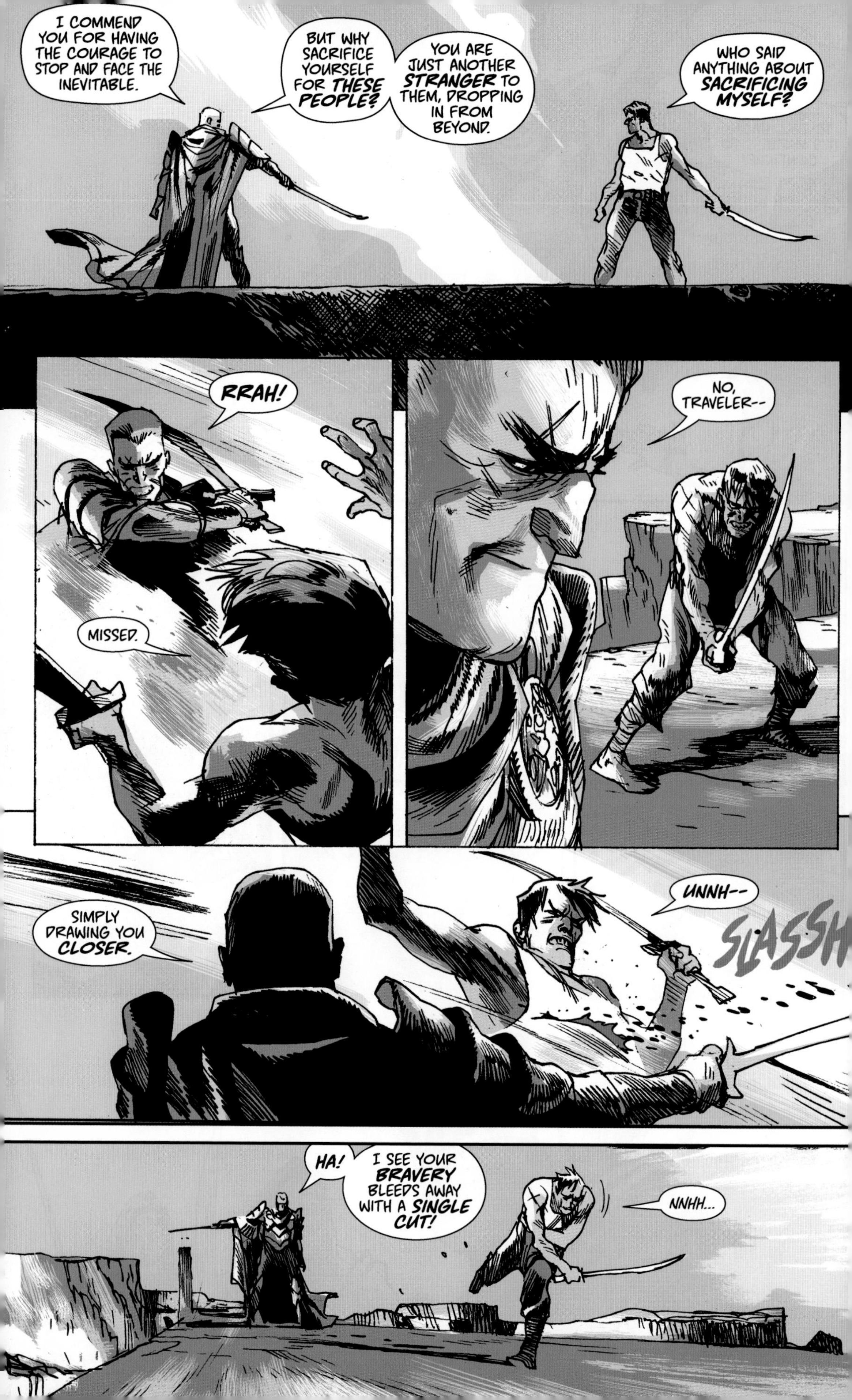
I COMMEND YOU FOR HAVING THE COURAGE TO STOP AND FACE THE INEVITABLE.
BUT WHY SACRIFICE YOURSELF FOR THESE PEOPLE?
YOU ARE JUST ANOTHER STRANGER TO THEM, DROPPING IN FROM BEYOND.
WHO SAID ANYTHING ABOUT SACRIFICING MYSELF?
RRAH!
MISSED.
NO, TRAVELER--
SIMPLY DRAWING YOU CLOSER.
UNNH--
SLASSH
HA!
I SEE YOUR BRAVERY BLEEDS AWAY WITH A SINGLE CUT!
NNHH...

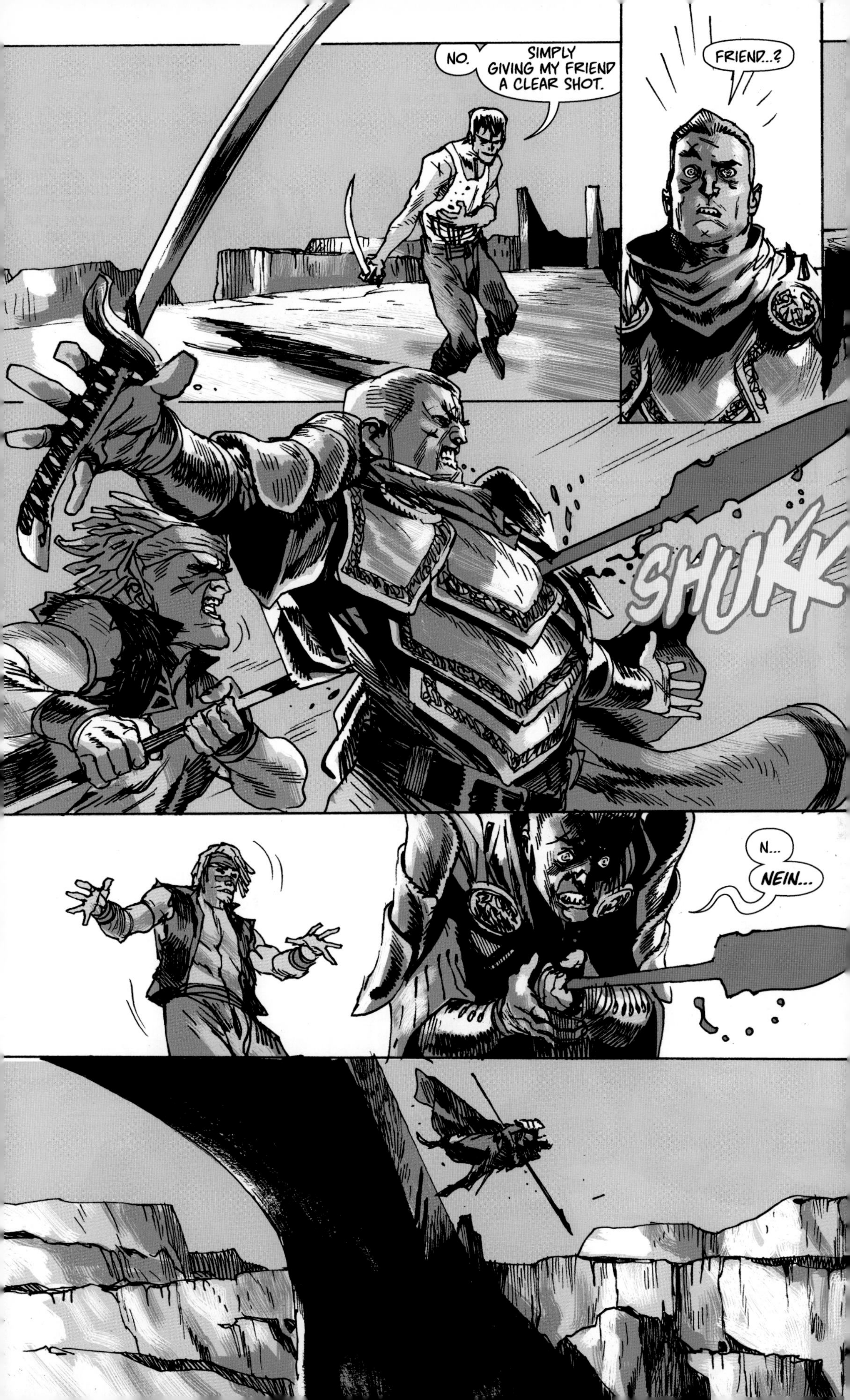
NO.
SIMPLY GIVING MY FRIEND A CLEAR SHOT.
FRIEND...?
SHUKK
N...
NEIN...

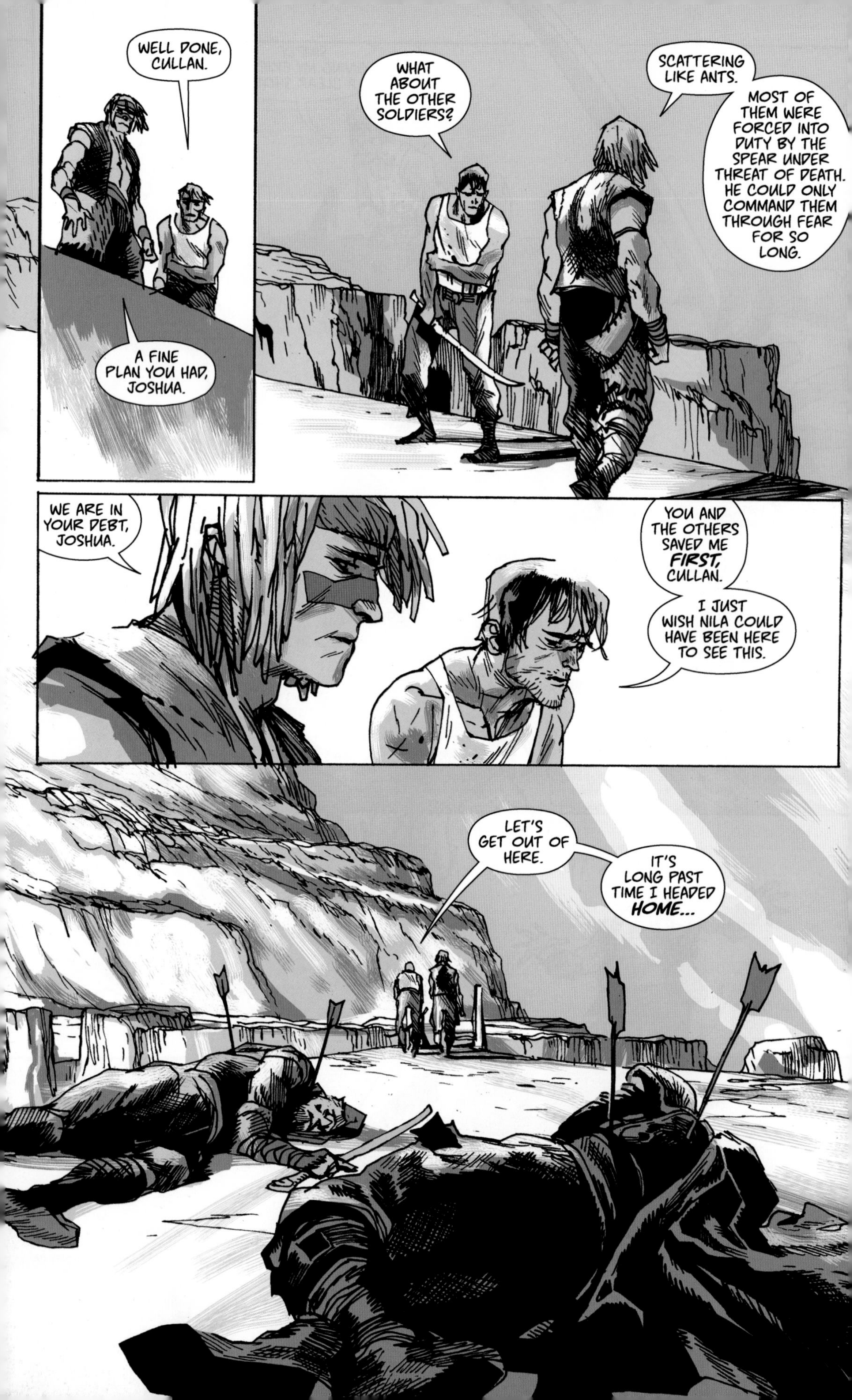
WELL DONE, CULLAN.
A FINE PLAN YOU HAD, JOSHUA.
WHAT ABOUT THE OTHER SOLDIERS?
SCATTERING LIKE ANTS.
MOST OF THEM WERE FORCED INTO DUTY BY THE SPEAR UNDER THREAT OF DEATH. HE COULD ONLY COMMAND THEM THROUGH FEAR FOR SO LONG.
WE ARE IN YOUR DEBT, JOSHUA.
YOU AND THE OTHERS SAVED ME FIRST, CULLAN.
I JUST WISH NILA COULD HAVE BEEN HERE TO SEE THIS.
LET'S GET OUT OF HERE.
IT'S LONG PAST TIME I HEADED HOME...

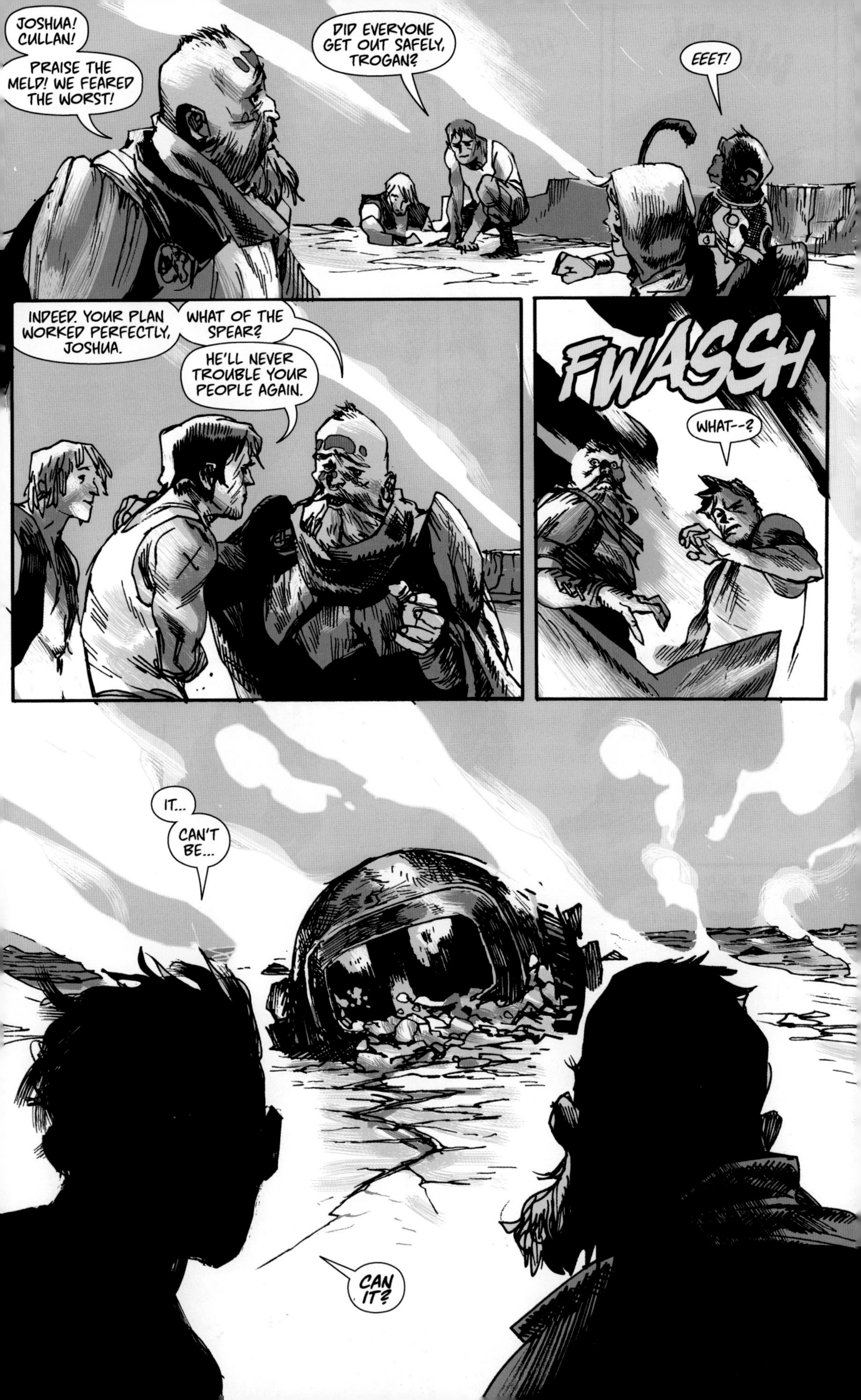
JOSHUA! CULLAN!
PRAISE THE MELD! WE FEARED THE WORST!
DID EVERYONE GET OUT SAFELY, TROGAN?
EEET!
INDEED. YOUR PLAN WORKED PERFECTLY, JOSHUA.
WHAT OF THE SPEAR?
HE'LL NEVER TROUBLE YOUR PEOPLE AGAIN.
FWASSH
WHAT--?
IT...
CAN'T BE...
CAN IT?

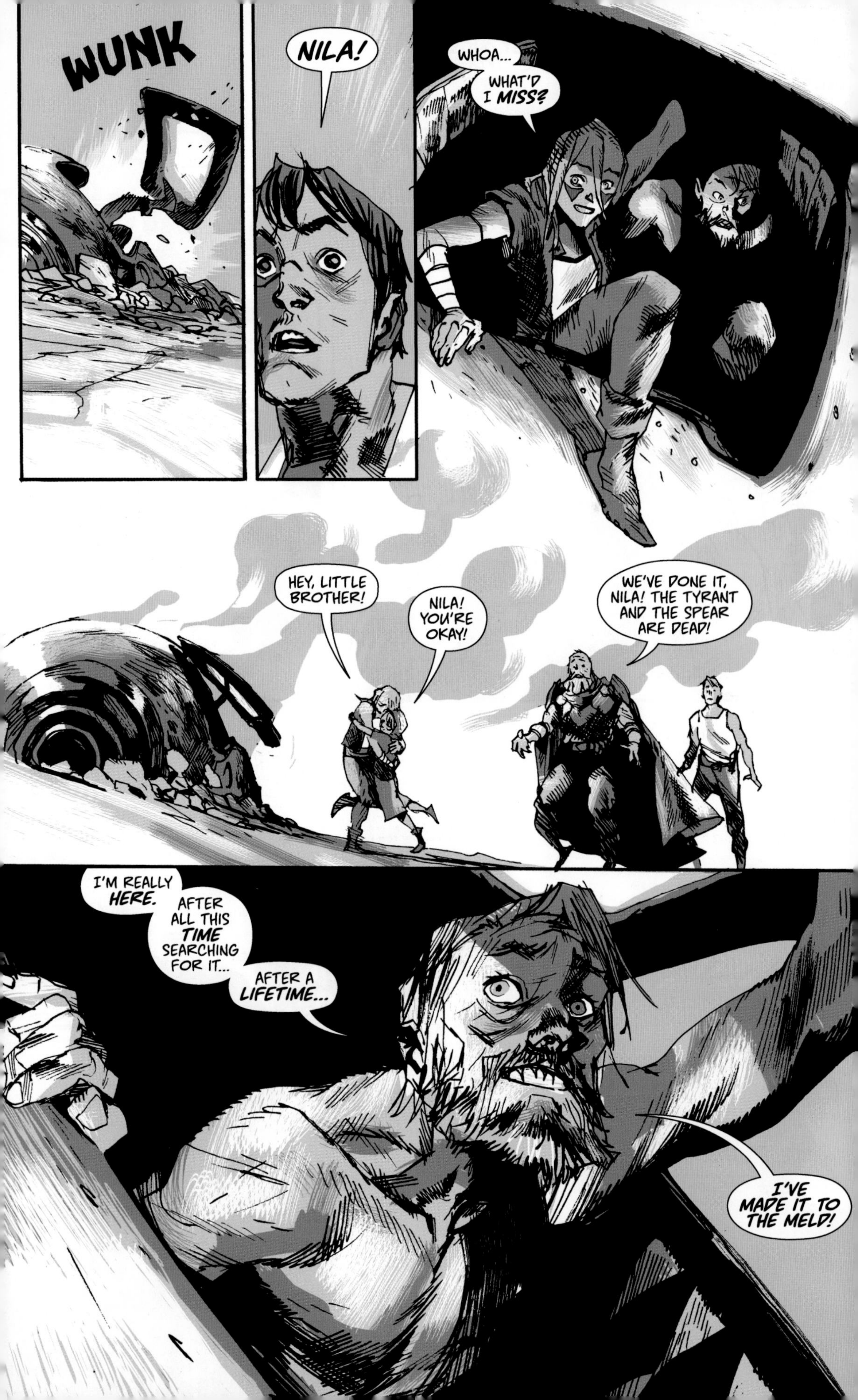
WUNK
NILA!
WHOA... WHAT'D I MISS?
HEY, LITTLE BROTHER!
NILA! YOU'RE OKAY!
WE'VE DONE IT, NILA! THE TYRANT AND THE SPEAR ARE DEAD!
I'M REALLY HERE.
AFTER ALL THIS TIME SEARCHING FOR IT...
AFTER A LIFETIME...
I'VE MADE IT TO THE MELD!

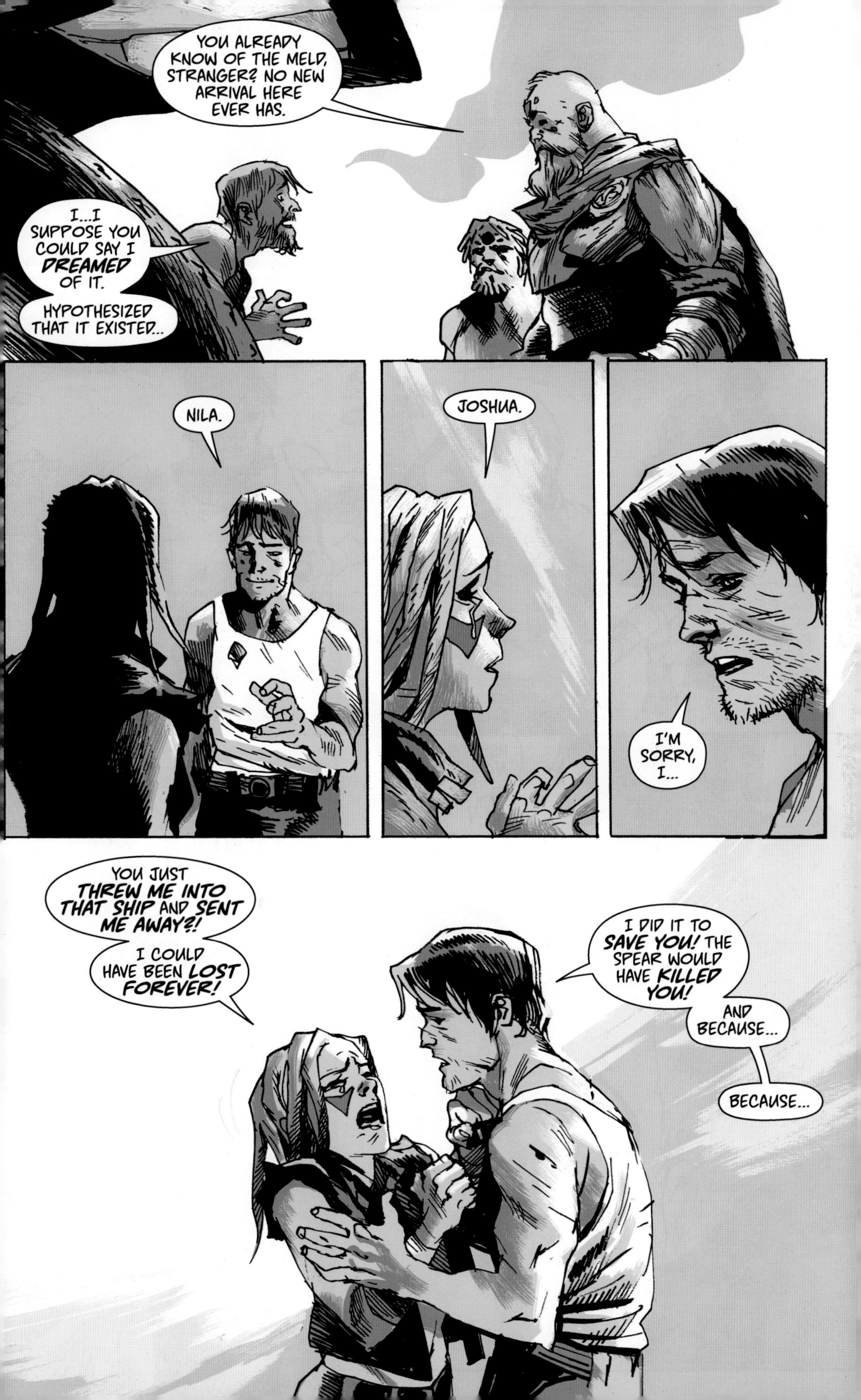
YOU ALREADY KNOW OF THE MELD, STRANGER? NO NEW ARRIVAL HERE EVER HAS.
I...I SUPPOSE YOU COULD SAY I *DREAMED* OF IT.
HYPOTHESIZED THAT IT EXISTED...
NILA.
JOSHUA.
I'M SORRY, I...
YOU JUST *THREW ME INTO THAT SHIP* AND *SENT ME AWAY?!*
I COULD HAVE BEEN *LOST FOREVER!*
I DID IT TO *SAVE YOU!* THE SPEAR WOULD HAVE *KILLED YOU!*
AND BECAUSE...
BECAUSE...

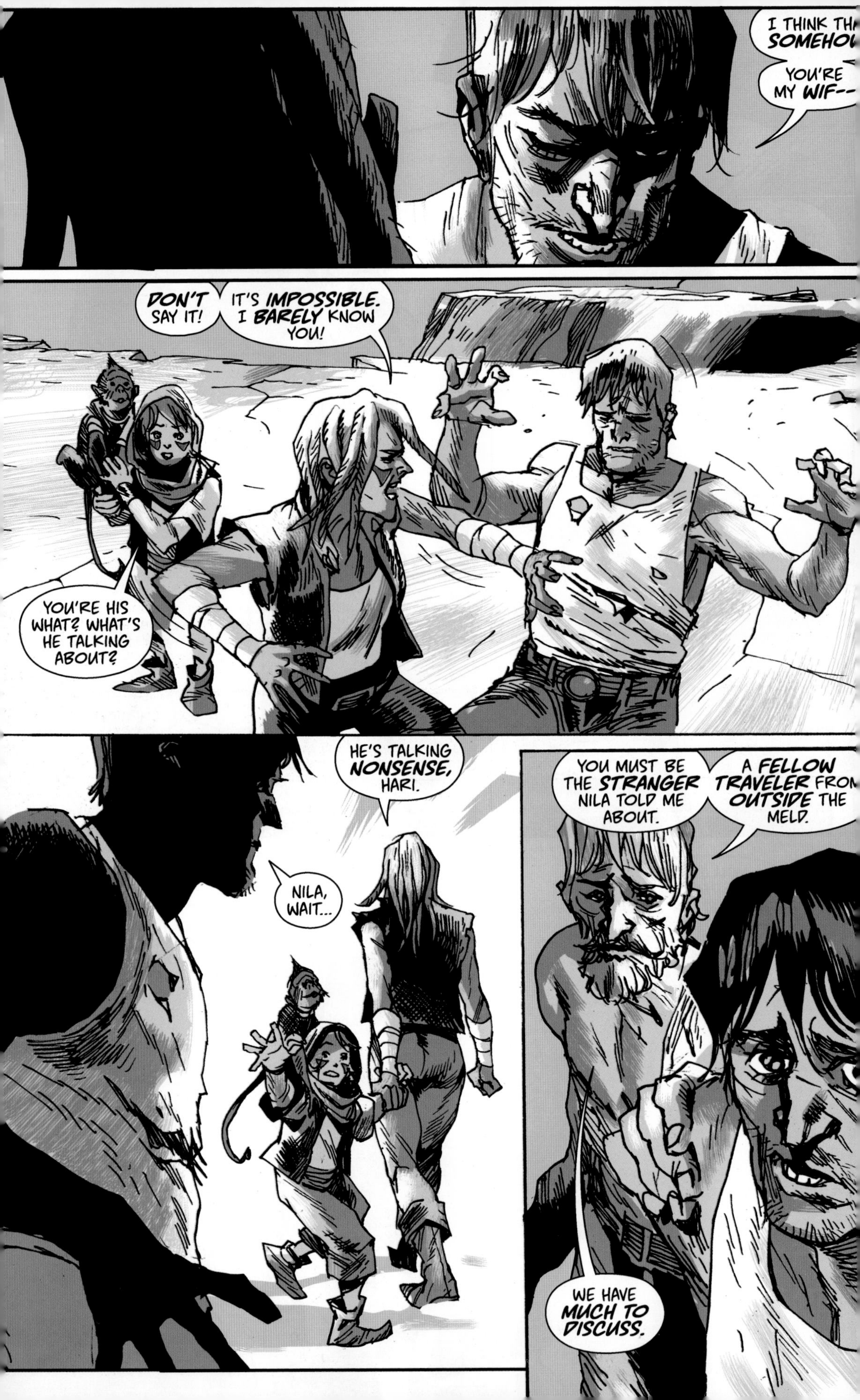
I THINK TH
SOMEHO
YOU'RE MY WIF--
DON'T SAY IT!
IT'S IMPOSSIBLE. I BARELY KNOW YOU!
YOU'RE HIS WHAT? WHAT'S HE TALKING ABOUT?
HE'S TALKING NONSENSE, HARI.
NILA, WAIT...
YOU MUST BE THE STRANGER NILA TOLD ME ABOUT.
A FELLOW TRAVELER FROM OUTSIDE THE MELD.
WE HAVE MUCH TO DISCUSS.

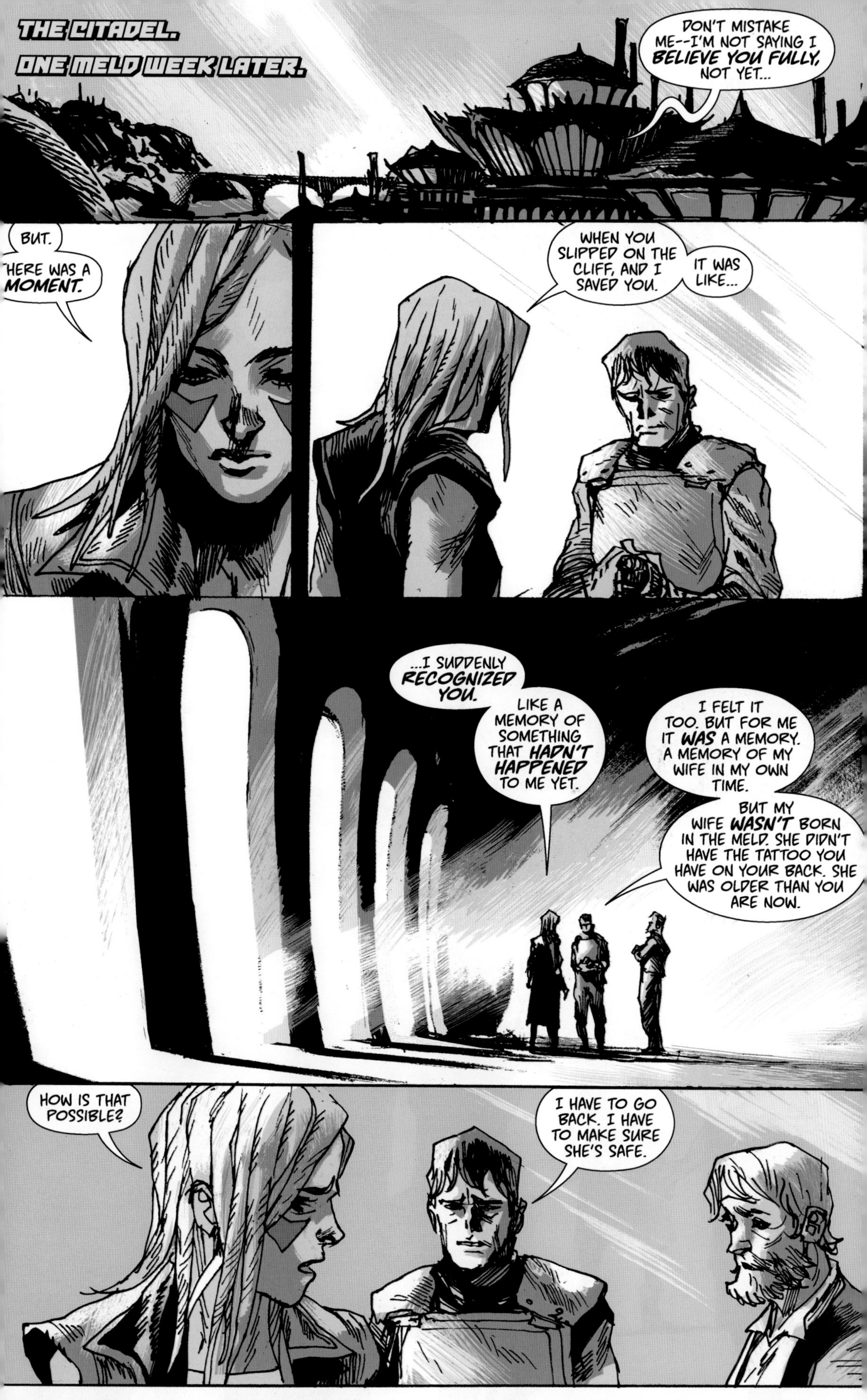
THE CITADEL.
ONE MELD WEEK LATER.
DON'T MISTAKE ME--I'M NOT SAYING I BELIEVE YOU FULLY, NOT YET...
BUT.
THERE WAS A MOMENT.
WHEN YOU SLIPPED ON THE CLIFF, AND I SAVED YOU.
IT WAS LIKE...
...I SUDDENLY RECOGNIZED YOU.
LIKE A MEMORY OF SOMETHING THAT HADN'T HAPPENED TO ME YET.
I FELT IT TOO. BUT FOR ME IT WAS A MEMORY. A MEMORY OF MY WIFE IN MY OWN TIME.
BUT MY WIFE WASN'T BORN IN THE MELD. SHE DIDN'T HAVE THE TATTOO YOU HAVE ON YOUR BACK. SHE WAS OLDER THAN YOU ARE NOW.
HOW IS THAT POSSIBLE?
I HAVE TO GO BACK. I HAVE TO MAKE SURE SHE'S SAFE.

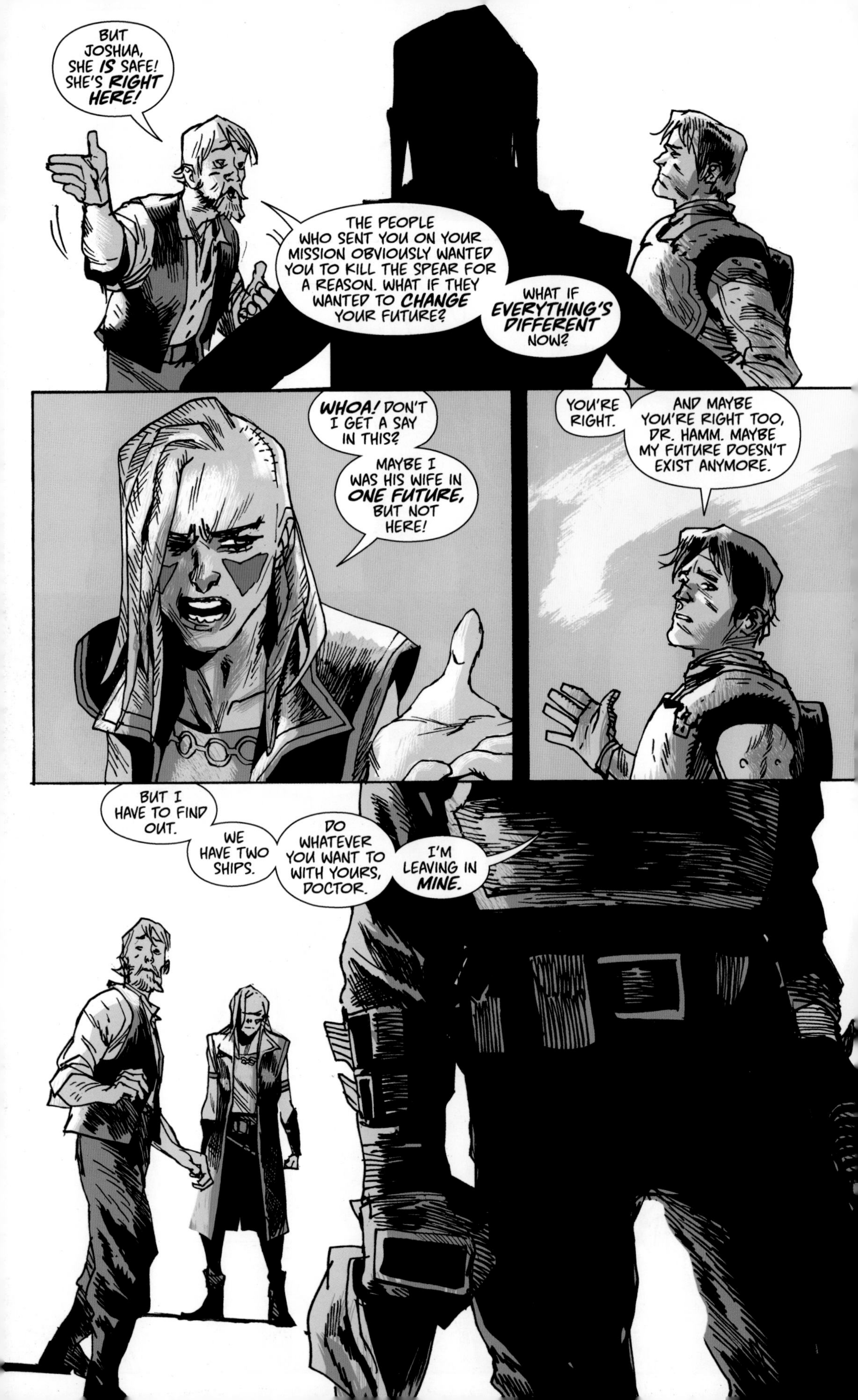
BUT JOSHUA, SHE IS SAFE! SHE'S RIGHT HERE!
THE PEOPLE WHO SENT YOU ON YOUR MISSION OBVIOUSLY WANTED YOU TO KILL THE SPEAR FOR A REASON. WHAT IF THEY WANTED TO CHANGE YOUR FUTURE?
WHAT IF EVERYTHING'S DIFFERENT NOW?
WHOA! DON'T I GET A SAY IN THIS?
MAYBE I WAS HIS WIFE IN ONE FUTURE, BUT NOT HERE!
YOU'RE RIGHT.
AND MAYBE YOU'RE RIGHT TOO, DR. HAMM. MAYBE MY FUTURE DOESN'T EXIST ANYMORE.
BUT I HAVE TO FIND OUT.
WE HAVE TWO SHIPS.
DO WHATEVER YOU WANT TO WITH YOURS, DOCTOR.
I'M LEAVING IN MINE.

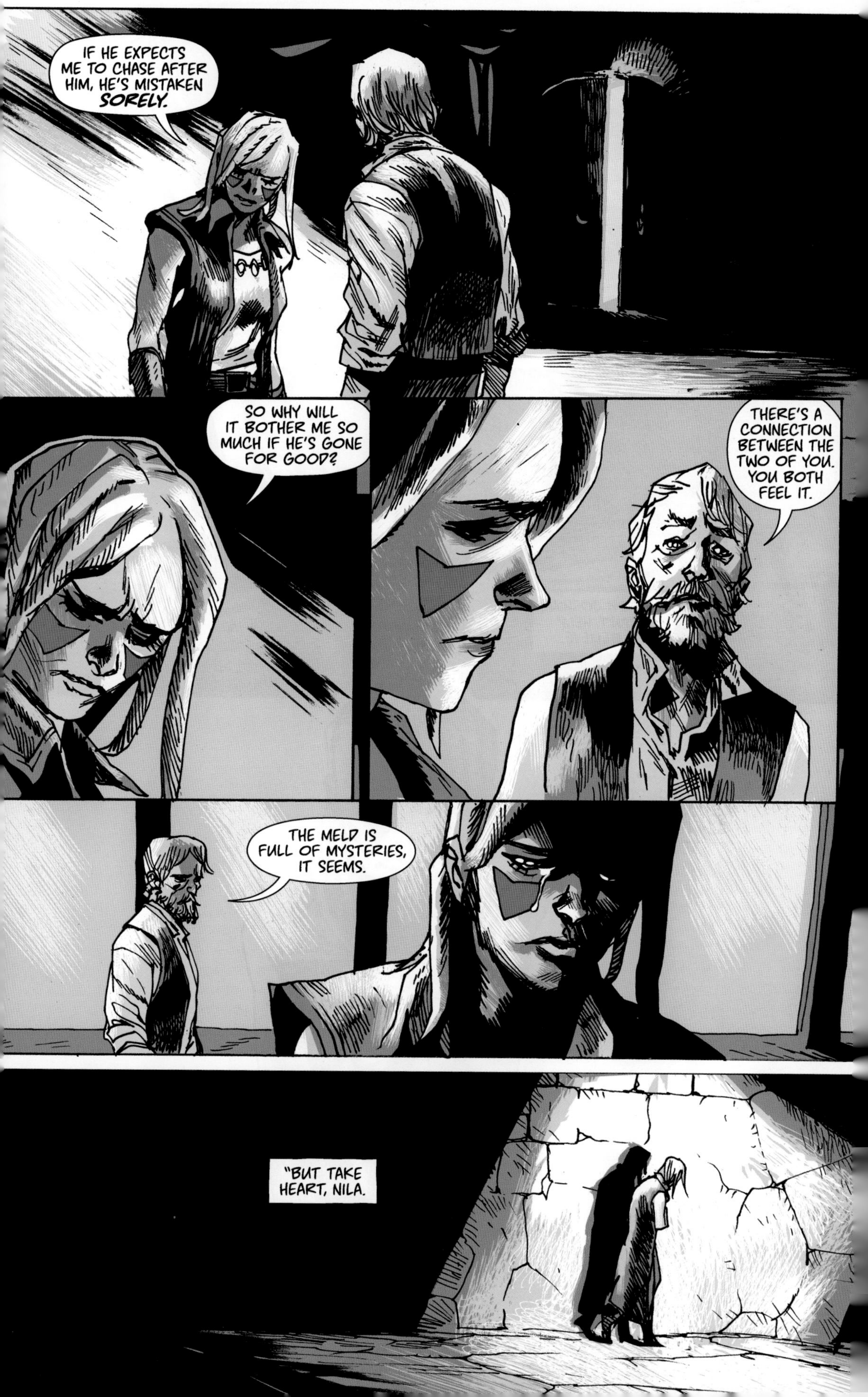
IF HE EXPECTS ME TO CHASE AFTER HIM, HE'S MISTAKEN SORELY.
SO WHY WILL IT BOTHER ME SO MUCH IF HE'S GONE FOR GOOD?
THERE'S A CONNECTION BETWEEN THE TWO OF YOU. YOU BOTH FEEL IT.
THE MELD IS FULL OF MYSTERIES, IT SEEMS.
"BUT TAKE HEART, NILA.

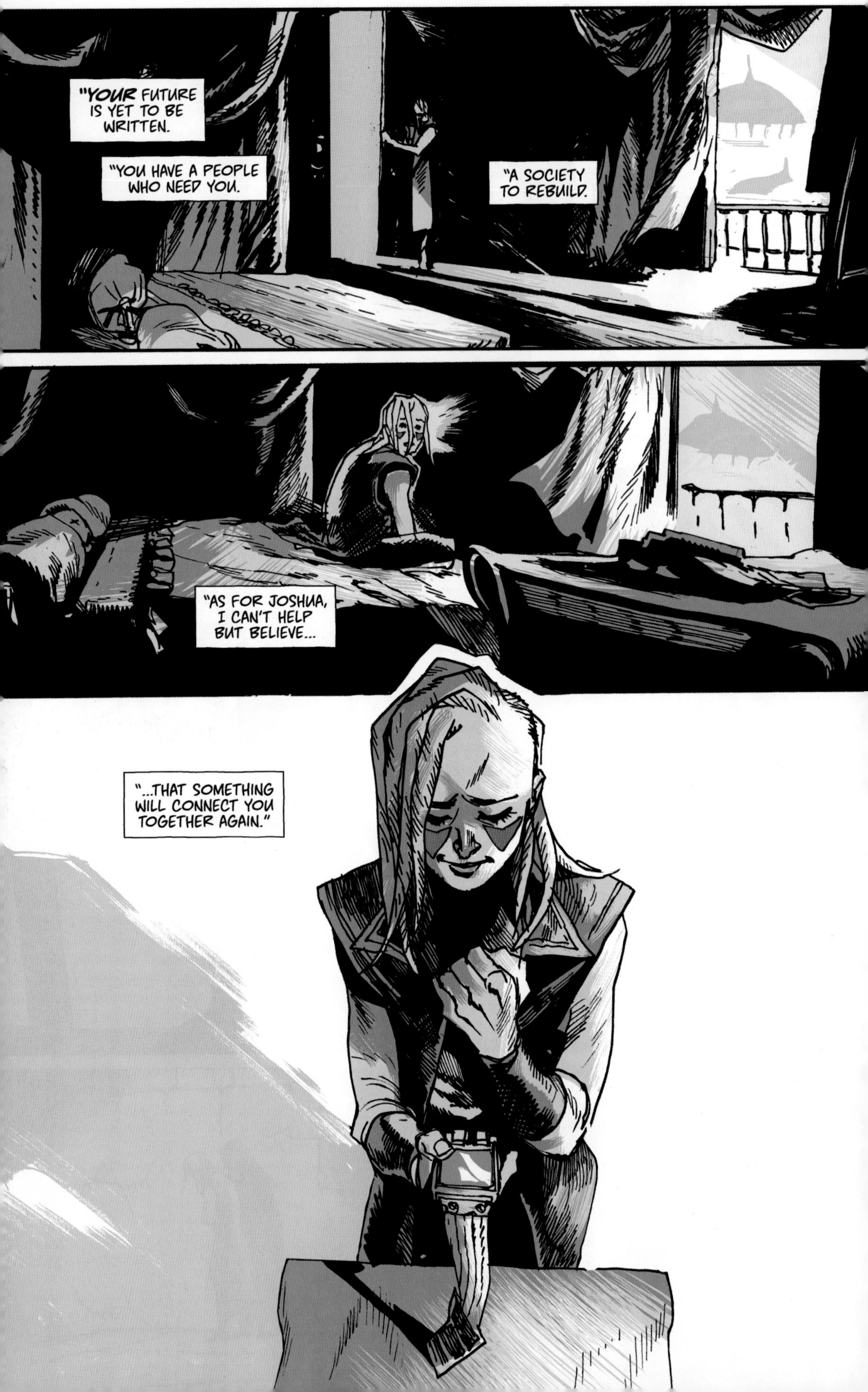
"YOUR FUTURE IS YET TO BE WRITTEN.
"YOU HAVE A PEOPLE WHO NEED YOU.
"A SOCIETY TO REBUILD.
"AS FOR JOSHUA, I CAN'T HELP BUT BELIEVE...
"...THAT SOMETHING WILL CONNECT YOU TOGETHER AGAIN."

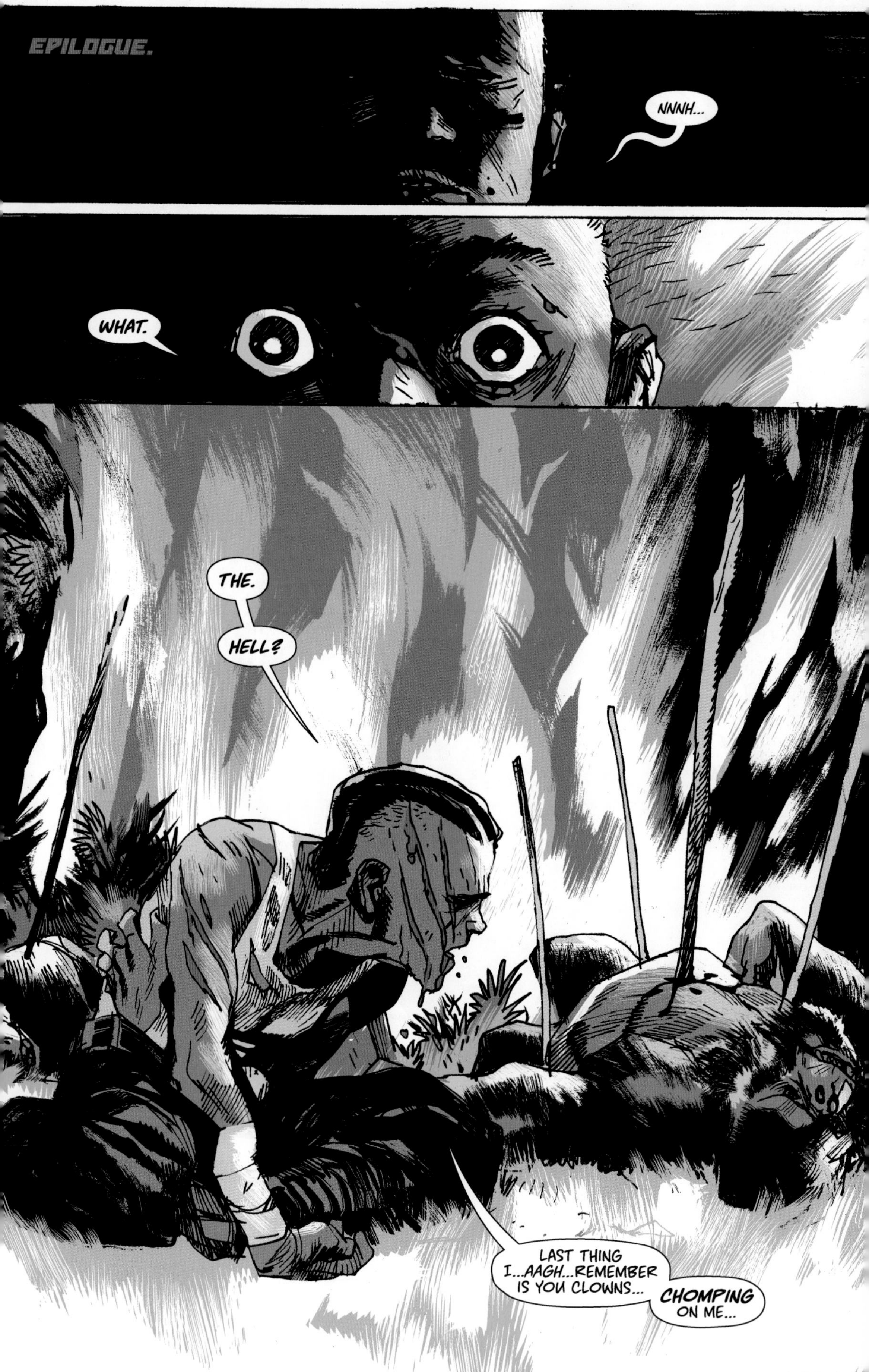
EPILOGUE.
NNNH...
WHAT.
THE.
HELL?
LAST THING I...AAGH...REMEMBER IS YOU CLOWNS... CHOMPING ON ME...

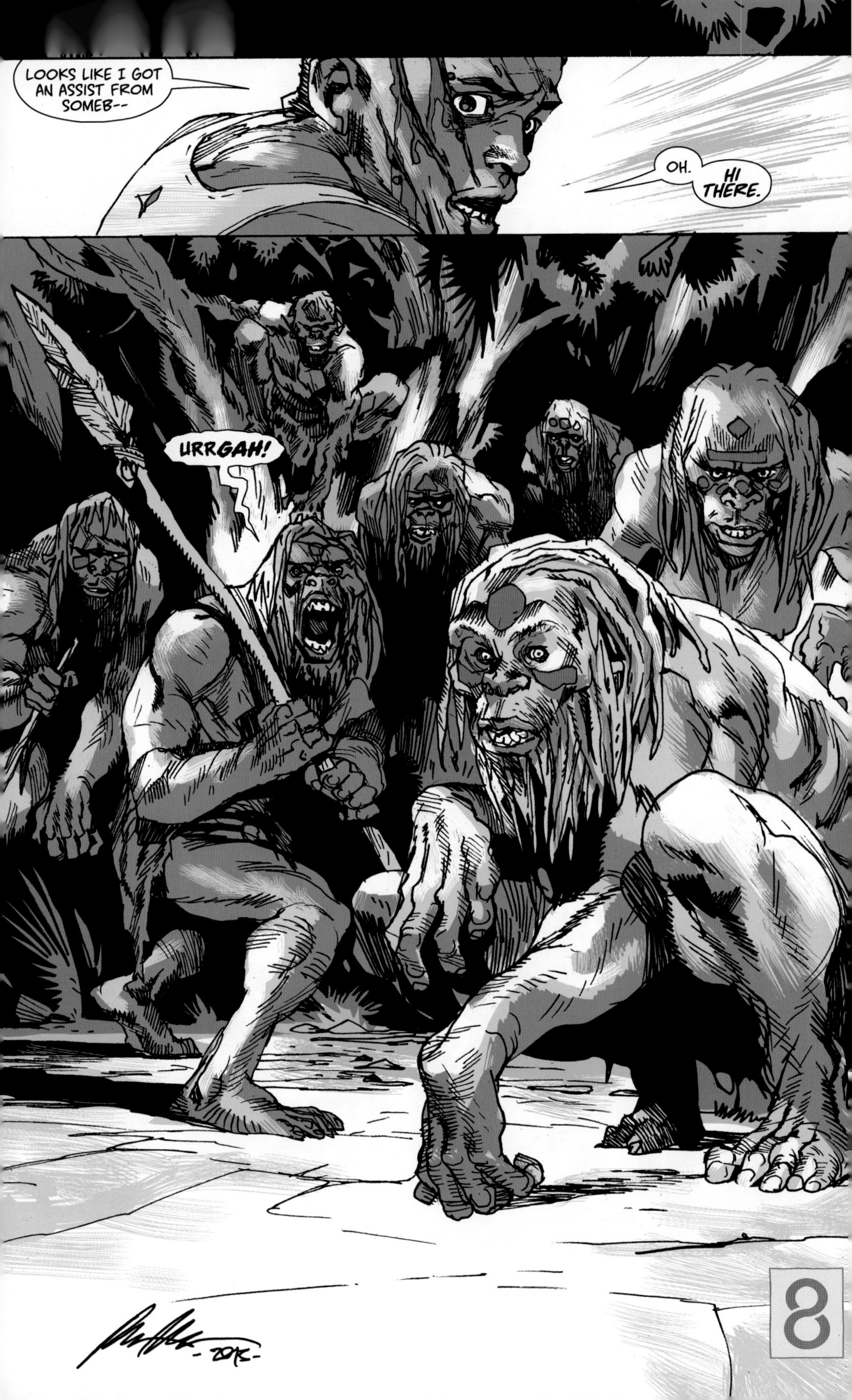
LOOKS LIKE I GOT AN ASSIST FROM SOMEB--
OH. HI THERE.
URRGAH!
8

THE MAKING OF EI8HT™

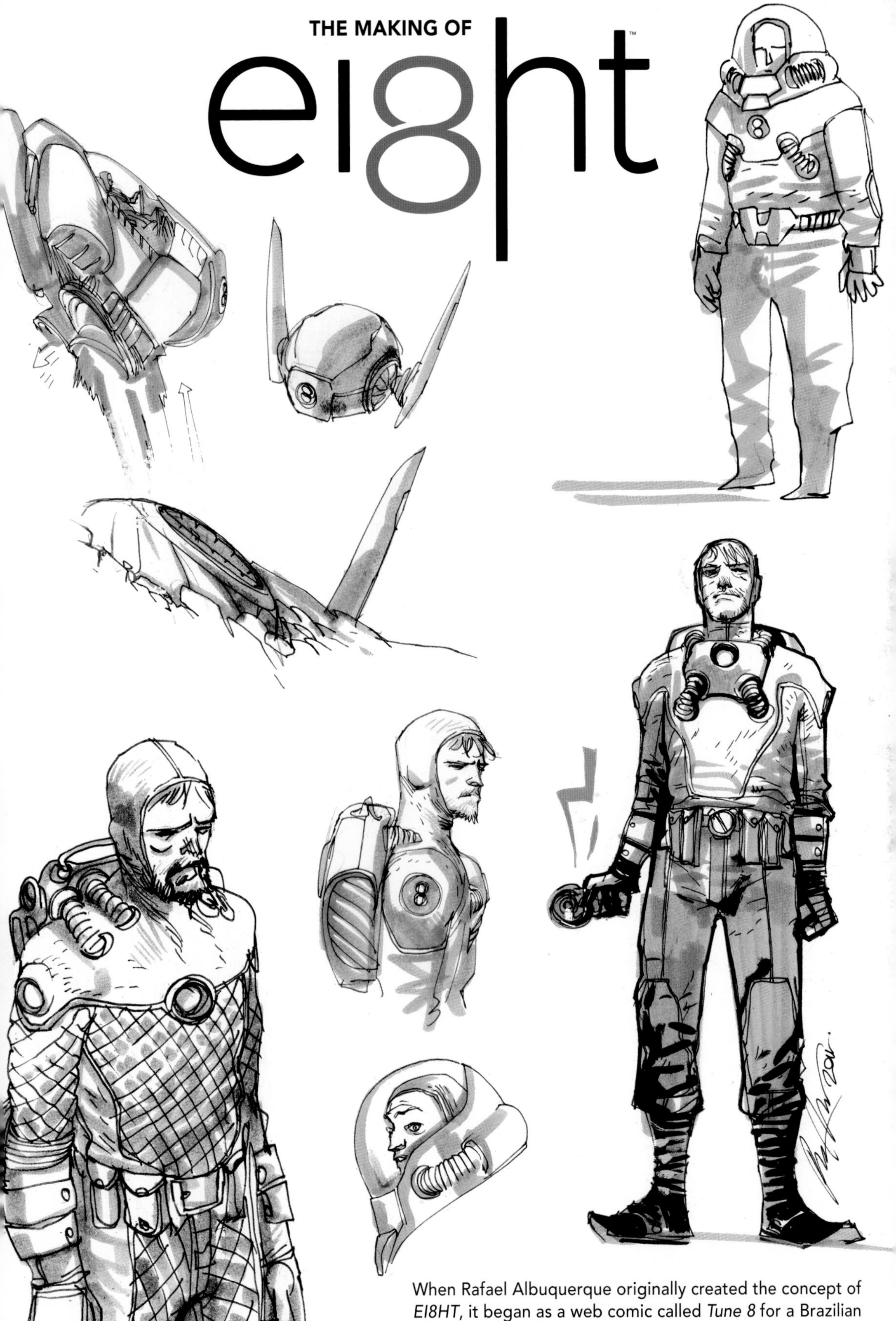

When Rafael Albuquerque originally created the concept of *EI8HT*, it began as a web comic called *Tune 8* for a Brazilian site. These sketches are the first concepts for Joshua and the ship in which he traveled to the Meld. The following page contains the updated character sketches for the new series.

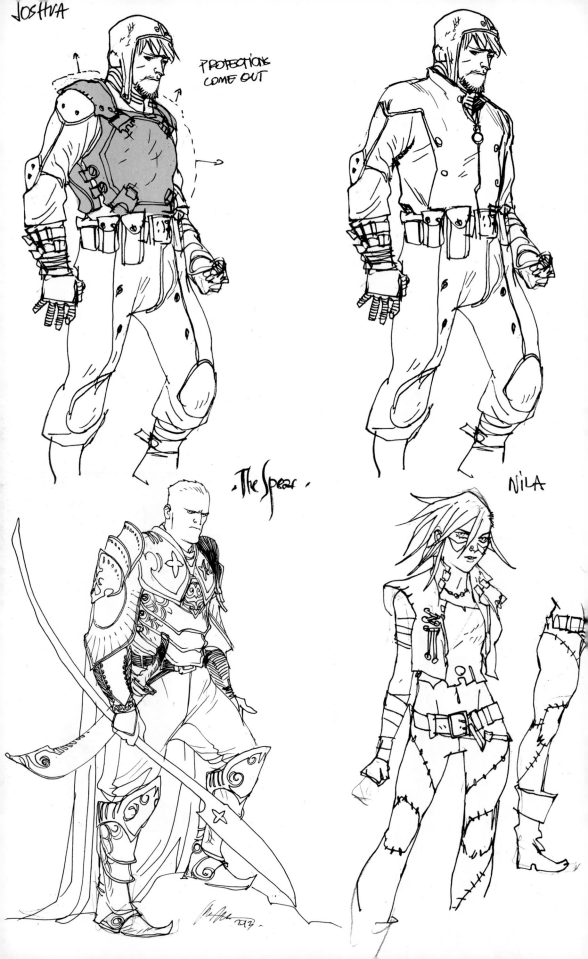

JOSHUA

PROTECTIONS
COME OUT

The Spear

NILA

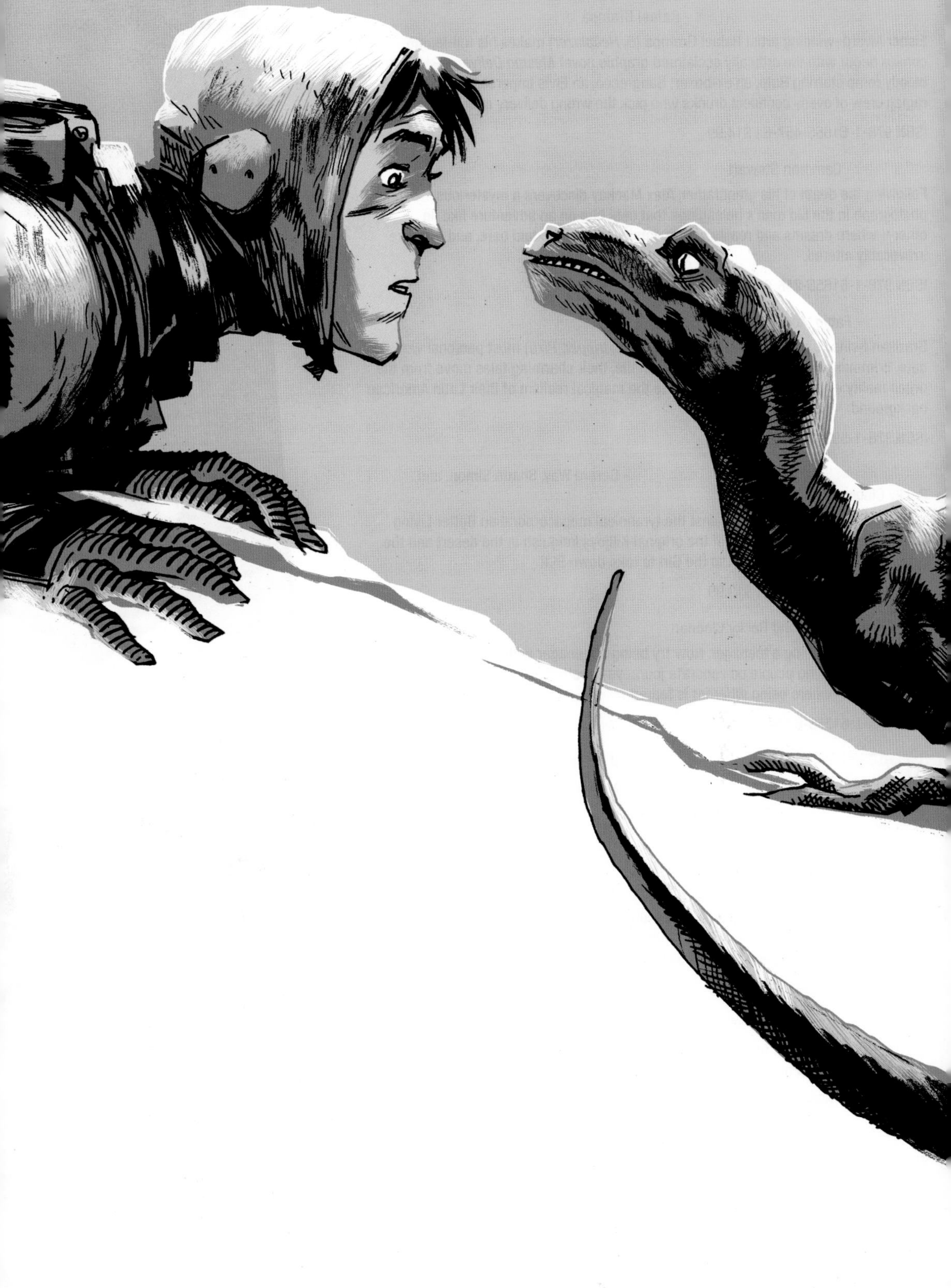

Second Printing Cover Art for *EI8HT* #1

CREATIVE GIANTS!

GET YOUR FIX OF DARK HORSE BOOKS FROM THESE INSPIRED CREATORS!

MESMO DELIVERY SECOND EDITION - Rafael Grampá

Eisner Award–winning artist Rafael Grampá (5, *Hellblazer*) makes his full-length comics debut with the critically acclaimed graphic novel *Mesmo Delivery*—a kinetic, bloody romp starring Rufo, an ex-boxer; Sangrecco, an Elvis impersonator; and a ragtag crew of overly confident drunks who pick the wrong delivery men to mess with.

ISBN 978-1-61655-457-6 | $14.99

SIN TITULO - Cameron Stewart

Following the death of his grandfather, Alex Mackay discovers a mysterious photograph in the old man's belongings that sets him on an adventure like no other—where dreams and reality merge, family secrets are laid bare, and lives are irrevocably altered.

ISBN 978-1-61655-248-0 | $19.99

DE:TALES - Fábio Moon and Gabriel Bá

Brazilian twins Fábio Moon and Gabriel Bá's (*Daytripper*, *Pixu*) most personal work to date. Brimming with all the details of human life, their charming tales move from the urban reality of their home in São Paulo to the magical realism of their Latin American background.

ISBN 978-1-59582-557-5 | $19.99

THE TRUE LIVES OF THE FABULOUS KILLJOYS - Gerard Way, Shaun Simon, and Becky Cloonan

Years ago, the Killjoys fought against the tyrannical megacorporation Better Living Industries. Today, the followers of the original Killjoys languish in the desert and the fight for freedom fades. It's left to the Girl to take down BLI!

ISBN 978-1-59582-462-2 | $19.99

DEMO - Brian Wood and Becky Cloonan

It's hard enough being a teenager. Now try being a teenager with *powers*. A chronicle of the lives of young people on separate journeys to self-discovery in a world—just like our own—where being different is feared.

ISBN 978-1-61655-682-2 | $24.99

SABERTOOTH SWORDSMAN - Damon Gentry and Aaron Conley

When his village is enslaved and his wife kidnapped by the malevolent Mastodon Mathematician, a simple farmer must find his inner warrior—the Sabertooth Swordsman!

ISBN 978-1-61655-176-6 | $17.99

JAYBIRD - Jaakko and Lauri Ahonen

Disney meets Kafka in this beautiful, intense, original tale! A very small, very scared little bird lives an isolated life in a great big house with his infirm mother. He's never been outside the house, and he never will if his mother has anything to say about it.

ISBN 978-1-61655-469-9 | $19.99

MONSTERS! & OTHER STORIES - Gustavo Duarte

Newcomer Gustavo Duarte spins wordless tales inspired by Godzilla, King Kong, and Pixar, brimming with humor, charm, and delightfully twisted horror!

ISBN 978-1-61655-309-8 | $12.99

SACRIFICE - Sam Humphries and Dalton Rose

What happens when a troubled youth is plucked from modern society and thrust though time and space into the heart of the Aztec civilization—one of the most blood-thirsty times in human history?

ISBN 978-1-59582-985-6 | $19.99

AVAILABLE AT YOUR LOCAL COMICS SHOP OR BOOKSTORE
To find a comics shop in your area, call 1-888-266-4226. For more information or to order direct: ON THE WEB: DarkHorse.com
E-MAIL: mailorder@darkhorse.com / PHONE: 1-800-862-0052 Mon.–Fri. 9 a.m. to 5 p.m. Pacific Time.
Mesmo Delivery™ © Rafael Grampá. Sin Título™ © Cameron Stewart. De:Tales™ © Fábio Moon & Gabriel Bá. The True Lives of the Fabulous Killjoys™ ©
Gerard Way & Shaun Simon. DEMO™ © Brian Wood & Becky Cloonan. Sabertooth Swordsman™ © Damon Gentry and Aaron Conley. Jaybird™ © Strip Art
Features. www.safcomics.com. Monsters!™ © Gustavo Duarte. Sacrifice™ © Sam Humphries & Dalton Rose. Dark Horse Books® and the Dark Horse logo
are registered trademarks of Dark Horse Comics, Inc. All rights reserved. (BL 5018)

DARK HORSE BOOKS